AGRICULTURAL TAXATION AND ECONOMIC DEVELOPMENT IN INDIA

AGRICULTURAL TAXATION
AND
ECONOMIC DEVELOPMENT
IN INDIA

E. T. MATHEW

ASIA PUBLISHING HOUSE
NEW YORK

PRINTED IN INDIA

BY A. K. MUKERJI AT THOMSON PRESS (INDIA) LTD., FARIDABAD, (HARYANA)
AND   PUBLISHED   BY   P. S. JAYASINGHE,   ASIA   PUBLISHING   HOUSE,
29 EAST 10TH STREET, NEW YORK, N.Y. 10003

To
MY PARENTS

PREFACE

THIS study is designed to investigate the role of agricultural taxation in the financing of India's economic development. The entire data for the work were collected while I was studying in the United States. After my return to India, the work could not be brought up to date owing to other preoccupations. However, it is now published without substantial modification since it is hoped that the work will be of interest to students of India's development problems.

An earlier version of the work was approved for the degree of Doctor of Philosophy by the Graduate School of the Vanderbilt University in January 1964. I owe a great debt of gratitude to Professor Rudolph C. Blitz who guided my research for the most part. My sincere thanks are also due to Professors Nicholas Georgescu-Roegen, William H. Nicholls, Anthony M. Tang, Millard F. Long, and John A. Brittain, all of Vanderbilt Economics Faculty, for their thoughtful suggestions and valuable criticisms. Professor Rendings T. Fels, Chairman of the Department of Economics, took a keen interest in my work. I am greatly indebted to the Graduate Program in Economic Development, Vanderbilt University, for the Ford Economic Fellowship I received during the period of the research and the preceding graduate work at Vanderbilt. I am keenly aware of my debt to Professor John F. Due, of the University of Illinois, who read the whole doctoral dissertation and made several suggestions for improvement. All of these, however, could not be carried out owing to various limitations. Needless to say, I bear full responsibility for what has finally appeared.

My colleagues in the Department of Economics, Kerala University, have always given me encouragement. Especially, I must thank Professor V. R. Pillai for his unfailing help and affection. Finally, I shall be failing in my duty if I do not acknowledge the profound debt I owe my wife, Elizabeth Mathew. Herself a graduate student at Venderbilt, this work would not have materialized but for her constant encouragement and assistance.

Trivandrum (Kerala)   E. T. MATHEW

CONTENTS

I. INTRODUCTION   1

II. PRESENT STATUS OF AGRICULTURAL TAXATION
IN INDIA   7

III. BURDEN OF AGRICULTURAL TAXATION   19

IV. AGRICULTURAL TAXATION VERSUS NONAGRICUL-
TURAL TAXATION   50

V. AGRICULTURAL TAXATION IN RELATION TO
NATIONAL GOALS   81

VI. TOWARDS AN IMPROVED SYSTEM OF AGRICULTURAL
TAXATION IN INDIA—(1) A CRITICAL REVIEW OF THE
EXISTING SYSTEM   109

VII. TOWARDS AN IMPROVED SYSTEM OF AGRICULTURAL
TAXATION IN INDIA—(2) RECOMMENDATIONS FOR
REFORM   141

VIII. SUMMARY AND CONCLUSIONS   151

APPENDIXES   169

BIBLIOGRAPHY   195

INDEX   201

CHAPTER I

INTRODUCTION

THIS study attempts to investigate the role of agricultural taxation in financing India's economic development. This writer believes that such a study is especially valuable in view of the dearth of domestic resources faced by the Government of India in the financing of its Five Year Plans. The investigation will concern itself with the following questions: (1) An estimation of the burden of taxation of the agricultural sector in terms of total and per capita tax as well as per capita tax as a proportion of per capita income. (2) A comparison of the agricultural sector's contribution to governmental revenue with that of the nonagricultural sector. While it appears legitimate to compare the tax contributions, no conclusive comparisons can be made about the relative tax burdens of the two sectors because of the difference in their income levels. To the extent that comparisons are made about relative tax burdens, they will be intra-sectoral and not inter-sectoral. (3) An examination of agricultural taxation in relation to national goals. (4) An appraisal of the existing system of agricultural taxation from the point of view of financing economic development. (5) Policy recommendations in the light of the findings under (1) to (4).

According to the programme of planned economic development accepted by the Government of India, "the public sector is expected to grow both absolutely and in comparison and at a faster rate than the private sector."[1] This means that more and more investment will be directly undertaken by the government. The proportion of investment in the public sector increased from 46 per cent of the total investment during the First Plan to 54 per cent in the Second Plan, and in the Third Plan it is expected to increase to 61 per cent.[2] To enable the government to undertake investment of such growing magnitude, it is necessary that an increasingly larger share of the

1 Government of India, Planning Commission, *Third Five Year Plan* (New Delhi: Government of India Press, 1961), p. 7.

2 *Ibid.*, pp. 32, 59.

increase in the amount of investment funds should be channelled through the government. Every effort, thus, needs to be made to increase the financial resources of the government. This study addresses itself to this problem.

From the very beginning the implementation of India's Five Year Plans has suffered on account of inadequate domestic resources. Modest as the growth targets have been, the situation in respect of internal resources has not improved even after a decade of planning. While 90 per cent of the public sector outlay was raised internally during the First Five Year Plan, the proportion of domestic resources was only 76 per cent during the Second Five Year Plan.[3] It is estimated that, during the Third Plan, internal resources will finance only 63.3 per cent of the outlay in the public sector.[4] This declining trend in the proportion of domestic resources used to finance economic development is contrary to what one would normally expect in a developing economy. One of the reasons for the government's failure to raise adequate domestic resources is that it has not effectively tapped every possible source of revenue. In this study we shall discuss this problem in relation to the agricultural sector. While the government has been investing increasingly larger amounts in agriculture,[5] it has not made a parallel effort to tax away a substantial portion of the marginal increment in the agriculturists' income.

Throughout this study we take the basic pattern of the Five Year Plans—approach, objectives, targets, etc.—as given. In particular, our analysis and recommendations will be with special reference to the Third Five Year Plan. With another plan or no plan at all, other recommendations may be appropriate.

Underdeveloped economies are characterized by the predominance of agriculture as the principal means of livelihood. In these economies, 50 to 80 per cent of the labour force is engaged in agricultural production and from 40 to 60 per cent of the national income is produced in agriculture. The agricultural sector is thus the largest and the most important segment of the economy in these countries. The study of agricultural taxation is very important if only by virtue

3 *Ibid.,* p. 33.

4 *Ibid.,* p. 100.

5 The investment in agriculture and community development, and in major and minor irrigation, totalled Rs 6010 million during the First Plan, and Rs 9500 million during the Second Plan. In the Third Plan it is proposed to spend Rs 17180 million on this sector. (*Third Five Year Plan,* pp. 33, 58.)

of the fact that the agricultural sector is so large. It is, however, a neglected topic. The importance of the study of agricultural taxation, thus, derives from the fact that in underdeveloped economies agriculture is the most important sector of the economy, no matter what one thinks the relative roles of agriculture and of manufacturing industry and commerce should be in the context of long-run economic development. In spite of the great strides India has taken in the fields of industry and commerce since Independence, agriculture still remains the most important segment of the economy. During the period 1948-49 to 1960-61, the share of agricultural production in national income has varied from a high of 51.3 per cent in 1950-51 to a low of 45.3 per cent in 1955-56.[6]

While there are historical precedents for heavy and almost exclusive taxation of agriculture to finance economic development, it needs to be added that these precedents have only very limited application to the Indian case. In the past, the Soviet Union and Japan have resorted to very extensive taxation of the agricultural sector—the former in the form of compulsory deliveries of grains by the collectives and the latter through heavy land taxes—to finance economic development. Although the Soviet Union has achieved a rapid growth of the industrial sector, the chronic deficiencies of the agricultural sector make it clear that Soviet agricultural policy, and this includes agricultural taxation, cannot serve as an example to be emulated by India. The Japanese policy of agricultural taxation, on the other hand, is a well-known success story and, therefore, an attractive example which underdeveloped countries may want to follow. However, upon careful reflection, it becomes apparent that the Japanese lesson needs to be qualified substantially when applied to India. Japanese agriculture was generally in a very prosperous state when the Meiji land tax[7] was enacted in 1873, whereas much of Indian agriculture is today in a state of extreme poverty. Because of this difference this study will in the end recommend reforms which will greatly lessen the burdens of the impoverished sections of Indian agriculture and will try to increase the incentives for these groups, at the same time suggesting a progressive system of taxation for

6 Government of India, Cabinet Secretariat (Department of Statistics), *Estimates of National Income, 1948-49 to 1960-61* (New Delhi: Government of India Press, 1962), p. 3.

7 For details, see Kazushi Okhawa and Henry Rosovsky, "The Role of Agriculture in Modern Japanese Economic Development," *Economic Development and Cultural Change* (Vol. IX, No. 1, Part II, October 1960), pp. 43-67.

agriculture, which may approximately double the yield from the land tax.

Other examples, though less impressive, are not hard to find. For instance, in the United States and Canada, property taxes have played a decisive role in the financing of education by local governments. The property tax yields 87 per cent of the tax revenue of the local governments in the United States and about 85 per cent in Canada.[8] This situation in the United States and Canada may be compared to the situation which obtains in Latin America generally. There, it is pointed out, local governments are financially starved.

Insufficient capital is one of the crucial factors resulting in underdevelopment.[9] In the absence of adequate voluntary savings, taxation, which represents forced savings, is the most effective, and perhaps the only, alternative available to the governments of the developing countries. The agricultural sector, being the largest segment of the economy, must, therefore, bear a substantial portion of the cost of economic development. It may be further noted that in many underdeveloped economies it is often not the insufficiency of savings but the behaviour of savings which constitutes the real problem. Referring to the problem of inadequate capital encountered by the leaders of the Industrial Revolution in England in its initial stage, Postan comments:[10]

> It can, indeed, be doubted whether there had ever been a period in English history when the accumulated wealth of landlords and merchants, of religious and educational institutions would have been inadequate for this purpose. What was inadequate was not the quantity of stored-up wealth, but its behaviour. . . . Much of the savings was hoarded. . . . In spite of the fact that rural England had long been familiar with the new financial methods, surprisingly little of her wealth found its way into the new industrial enterprises, where the shortage of capital must have been acute, and the risks, even as they might appear to the inventor, not immoderate.

As with England in the early period of the Industrial Revolution, so

8 John F. Due, *Government Finance* (Homewood, Illinois: Richard D. Irvin, Inc., 1959), p. 385.

9 Ragner Nurkse, *Problems of Capital Formation in Underdeveloped Countries* (Oxford: Basil Blackwell, 1953), p. 1.

10 M.M. Postan, "Recent Trends in the Accumulation of Capital," *The Economic History Review* (Vol. VI, No. 1, October 1935), p. 2.

with India in the present day, this statement is largely true. It is estimated that hoards of gold in India amounts to about Rs 40 billion ($ 8.42 billion) at current domestic prices and to Rs 18 billion ($ 3.8 billion) at the international prices.[11] Much of these hoards of gold is concentrated in the rural sector.[12] Such conditions as these only strengthen the case for increased taxation, especially of the rural sector, in India.

Agricultural taxation plays a twofold role in the process of economic development. In the first place, it provides the government with financial resources for carrying out developmental expenditures. But it also serves another very important objective—in most cases a far more vital objective—by supplying the rest of the economy with a larger food surplus. The latter aspect has been seldom emphasized in the general literature. A marginal increase in agricultural productivity need not result in increased marketed surplus, since the agricultural producers may retain for their own consumption the entire increment in output. This proposition has special validity in underdeveloped economies where the existing levels of consumption are pitifully low. To quote Kaldor:[13]

As development proceeds, the proportion of the working population engaged in producing food for domestic consumption is steadily reduced, and the proportion engaged in manufacturing, commerce and services is steadily increased. In order to make this possible the proportion of food produced on the land which is *not* consumed by the food producers must steadily increase; this in turn inevitably involves that each family engaged in food production should sell a steadily larger part of its output for consumption outside the agricultural sector. Unless this happens it is impossible for the non-agricultural sector to expand so as to occupy an increasing proportion of the community's manpower. Such an expansion of the "agricultural surplus" cannot be relied upon to arise automatically as part of the over-all process of growth in the economy. Economic incentives do not operate in the same

11 *Indian Finance* (January 12, 1963), p. 81.

12 *Cf.* P.G. Kesava Panikar, *An Essay on Rural Savings in India* (unpublished Ph. D. dissertation, Vanderbilt University, 1959), pp. 134-6.

13 Nicholas Kaldor, "The Role of Taxation in Economic Development" (paper presented at the International Congress on Economic Development held under the auspices of the International Economic Association at Vienna, Austria, August 30-September 6, 1962), p. 7.

way in the "subsistence sector" as in the case of industry and commerce. A shortage of food is not likely to call forth increased production; a rise in the price of locally produced food may even lead to a *decrease* of the amounts which are offered for sale since it may cause the agricultural families to reduce their amount of work (or increase their own consumption) if their own needs for things which can only be procured with money can now be satisfied in exchange for a smaller quantity of food stuffs.

Kaldor, therefore, argues that the taxation of agriculture "has a critical role to play in the acceleration of economic development since it is only *the imposition of compulsory levies on the agricultural sector itself* which enlarges the supply of savings for economic development."[14]

In conclusion, we may emphasize that what we have to say about agricultural taxation in this study does not really stand or fall with any particular view regarding the share of agriculture in the labour force of the country during the process of economic development. Regardless of what proportion of the labour force will be engaged in agricultural production in India, say, twenty-five years from now, agricultural taxation must play a key role so long as agriculture is the largest segment—in terms of its contribution to national income—of the economy.

14 *Ibid.*, p. 8.

CHAPTER II

PRESENT STATUS OF AGRICULTURAL TAXATION IN INDIA

THE purpose of this chapter is to give a systematic account of the different taxes borne by the agriculturists in India. The term "agricultural taxation" as used in this study includes not only taxes paid by the agriculturists in their role as agricultural producers, but also those borne by them in other capacities, e.g. as consumers, owners of wealth, etc.

Direct taxes on agriculture consist of the land tax, traditionally called land revenue, and agricultural income tax. These may be called "agricultural taxes proper." Other direct taxes include estate duty, wealth tax, expenditure tax, gift tax, and stamps and registration. Under indirect taxes (taxes on commodities and services) we may mention excise duties, the general sales tax, import duties, entertainment tax, electricity duty, motor vehicles tax, sales tax on motor spirit, etc. Of the various taxes affecting the agricultural sector, land revenue, agricultural income tax, the general sales tax, entertainment tax, electricity duty, sales tax on motor spirit, and motor vehicles tax are levied, collected, and the proceeds retained by the state governments. Excise duties are levied and collected by both the central and state governments. But a portion of the revenue from the central excise duties is distributed among the states. In the case of stamps and registration, these are levied and collected by both the state and central governments. Expenditure tax, gift tax, and wealth tax are exclusively central taxes. In the case of estate duty, the tax is levied and collected by the central government, but the state governments receive a portion of the revenue collected. Import duties are exclusively central taxes.

For the purpose of this study we shall include under agricultural taxation all the relevant central (federal) and state taxes. We will not take into account local taxation since we do not have enough data on local taxes, especially in the rural sector. This, however, should not be considered a serious omission since it is known that local taxation within the rural sector is negligible.

7

LAND REVENUE

Land revenue has been traditionally the most important tax on agricultural land. Though its relative importance has greatly declined in recent times as a result of inflation and also due to the introduction and extension of many new levies, it is still the most important tax on agriculture. Under the Constitution of India, land revenue is levied and collected by the state governments. In 1958-59, land revenue accounted for 8.47 per cent of the combined revenue of the central and state governments.[1] The rapid decline in the relative importance of land revenue as a source of revenue is brought out by the fact that in 1950-51 land revenue formed 66.5 per cent of the combined revenue receipts of the central and state governments.[2]

Land revenue is the oldest tax in India. The foundations of the modern land revenue system were laid by Akbar (1556-1605), the great Moghul emperor of India, with the help of his famous revenue minister, Raja Todar Mal. Land revenue was fixed as a percentage of the gross produce. In calculating the gross produce, differences in soil and fertility were taken into account. With the decline of the Moghul Empire, the middlemen employed to collect the land revenue became stronger, and in course of time became "zamindars" or owners of land. The East India Company conferred greater status and legality on the zamindars. The Company under Lord Cornwallis decided in 1793 in favour of a "Permanent Settlement" of land revenue in the areas now covered by Bengal, and parts of Bihar and Orissa. Under the permanent settlement, land revenue was fixed permanently.[3] Land revenue was fixed at nine-tenths of the rental.[4] The zamindars were thus assured of the benefits of any future increments in the value of, and income from, land. Since the permanent settlement ensured a regular inflow of revenue, the East India Company later extended it to many other parts of the country. When the Company's rule was, however, securely established, it was thought that the state would benefit more from periodical settlements. There were two types of such settlements, "mahalwari" and "ryotwari."[5]

1   Reserve Bank of India, *Report on Currency and Finance for the Year* 1961-62 (Bombay, 1962), Statements 56 and 60.

2   Government of India (Finance Ministry), *Report of the Taxation Enquiry Commission,* 1953-54 (New Delhi: Government of India Press, 1955), Vol. III, p. 216.

3   Romesh Chunder Dutt, *The Economic History of India* (Delhi: Government of India Press, 1960), Vol. I, pp. 58-68.

4   *Ibid.,* p. 62.

5   For details, see *ibid.,* pp. 83-139.

In the former case, settlement was concluded with village communities according to which the villagers were held jointly and severally responsible for the payment of land revenue. The land revenue was initially fixed at 83 per cent of the rental of the estate.[6] In the latter case, land revenue was directly settled with individual farmers. The land revenue was fixed at 45-55 per cent of the gross produce.[7] In these cases the assessments were not fixed in perpetuity but for a definite period, varying from fifteen to forty years.

Impact of Land Reforms on Land Revenue. Under the land reforms implemented in India since the attainment of independence, intermediaries between the state and the tiller of the soil were abolished in most cases. The "zamindari" system has disappeared and along with it the permanent settlement of land revenue. Where tenancy exists, the tenant is assured security of tenure. These changes have had some impact on the land revenue system. Receipts from land revenue increased from Rs 515.8 million in 1950-51 to Rs 957.5 million in 1959-60.[8] This substantial rise in the proceeds from land revenue is largely accounted for by the fact that the payments which formerly went to the landlords or other intermediaries now go directly to the government.[9] Thus, in a real sense, the increase in the receipts from land revenue in the recent past does not indicate increased taxation of the agriculturists; it is only a conversion of rents into land revenue.

In assessing the land revenue, different states have in the past adopted different bases.[10] In Punjab, Uttar Pradesh, and Madhya Pradesh, and in some parts of Bihar, Orissa, and West Bengal, assessment of land revenue is based on the "net assets," determined by estimating the gross produce, valued at the average price of the crop for a specified period and deducting the landlord's estimated costs. In Madras the assessment is based directly on the value of the net produce. Gross produce is the basis of assessment in Assam. In Bombay and Mysore, and in certain other parts of India, the standards to be used by the assessing officers in determining the basis of

6 *Ibid.,* p. 138.

7 *Ibid.,* p. 110.

8 Reserve Bank of India, *Report on Currency and Finance for the Year* 1961-62, Statements 56 and 60.

9 See R.N. Tripathy, *Fiscal Policy and Economic Development in India* (Calcutta: The World Press Private Ltd., 1958), pp. 124-32.

10 For details, see Government of India, *Report of the Taxation Enquiry Commission,* Vol. III, pp. 185-6.

assessment are not fixed by law: they are left to the judgment of the assessing officers.

Since there has been no regular periodical revision of the land revenue assessment in the last few decades, the above-mentioned bases have fallen into disuse and thus lost their practical validity. Thus the land revenue has, in practice, become a crude acreage tax.

According to the land revenue laws, where assessment is based on net assets or net produce, the maximum limits on the rates of land revenue vary from 25 per cent to 50 per cent. Where the gross produce is the base, the rate of tax varies from one-tenth to one-fifth of the gross produce. Where zamindari tenure has been abolished, the rate generally amounts to 100 per cent of the settled rental value, since rent formerly paid to the zamindars is now paid directly to the state as land revenue.

AGRICULTURAL INCOME TAX

Agricultural income tax, like land revenue, is levied and collected by the state governments. Bihar was the first state in India to levy a tax on agricultural income in 1938. In most cases it was the existence of big landlords or of large plantations that drew the attention of the state governments to the desirability of levying this tax.[11]

Agricultural income tax plays only a minor role in the agricultural tax system of India. The revenue from this source in 1959-60 was Rs 89.2 million which formed 1.5 per cent of the tax revenue and one per cent of the total revenue of the states.[12] This compares quite unfavourably with the corresponding figure for land revenue. Total receipts from land revenue (excluding territories directly administered by the central government) in 1959-60 was Rs 951.5 million which accounted for 16.5 per cent of the tax revenue and 10.4 per cent of the total revenue of the states.[13] It may be further pointed out that three states (out of a total of fifteen states)—Assam, Kerala, and Madras—account for the bulk of the receipts from agricultural income tax. Out of a total revenue of Rs 89.2 million from this tax, these states accounted for Rs 60.9 million (i.e. 68 per cent).[14]

The exemption limits and the rates of the tax have in no state

11 *Ibid.*, p. 199.
12 Figures based on Statement 60, *Report on Currency and Finance*, 1961-62.
13 *Ibid.*
14 *Reserve Bank of India Bulletin,* June 1961, pp. 871-8.

remained constant. In a few states like Kerala and Assam, agricultural incomes are also subject to a "super tax." In Kerala, for example, the highest rate of agricultural super tax is 31 paise in the rupee (1 rupee = 100 paise) for companies and 34 paise in the rupee for individuals and families.[15] In Assam, super tax is applied to agricultural incomes over Rs 20000 per annum, bringing the total incidence to 35-50 paise in the rupee.[16] The exemption limit is Rs 3000 in Bihar, Jammu and Kashmir, and Madras, Rs 3600 in Kerala, Rs 5000 in Orissa, and Rs 6000 in Rajasthan. Incomes are arranged in class intervals and progression is introduced. The marginal rate of tax goes up to 50 per cent as in the case of Assam.

Apart from levels of income which are exempt, there are also types of agricultural incomes which are exempt from agricultural income taxation, such as any income derived from a house or building which is in actual use of the agriculturist, or income derived from property held under trust, etc.[17]

OTHER DIRECT TAXES

Land revenue together with agricultural income tax represents agricultural taxes proper. However, since in this study we are interested in the total tax burden of the agricultural sector, we have also to take into account other taxes falling on the agriculturist. These taxes with the exception of stamps and registration are new levies.[18]

These new levies—expenditure tax, gift tax, estate duty, and wealth tax—do not yet play any significant role in the Indian tax system. The combined receipts from these taxes amounted to only Rs 166.2 million in 1959-60, which was less than 3 per cent of the tax revenue of the Government of India during the same year.[19] Since the exemption limits of these taxes are very high, the amount collected from the agriculturists cannot be significant. Furthermore,

15 Reserve Bank of India, *Report on Currency and Finance*, 1960-61 (Bombay, 1961), p. 92.

16 Reserve Bank of India, *Report on Currency and Finance*, 1961-62 (Bombay, 1962), p. 93.

17 Government of India, *Report of the Taxation Enquiry Commission*, Vol. III, p. 202.

18 The expenditure tax and the gift tax came into force in 1958, estate duty in 1953, and wealth tax in 1957.

19 It may be noted that, of these taxes, expenditure tax, gift tax, and wealth tax are levied and collected by the central government, and also the proceeds are retained by them. In the case of estate duty, however, the tax is levied and collected by the central government, but most of the net proceeds is distributed among the states.

agriculturists are granted certain special exemptions. For instance, agricultural land has been, up till now, exempt from estate duty. Similarly, agricultural land and growing crops, and standing trees on such lands, are exempt from wealth tax. Also, tools and implements used for the raising of agricultural products are exempt.

In sharp contrast to the above direct taxes, the receipts from stamps and registration have been quite substantial. These taxes are levied and collected by both the central and state governments. In the case of certain stamp duties, the taxes are levied by the central government but the proceeds are collected and retained by the states. Revenue from this levy comes mainly from three sources: the sale of judicial stamps, court fee stamps, and registration of documents. The central government receives very limited revenue from stamps and registration whereas the state governments derive considerable revenue. In 1959-60, the central and the state governments realized Rs 33.5 million and Rs 406.9 million respectively.[20]

We have not tried to show how much of the revenue from the above taxes comes from the agricultural sector. We will address ourselves to this task in the following chapter.

TAXES ON COMMODITIES AND SERVICES (INDIRECT TAXES)

Among the indirect taxes which affect the agriculturists as consumers, excise duties and the general sales tax are the most important. Import duties used to be significant till a few years back, but their relative importance has greatly declined in recent years. As between the rural and urban sectors, the import duty affects the latter much more than the former, since it is the government's policy to levy prohibitive rates of duty on "luxury" items of import.

By far the major portion of the excise duties is levied and collected by the central government. However, 20 per cent of the net proceeds of the central excise duties is distributed among the states.[21] State excise duties which are levied exclusively on alcoholic beverages and narcotics are relatively insignificant. While the revenue from central excise duties was Rs 3606.5 million in 1959-60, that from state excise duties was only Rs 496.0 million in the same year.[22] During the

20 Reserve Bank of India, *Report on Currency and Finance,* 1961-62, Statements 56 and 60.

21 Government of India, *Report of the Finance Commission* 1961, p. 22.

22 Reserve Bank of India, *Report on Currency and Finance,* 1961-62, Statements 56 and 60.

financial year 1962-63, forty-seven categories of commodities were subject to central excise duties, the most prominent of which, from the point of view of revenue, were tobacco, sugar, motor spirit, cotton cloth, matches, refined diesel oils and vaporising oils, industrial fuel oils, and cement.[23]

Sales tax is a comparatively new levy, though an increasingly important one. It is levied and collected by states. The first state to impose a general sales tax was Madras in 1939. Since 1957-58, the revenue from the general sales tax has exceeded that from land revenue. Broadly speaking, states which have enjoyed a substantial urban trade and significant industrial and manufacturing activities have tended to adopt a single-point tax imposed only at one point. On the other hand, states with predominantly rural economies have generally adopted multi-point sales taxes. In the case of inter-state commerce, the sales tax is levied by the central government.

Revenue from import duties has been steadily increasing during the last few years. It rose from Rs 1077.0 million in 1950-51 to Rs 1788.5 million in 1961-62 (budget estimates). However, their relative importance as a source of revenue has markedly fallen, since in recent years greater reliance has been placed on central excise duties. Import duties are levied on several items of goods including both consumption and capital goods. Luxury consumption goods are taxed at penal rates.

Besides excise duties, general sales tax, and import duties, there are a few other taxes which are of relatively minor importance. Among them, sales tax on motor spirit and motor vehicles tax are the most prominent; their relative importance has been growing recently.

Trends in the Yields and Relative Importance of Central and State Taxes. We may conclude this chapter with a brief examination of the trend in revenue yields of the different taxes and also their relative places in the system of taxation. Table 1 shows the combined tax revenue receipts of the central and state governments for over a decade from 1950-51. We observe that the revenue from all the taxes listed in this table except wealth and gift taxes has recorded an increase during the period 1950-51 to 1961-62. The annual rate of increase in revenue has been negligible in respect of estate duty (0.6 per cent) and state excises (0.9 per cent). The increase in respect of expenditure tax (6.3 per cent), agricultural income tax (9.3 per cent), land revenue (8.4 per cent), import duties (5.5 per cent), entertainment

---

23 Reserve Bank of India, *Report on Currency and Finance*, 1961-62, Statement 57.

TABLE I

COMBINED TAX REVENUE RECEIPTS OF THE CENTRE AND THE STATES FOR THE PERIOD 1950-51 to 1961-62

(in million Rs)

Head of revenue	1950-51	1951-52	1952-53	1953-54	1954-55	1955-56
Agricultural income tax	40.9	43.3	40.6	37.7	47.7	57.4
Expenditure tax	—	—	—	—	—	—
Estate duty	—	—	—	—	—	18.1
Tax on wealth	—	—	—	—	—	—
Gift tax	—	—	—	—	—	—
Stamps and registration	275.0	274.4	273.2	292.0	286.7	298.3
Land revenue	515.8	508.4	578.4	714.9	730.3	812.1
Customs: import duties (gross)	1077.0	n.a.	1180.7	1196.0	1410.6	1279.8
Central excise duties	675.4	857.8	830.3	949.8	1082.2	1452.5
State excises	473.2	494.1	463.0	446.6	445.6	434.9
General sales tax	559.9	544.0	512.1	583.3	663.9	682.8
Sales tax on motor spirit	35.9	45.3	59.9	73.5	72.7	83.0
Motor vehicles taxes	87.5	100.9	116.5	136.7	136.7	143.9
Tax on railway fares	—	—	—	—	—	—
Entertainment tax	58.8	63.9	61.4	58.8	62.2	65.0
Electricity duties	31.3	33.9	34.2	47.6	52.4	56.3
TOTAL TAX REVENUE	6280.1	7410.4	6751.5	6780.3	7213.7	7610.0

TABLE I (Contd.)

Head of revenue	1956-57	1957-58	1958-59	1959-60	1960-61	1961-62
Agricultural income tax	57.3	78.0	84.2	89.2	84.8	86.7
Expenditure tax	—	—	6.4	7.9	9.0	8.0
Estate duty	21.1	23.1	27.0	29.1	30.0	30.0
Tax on wealth	—	70.4	96.7	121.1	75.0	70.0
Gift tax	—	—	9.8	8.1	8.0	8.0
Stamps and registration	320.7	364.0	389.4	440.4	445.2	476.0
Land revenue	932.0	880.7	923.8	957.5	985.5	1037.3
Customs: import duties (gross)	1405.2	1509.4	1165.3	1358.2	1468.8	1788.5
Central excise duties	1994.3	2736.2	3129.4	3606.5	3949.8	4371.4
State excises	427.6	460.2	469.4	496.0	495.9	524.0
General sales tax	706.6	1073.7	1116.8	1243.7	1339.1	1403.0
Sales tax on motor spirit	87.3	98.5	121.9	124.6	150.8	158.9
Motor vehicles tax	149.8	211.3	244.6	263.8	297.8	308.3
Tax on railway fares	—	48.1	108.8	130.6	137.5	—
Entertainment tax	65.3	85.6	106.5	113.2	115.5	122.9
Electricity duties	58.1	71.5	105.1	119.7	115.1	122.9
TOTAL TAX REVENUE	8604.9	10473.1	10901.2	12198.6	12910.9	13795.6

SOURCE: (1) Reserve Bank of India, *Report on Currency and Finance*, 1960-61, Statements 57 and 61. (2) Reserve Bank of India, *Report on Currency and Finance*, 1957-58, Statements 58 and 61. (3) Tripathy, *Fiscal Policy and Economic Development*, pp. 126-7.

NOTE: (1) The revenue figures for 1955-56 give the accounts for the Centre and revised budget estimates for the states. The 1956-57 figures give accounts for the Centre and budget estimates for the states. The 1960-61 figures for both the Centre and the states are revised budget estimates. The figures for 1961-62 represent budget estimates for both the Centre and the states. (2) — means the tax did not exist in that year. (3) n.a. means the figure is not available for that year.

TABLE 2

PERCENTAGE-WISE CONTRIBUTION OF INDIVIDUAL TAXES TO THE COMBINED TAX REVENUE OF THE CENTRAL AND STATE GOVERNMENTS, 1950-51 to 1961-62

Head of revenue	1950-51	1951-52	1952-53	1953-54	1954-55	1955-56
Agricultural income tax	0.65	0.58	0.60	0.56	0.66	0.75
Expenditure tax	—	—	—	—	—	—
Estate duty	—	—	—	—	—	—
Wealth tax	—	—	—	—	—	—
Gift tax	—	—	—	—	—	—
Stamps and registration	4.38	3.70	4.05	4.31	3.97	3.92
Land revenue	8.21	6.86	8.57	10.54	10.12	10.67
Customs: import duties	17.15	n.a.	17.49	17.64	19.55	16.82
Central excises	10.75	11.58	12.30	14.01	15.00	19.09
State excises	7.53	6.67	6.86	6.59	6.18	5.71
General sales tax	8.92	7.34	7.58	8.60	9.20	8.97
Sales tax on motor spirit	0.57	0.61	0.89	1.08	1.01	1.09
Motor vehicles tax	1.39	1.36	1.73	2.02	1.90	1.90
Tax on railway fares	—	—	—	—	—	—
Entertainment tax	0.94	0.86	0.91	0.87	0.86	0.85
Electricity duties	0.50	0.46	0.51	0.70	0.73	0.74

TABLE 2 (Contd.)

Head of revenue	1956-57	1957-58	1958-59	1959-60	1960-61	1961-62
Agricultural income tax	0.67	0.74	0.77	0.73	0.66	0.63
Expenditure tax	—	—	0.06	0.06	0.07	0.06
Estate duty	0.25	0.22	0.25	0.24	0.23	0.22
Wealth tax	—	0.67	0.89	0.99	0.58	0.51
Gift tax	—	—	0.09	0.07	0.06	0.06
Stamps and registration	3.73	3.48	3.57	3.61	3.45	3.45
Land revenue	10.83	8.41	8.47	7.85	7.63	7.52
Customs : import duties	16.33	14.41	10.69	11.13	11.38	12.96
Central excises	22.13	26.13	28.70	29.56	30.60	31.69
State excises	4.97	4.39	4.31	4.07	3.84	3.80
General sales tax	8.21	10.25	10.24	10.20	10.37	10.17
Sales tax on motor spirit	1.01	0.94	1.12	1.02	1.17	1.15
Motor vehicles tax	1.74	2.02	2.24	2.16	2.31	2.23
Tax on railway fares	—	0.46	1.00	1.07	1.06	—
Entertainment tax	0.76	0.82	0.98	0.93	0.89	0.89
Electricity duty	0.68	0.68	0.96	0.98	0.89	0.89

NOTE: This table is based on Table 1.

tax (9.1 per cent), and stamps and registration (6.1 per cent) is quite substantial. The most spectacular growth in revenue, however, has been in the case of central excise duties (45.6 per cent), the general sales tax (12.6 per cent), sales tax on motor spirit (28.6 per cent), tax on railway fares (46.5 per cent), electricity duty (24.4 per cent), and motor vehicles tax (21.0 per cent). If we leave out the tax on railway fares which was abolished four years after its introduction, the most impressive growth has been in the case of central excise duties. In fact, central excise duties have emerged as the most important tax in India during the last decade. Receipts from this item accounted for 37.1 per cent of the combined tax revenue of the central and state governments in the budget estimates for 1961-62. There is no other tax in India which is even a close second to the central excise duties.

We may also examine the relative importance of the different taxes. The percentage-wise contribution of each tax to the combined tax revenue of the central and state governments is presented in Table 2. We observe that the relative contributions of agricultural income tax, expenditure tax, estate duty, wealth tax, gift tax, stamps and registration, land revenue, general sales tax, entertainment tax, and electricity duties have remained more or less the same over the period 1950-51 to 1961-62. The relative importance of import duties and state excise taxes has greatly declined during the same period. Finally, central excise duties, sales tax on motor spirit, and motor vehicles tax have grown considerably in their relative contributions.

CHAPTER III

BURDEN OF AGRICULTURAL TAXATION

No study of taxation is complete without an inquiry into its burden. As the Harvard Conference on Agricultural Taxation (1954) emphasized, "A study of incidence is considered a necessary first step in any broader analysis of taxation effects, be it in connection with incentives, resource transfers, taxable capacity, or equity."[1] Unless one knows how lightly or how heavily agriculture is taxed, one cannot offer any policy recommendations for the improvement of the agricultural tax system.

In the case of India, as the Taxation Enquiry Commission (1953-54) pointed out, there has been no comprehensive inquiry into the burden of taxation.[2] This is especially true of the agricultural sector. The Taxation Enquiry Commission itself made some estimates,[3] but they were of a very rough and incomplete nature. The study of the burden of taxation, however, is "one of the most complicated subjects in economic science."[4] As in the case of most underdeveloped economies, the paucity of adequate data is an extremely serious handicap facing any research worker undertaking such a study on India. Officially published data are too aggregative to be readily used. Besides the official statistics, the only other information available is that provided by the National Sample Survey in their studies on consumer expenditure pattern. Even these data need to be processed further before they could be used in the study of incidence. Moreover, they suffer from several limitations arising from the direct interview method on a national scale and from the

---

1 Harvard Law School, International Program in Taxation, *Papers and Proceedings of the Conference on Agricultural Taxation and Economic Development,* January-February 1954 (Cambridge, Mass.: Harvard University Press, 1954), p. 51.

2 Government of India, Ministry of Finance, *Report of the Taxation Enquiry Commission,* 1953-54 (New Delhi: Government of India Press, 1955), Vol. I, p. 45.

3 *Ibid.,* pp. 63-81.

4 Edwin R.A. Seligman, *The Shifting and Incidence of Taxation* (New York: Columbia University Press, 1932), p. 1.

general underdevelopment of the economy.[5] However, the National Sample Survey data are the only comprehensive and reliable information available to us. Hence, we may be justified in making the best possible use of them, being at the same time aware of their imperfections and limitations.

As will be clear from the following discussion on definitions and concepts, the term "incidence" has different meanings for different economists. To avoid any likely confusion, we may instead use the term "burden of taxation" which refers to the "social accounting calculation of the proportion of people's incomes paid over to taxing authorities in a defined period."[6] In this chapter we shall try to estimate the burden of agricultural taxation in India.

DEFINITIONS AND CONCEPTS

(1) *Incidence.* Edwin R. A. Seligman makes a distinction between the shifting of a tax and its incidence. The person who originally pays the tax may not be the one who bears its burden finally. This process of the transfer of a tax is called the "shifting of the tax," while the settlement of the burden on the ultimate taxpayer is called the "incidence of the tax."[7] Whenever the total tax is shifted, there is no incidence on the person who pays it initially; there is only an "impact" of the tax. Thus, according to Seligman, we have here three concepts—the impact, the shifting, and the incidence of a tax, which correspond respectively to the imposition, the transfer, and the settling or coming to rest of the tax. Seligman warns that impact should not be confused with incidence.

Bent Hansen has called the above approach the "neo-classical partial incidence theory."[8] In his words:

It is based on the usual partial theory of price formation. The shape of the demand and supply curves (cost curves) is decisive for the extent to which the tax in question leads to an increase in price, and also for the other effects of the tax (capitalization of the tax, etc.).[9]

5 *Taxation Enquiry Commission Report,* Vol. I, p. 48.

6 Ursula K. Hicks, "The Terminology of Tax Analysis," in American Economic Association, *Readings in the Economics of Taxation* (Homewood, Illinois: Richard D. Irwin, Inc., 1959), p. 225.   7 Seligman, *op. cit.*, p. 1.

8 Bent Hansen, *The Economic Theory of Fiscal Policy* (English edition) (London: Allen and Unwin, Ltd., 1958), pp. 90-100.   9 *Ibid.*, p. 90.

Hansen does not agree with the narrow sense in which the term "incidence" is used by the neo-classical economists. The latter make a distinction between the incidence of taxes and their effects. To quote Seligman:

> A tax may have a great many effects. It may diminish industry and impoverish individuals; it may be an unmitigated curse to society; it may be a necessary evil; it may be an unqualified boon to the community regarded as a whole.... With the wider questions of the general effects of taxation the student of incidence does not primarily busy himself.... The shifting is the process; the incidence is the result; the changes in the distribution of wealth are the effects.[10]

To avoid the anomaly of having to make a distinction between the incidence and "other" effects of the tax, Bent Hansen suggests that we can speak of incidence in a more general sense meaning the "effect of a certain fiscal policy measure, other things being equal, upon the real incomes in society in the long or short run."[11]

Richard Musgrave follows more or less the same approach as Bent Hansen. Musgrave interprets incidence as the "change in distribution that results from particular changes in budget policy."[12] Having defined incidence thus, Musgrave goes on to define what is meant by change in distribution. In any exchange economy, each individual is linked with the market in two ways. He is affected on the "sources" side through the price he obtains from the sale of his services; and on the "uses" side he is affected through the price he must pay for the products he buys. When a change in budget policy is made, he may find his position changed on both sides of his accounts. Depending on the particular case, one or the other change may be more important. In a community composed of many individuals, however, it is neither feasible nor necessary to develop a measure of change in the state of distribution that allows for changes in the position of each individual. Hence, Musgrave suggests, some grouping must be made. The question is how the relevant groups should be defined. The classical economists followed the grouping based on distributive shares or types of factor incomes. Musgrave argues that,

10 Seligman, *op. cit.,* p. 14.

11 Hansen, *op. cit.,* p. 93.

12 Richard A. Musgrave, *The Theory of Public Finance* (New York: McGraw-Hill Book Company, Inc., 1959), p. 217.

with the development of a more generalized theory of factor pricing, the distinction between particular shares has lost much of its analytical sharpness. Also, the social significance of distribution by factor shares has declined. For example, incomes from labour broadly defined accrue to recipients at high as well as low points in the income scale, and there is a growing tendency for people to receive incomes from a variety of sources.[13] Accordingly, Musgrave defines incidence as referring to changes in the distribution of income by size brackets and not by factor shares.

Before we proceed further with the discussion of incidence, let us pause for a moment and examine briefly which grouping is relevant for India. For a country like the United States there is certainly considerable merit and substance in Musgrave's reasoning. In the United States one comes across very rich landowners as well as very poor, very well-to-do skilled workers as also labourers who earn very little. The classification of recipients of income into landowners and labourers, for example, does not have any precise meaning in such a context. On the other hand, it is not entirely so in an economy like that of India. India is going through a period of economic transition at present. Up till recently, the landlord class used to be very prosperous. With the nationwide land reform legislation the situation has changed considerably. The process of implementation of land reforms being not yet complete, there is still some relevance for a grouping on the basis of distributive shares. Also, the economically deplorable condition of agricultural labour, the majority of whom are landless, adds strength to this approach. Under the circumstances, there is some logic in favour of both the approaches, namely, grouping of the agricultural population on the basis of distributive shares and grouping on the basis of income by size brackets. It may be noted that the Taxation Enquiry Commission appointed by the Government of India in April 1953 to conduct a comprehensive inquiry into taxation considered the income basis more relevant. The Commission said:

> The occupational group, however, does not form a homogeneous economic class by income, and, therefore, does not indicate ability to pay tax. There is little in common, for example, from the point of view of tax policy between an owner cultivator with an annual

13 Note that Musgrave has in mind primarily conditions in the United States or probably Western Europe. What he says about distributive shares may not be completely applicable to India.

family income, say, of less than Rs 500 and another with such income above Rs 3000.... The fundamental basis of classification of the population relevant to a study of tax incidence, we believe, therefore, is income.[14]

To the extent the available data permit, we shall try to have both the approaches, since it will give a global picture of the agricultural sector.

To go back to our main line of discussion, what precise meaning shall we give to the concept of incidence—the Seligman approach or Hansen-Musgrave approach? While we are interested in the shifting and incidence of a tax in the Seligman sense, the most important and crucial question is how a tax affects the different parts of the economy, and what is the final result. The dilemma is solved by Musgrave himself. He has "rehabilitated" the concept of shifting by endowing it with a somewhat different meaning. He distinguishes between "effective incidence" and "impact" incidence. Effective incidence refers to "the actual change in distribution that results as a given tax is imposed or tax substitution is made";[15] impact incidence refers to "the change that would result if the income position of a new tax-payer were reduced by the amount of tax addition, or if the income position of a former taxpayer were improved by the amount of tax remission, while the positions of all others remained unchanged." [16] Impact incidence is on whoever is liable for payment under the law; if the seller can raise his price or cut other factor payments, effective incidence differs from impact incidence and shifting has occurred. In the case of a sales tax, for example, if the tax is paid by the consumer of the goods, according to our definitions, the impact incidence is on the seller since he is liable for payment of the sales tax under the law, and the effective incidence is on the consumer or the buyer of the article.

At this stage of our discussion we may introduce a third concept relating to incidence, namely, "formal incidence." The term has been used by Ursula Hicks in bringing out the distinction between formal incidence and effective incidence. She defines formal incidence as "the proportion of people's incomes which goes not to provide the incomes of those who furnish them with goods and services, but is paid

---

14 Government of India (Ministry of Finance), *op. cit.*, p. 46.
15 Musgrave, *op. cit.*, p. 230.
16 *Ibid.*

over to governing bodies to finance collective satisfactions."[17] The same idea is conveyed in a more straightforward and explicit fashion by the Taxation Enquiry Commission. They define formal incidence as "the money burden of taxes as resting with the subject on whom the burden is *intended* by the taxing authority to fall; the amount paid in tax is thus measured as per cent of income of different income groups."[18] Underlying this definition is the assumption that the incidence of direct taxes rests with those who initially pay the tax, while that of indirect taxes is borne by consumers of taxed commodities. It is obvious that the concept of formal incidence thus defined is different from the concept of impact incidence as defined by Musgrave. If we may put it so, formal incidence is an advance step from impact incidence. As far as the concept of effective incidence is concerned, there is very little difference between Musgrave's definition and that of Ursula Hicks. She says:

In order to discover the full economic consequences of a tax we have to draw and compare two pictures—one of the economic set-up (distribution of consumers' wants and incomes, and allocation of factors), as it is with the tax in question in operation; the other of a similar economic set-up, but without the tax. It is convenient to call the difference between these two pictures the Effective Incidence of the tax.[19]

In this study we shall be mainly concerned with the burden of taxation of the agricultural sector in the sense of formal incidence of taxation. The reason for focusing attention on formal incidence is that we are interested in arriving at a quantitative estimate of the burden of taxation. As we have noted earlier, effective incidence cannot be statistically calculated. The concept of effective incidence is analytical. As Ursula Hicks points out, "The analytical concept is essentially hypothetical. It is a comparison of two complete economic situations, one with a particular tax in force, the other without it. One of these set-ups will normally be imaginary, although statistical data on past changes are not entirely lacking."[20] On the other

---

17 Ursula K. Hicks, *Public Finance* (Cambridge: Cambridge University Press, 1946), p. 158.

18 Government of India (Ministry of Finance), *op. cit.*, p. 45.

19 Hicks, *Public Finance*, p. 159.

20 Hicks, *Readings in the Economics of Taxation*, pp. 224-5.

hand, formal incidence which is "the social accounting calculation of the proportion of people's incomes paid over to taxing authorities in a defined period"[21] can be measured with a fair degree of statistical accuracy and completeness. Therefore, as far as measurement is concerned, we shall measure formal incidence; for the rest, we shall try to draw whatever conclusions we can about effective incidence.

(2) *Gross and Net Burden of Taxation.* The government is not only a revenue-raising authority, but also a revenue-spending institution. If the agriculturists only paid taxes but did not receive anything back from the government, their gross and net burden of taxation would be equal. But in actual practice the government, through public expenditure and transfer payments, returns a part of the revenue to them. Thus, in estimating the net burden of the taxation of agriculture, we have to deduct from the gross burden the benefits which the agricultural sector receives from the government.

Walter Heller has aptly made a distinction between negative taxes and positive taxes.[22] Negative taxes represent the benefits enjoyed by the taxpayers, and positive taxes mean taxes in the ordinary sense. He points out:

> To determine the net fiscal burden or advantage of the agricultural sector clearly requires that "negative taxes" and related measures be taken into account side by side with positive taxes and related measures. Thus, transfer payments in the form of relief, social security and similar government disbursements to the agricultural population enter the balance.[23]

In this study we shall attempt to estimate both the gross and net fiscal burdens of the agricultural sector.

(3) *Producers' Taxes and Consumers' Taxes.* There are certain taxes which the agriculturists pay in their capacity as producers. Agricultural income tax is a typical example. Land revenue, if based on produce, is another example. On the other hand, there are several taxes which agriculturists pay irrespective of whether they are producers or not. These taxes are paid by the agriculturists in their role as consumers of goods and services. Sales tax is a good example of such a tax. In estimating the tax burden of the agricultural sector, we shall include all the taxes paid by the agricultural sector—those

21 *Ibid.*, p. 224.
22 Harvard Law School, *Papers and Proceedings*, pp. 117-71.
23 *Ibid.*, p. 130.

taxes paid by the agriculturists as producers and those paid as consumers.

ESTIMATES OF AGRICULTURAL TAX BURDEN

Measurement of Tax Burden

There are three measures of tax burden, namely: (1) total tax collection, (2) per capita tax, and (3) tax as a per cent of income. At a later stage in our study we shall compare the tax burden of the agricultural sector with that of the nonagricultural. Wherever possible we shall also be interested in comparing the agricultural tax burden of one state with that of others.

It would be beyond the scope of a study like this to estimate the burden of each individual tax, of which there are many, for a number of years. We do not have adequate data relating to all the important variables for a number of years. Hence for the purpose of this study the year 1958-59 is chosen. It seems to be the most suitable period from the point of view of availability of information. The year refers to the fiscal year which is a twelve-month period from April 1 to March 31.

Burden of Direct Taxes on Agriculture

(1) *Land Revenue.* Land revenue is as important to the agricultural sector as income tax is to the nonagricultural. Before we can have an estimate of the burden of land revenue, we need to undertake certain preliminary calculations. The 1961 census data provide us with the rate of growth of the population for the whole of India and for each state during the decade 1951-61. Assuming that the rate of growth of population has been uniform over the entire decade, we could estimate the population for 1958-59 through interpolation, for all India as well as for each state. The 1961 census provides also the statewise and national distribution of rural and urban population. The proportion of rural population in the nation decreased from 82.62 per cent of the total population in 1951 to 82.16 per cent in 1961. There has been, thus, a slight decline in the proportion of rural population. Assuming that the decline has been uniformly spread over the decade, we could estimate the proportion of rural population for 1958-59 through interpolation. We may also assume that there has been a similar decline in the proportion of rural population in each state. Further we assume that the proportion of agricultural population in total population remained roughly constant at 69.85 per cent throughout the decade. Finally, we assume that 10 per cent of the

urban population derive their main income from agriculture. This assumption is made on the basis of the finding of the Rural Credit Survey in 1954 that 12 per cent of the urban population were agriculturists.[24] For the purpose of our calculations we assume that, as a result of land reforms, this proportion has declined to 10 per cent. On these grounds, we have estimated the agricultural population of India and of each state for the year 1958-59.[25] Table 3 presents the burden of land revenue for the year 1958-59.

For the whole of India, including the state of Jammu and Kashmir and territories under the direct administration of the Government of India, per capita land revenue in 1958-59 was Rs 3.16. Among the states, the per capita burden varied from Rs 1.41 in Kerala to Rs 4.88 in Rajasthan. The national average of per capita land revenue formed 1.5 per cent of per capita income. For states, the proportion varied from 0.7 per cent in Punjab to 2.7 per cent in Rajasthan. Viewed against the fact that land revenue is the most important direct tax on agriculture, the national average of 1.5 per cent is too small.

Land revenue is a tax levied on agricultural land and is supposed to be paid out of the yield from cultivating the land. Hence, it may be interesting to find out the burden of land revenue per acre of sown area.

Land revenue per acre of net sown area for the whole of India in 1958-59 was Rs 2.85. The per acre burden of states varied from Rs 1.73 in the case of Orissa to Rs 5.82 in Bihar. It is, however, important to note that, since the net sown area does not include the area under tree crops and groves, the per acre land revenue figures we have calculated are overstated. Further, if we include all land which could be utilized for one purpose or another, the per acre burden of land revenue will be still smaller.

(2) *Agricultural Income Tax.* All the states of the Indian Union with the exception of Punjab and Gujarat levy a tax on agricultural

24 Reserve Bank of India, *All India Rural Credit Survey,* Vol. II, *The General Report* (Bombay, 1954), p. 20.

25 We may present the population distribution of India (percentage-wise) for the year 1958-59 in the form of a "contingency" table as follows:

	Agricultural	Nonagricultural	Total
Rural	68.081	14.190	82.271
Urban	1.773	15.956	17.000
TOTAL	69.854	30.146	100.000

TABLE 3
BURDEN OF LAND REVENUE, 1958-59

State	Estimated agricultural population (millions)	Per capita land revenue [a] (in Rs)	Per capita income [b] (in Rs)	Per capita land revenue as percentage of per capita income
Andhra Pradesh	24.4346	3.413	205.94	1.66
Assam	8.7118	2.823	256.84	1.10
Bihar	33.8737	3.381	177.88	1.90
Bombay	36.7352	3.642	150.49	2.42
Kerala	11.6396	1.405	125.77	1.12
Madhya Pradesh	22.0859	3.797	273.39	1.39
Madras	21.0067	2.290	175.39	1.31
Mysore	14.7106	2.991	156.24	1.27
Orissa	13.5100	1.774	151.01	1.18
Punjab	12.8302	2.903	414.82	0.70
Rajasthan	13.5182	4.880	179.73	2.72
Uttar Pradesh	52.5007	3.527	233.01	1.51
West Bengal	21.7136	3.091	210.02	1.47
INDIA	292.2124	3.161	213.54	1.48

SOURCE: (1) Government of India (Publications Division, Ministry of Information and Broadcasting), *India* 1959 (Delhi: National Printing Works, 1959), pp. 400-67. (2) Reserve Bank of India, *Report on Currency and Finance*, 1961-62 (Bombay, 1962), Statements 56 and 60. (3) *Reserve Bank of India Bulletin*, June 1961, p. 901. (4) K. N. Raj, "Some Features of Economic Growth of the Last Decade in India," *Economic Weekly* (February 4, 1961), p. 265.

NOTE: (a) The land revenue figures for the states represent "Revised budget estimates." Figures of actual receipts (accounts) could not be had. This, however, is not a serious deficiency since usually the actual receipts differ from the revised budget estimates by less than one per cent. The land revenue figures for all India represent actual receipts.

(b) Per capita income is derived by dividing total income (net) from agriculture by the agricultural population. This procedure, though widely followed by economists and statisticians in India, is not quite valid because the agriculturists may derive part of their income from nonagriculture. (Definitionally, a person is an agriculturist if he derives more than 50 per cent of his income from agriculture.) Thus the income from agriculture is not the same as the agriculturists' income, the latter includes nonagricultural incomes also. However, in the absence of any better estimates, we may adopt the usual method, assuming that the agriculturists' nonagricultural income offsets the nonagriculturists' agricultural income.

income. Unlike in the case of land revenue, not all agriculturists who are owners of land pay an agricultural income tax; only those who

TABLE 4
BURDEN OF LAND REVENUE PER ACRE OF SOWN AREA, 1958-59

State	Land revenue (revised budget estimates) (million Rs)	Total cropped area (million acres)	Net area sown (million acres)	Land revenue per acre of net sown area (Rs)
Andhra Pradesh	83.400	29.872	27.302	3.05
Assam	24.596	6.003	5.118	4.81
Bihar	114.528	27.378	19.690	5.82
Bombay	133.783	70.673	67.438	1.98
Kerala	16.357	5.537	4.587	3.57
Madhya Pradesh	83.850	43.813	38.790	2.16
Madras	48.110	17.097	14.326	3.36
Mysore	44.000	26.031	25.142	1.75
Orissa	23.973	14.958	13.854	1.73
Punjab	37.252	24.527	18.488	2.01
Rajasthan	65.972	33.921	31.104	2.12
Uttar Pradesh	185.149	53.794	42.122	4.40
West Bengal	67.111	15.055	12.929	3.19
INDIA	923.800	372.762	324.123	2.85

SOURCE: (1) *Agricultural Situation in India* (November 1962), pp. 886-9. (2) Government of India, *India 1959*, pp. 400-67. (3) Reserve Bank of India, *Report on Currency and Finance*, 1961-62, Statements 56 and 60.

NOTE: (1) Land revenue figures for the states refer to revised budget estimates and for India to actual receipts.

(2) It will be noticed that there is a difference between total cropped area and net area sown. This arises from the fact that some lands are sown more than once a year. Net sown area—total cropped area—area sown more than once.

(3) It is important to note that the net sown area does not include land under miscellaneous tree crops and groves, which are an important source of income to the farmers in many states. In 1958-59, such lands amounted to 14.105 million acres for the whole of India.

earn not less than a certain minimum income, say, Rs 3500 a year, have to pay this tax. Obviously, such people form a very small proportion of the total agricultural population. Moreover, because of the problems involved in the enforcement of the tax, many agriculturists who ought to be paying this tax in virtue of their income do evade it. We shall return to this problem later. The burden of agricultural income is presented in Table 5.

For the whole country per capita agricultural income tax amounted to Rs 0.29 only in 1958-59. This certainly is an extremely negligible burden. Compared to the national average, the per capita burden of agricultural income tax was much higher in Assam (Rs 1.65), Kerala (Rs 1.99), Madras (Rs 0.84), and Mysore (Rs 0.54). However, in Andhra Pradesh, Bihar, Madhya Pradesh, Orissa, and Rajasthan, it was negligible, varying from Rs 0.01 to Rs 0.03. The rest of the states occupied an intermediate position.

TABLE 5
BURDEN OF AGRICULTURAL INCOME TAX, 1958-59

State	*Total revenue*	*Per capita tax (Rs)*	*Per capita tax as percentage of per capita income*
Andhra Pradesh	0.50	0.020	0.10
Assam	14.40	1.653	0.64
Bihar	0.90	0.027	0.20
Bombay	—	—	—
Kerala	23.10	1.985	1.58
Madhya Pradesh	0.30	0.014	0.01
Madras	17.70	0.843	0.48
Mysore	8.00	0.544	0.35
Orissa	0.40	0.030	0.02
Punjab	—	—	—
Rajasthan	0.40	0.030	0.02
Uttar Pradesh	6.80	0.130	0.06
West Bengal	7.30	0.336	0.16
INDIA	84.20	0.288	0.13

SOURCE: *Reserve Bank of India Bulletin* (May 1958), pp. 512-6.

NOTE: (1) Total revenue figures for the states represent budget estimates and that for India, actual receipts. Figures for actual receipts of the states are not available. (2) No agricultural income tax existed in Bombay and Punjab during 1958-59.

Agricultural income tax formed only 0.13 per cent of income for the entire country in 1958-59. Most states—Uttar Pradesh, Rajasthan, Orissa, Madhya Pradesh, Bihar, and Andhra Pradesh—showed a percentage even lower. Only in one state, Kerala, was the percentage higher than one. Thus, in none of the states with the possible exception of Kerala could the percentage be said to be significant.

BURDEN OF NONAGRICULTURAL DIRECT TAXES

These taxes include expenditure tax, estate duty, wealth tax, gift tax, and stamps and registration. In estimating the burden of these levies we are faced with a difficult problem. The problem is: how much of the revenue from these taxes should be attributed to the agricultural sector and how much to the nonagricultural? Published (official) data provide us with only the total revenue figures for each tax. Obviously, there is no easy way of splitting them between the two sectors. Faced with this problem, we could, however, think of at least three alternative methods of splitting the revenue between the two sectors in respect of the first four taxes—expenditure tax, estate duty, wealth tax, and gift tax. First, we could distribute the revenue from these taxes between the two sectors on the basis of population. This is a very unsatisfactory method for obvious reasons. Second, the revenue could be apportioned between the agricultural and nonagricultural sectors in the ratio of the total income of the two sectors. This is a better procedure than the first, but not quite satisfactory since the total income of a sector is no accurate indication of how much tax it pays. This is because the exemption limits of these taxes are so high that only the very rich people are liable to pay these taxes.[26] A third alternative is to apportion the revenue between the two sectors in the ratio of the income of the upper-income groups within the farm and nonfarm households. This seems to be the most satisfactory method and hence we shall adopt this procedure for our purpose. It should, however, be pointed out that even this method is not completely satisfactory since none of the above taxes are based on incomes. But it is somewhat logical to assume that income is a good index of wealth. Similarly, it is more probable that people with higher incomes incur more expenditure than those with lower incomes and thus become liable to pay expenditure tax. Also it is not illogical to assume that the high-income groups make large gifts and not the low-income groups. In any case, in the absence of any better data, we have to rely on this method as the best approximation.

The data used for this method are taken from a study published by the Reserve Bank of India.[27] According to this study, during the period 1953-54 to 1956-57, the farm high-income group had an average total income (at current prices) of Rs 5670 million and the

26 An individual taxpayer has to spend a minimum of Rs 40000 on consumption expenditure in order to become liable to pay expenditure tax, has to pass on at least Rs 50000 (net) worth of property to make the successors liable for the estate duty, has to own wealth worth at least Rs 200000 to become liable for wealth tax, and has to make gifts worth at least Rs 50000 to be liable to pay gift tax. For "Hindu Un-divided" families the exemption limits are higher.

27 *Reserve Bank of India Bulletin* (September 1962), "Distribution of Income in the Indian Economy 1953-54 to 1956-57," pp. 1348-63.

nonfarm high-income group Rs 14570 million. Assuming that this ratio holds good for the year 1958-59 we may distribute the burden of these taxes between the agricultural and the nonagricultural sector in the ratio of the total incomes of the high-income farm households and the high-income nonfarm households. This is presented in Table 6.

TABLE 6

BURDEN OF NONAGRICULTURAL DIRECT TAXES, 1958-59

Type of tax	Total revenue (Rs million)	Share of agricultural sector (Rs million)	Per capita tax (Rs)	Per capita tax as percentage of per capita income
Expenditure tax	6.4	1.7929		
Estate duty	27.0	7.5651		
Wealth tax	96.7	27.0944		
Gift tax	9.8	2.7459		
TOTAL	139.9	39.1983	0.1341	0.063

SOURCE: (1) *Reserve Bank of India Bulletin* (September 1962), p. 1357. (2) Reserve Bank of India, *Report on Currency and Finance*, 1961-62, Statement 56.

We find that the per capita burden of the other direct taxes on the agricultural sector was only Rs 0.13 in 1958-59. This constitutes roughly 0.1 per cent of the sector's per capita income. Clearly the burden of these taxes on the agricultural sector is extremely negligible.

Among the nonagricultural direct taxes we have to consider the burden of one more tax, namely, stamps and registration. This is a tax on property and capital transactions. This levy does not fall on any one particular income group. Even transactions which involve nominal amounts have to bear a certain registration or stamp fee in order that the transaction may be legal. To give one simple example, the recipient of any payment over Rs 20 has to sign a receipt on which a "revenue" stamp of appropriate value is affixed so that the receipt may acquire legality. Because of the wider applicability of this tax, we cannot apply the technique which we used in the case of expenditure tax, wealth tax, etc.

How shall, then, we distribute the burden of "stamps and registration" between the two sectors? First, it seemed that, on the whole, more urbanized states had a higher per capita tax from this source. The states in which the three major cities of Bombay, Madras, and Calcutta are located showed a much higher per capita tax (see Table 1). In order to see how far this initial impression was correct, we tested if there was any correlation between the two variables. It was found that there is a significant[28] positive correlation (r–0.829) between them. A straight line relationship appeared adequate on the basis of the chart (see Fig. 1). Thus it was thought appropriate to distribute the tax between the urban and rural sectors on the basis of the linear regression[29]

$$t = a + bp_u$$

(where t = per capita tax and p_u = proportion of urban population), which when fitted gave

$$t = 0.178 + 3.819\, p_u.$$

Let us assume that this relationship is due almost entirely to the differential tax load of the two sectors. Now, when $a = t_r$ (rural per capita tax) and $b = t_u$ (i.e. urban per capita tax) $- t_r$, the above equation becomes an identity, $t = t_r + (t_u - t_r)p_u$, for each state with unknown parameters t_r and t_u. For each individual state and for the whole country, there is a particular set of numerical values for t_r and t_u which preserve this identity exactly. Our case for fitting the equation to cross-section data rests on the assumption that the ratio between t_r and t_u is approximately constant from state to state. In other words, the "structural relation" is assumed approximately constant, i.e. we are assuming that the entire pattern of the relationship between t and p_u can be adequately explained by a single pair of values for t_r and t_u. It may be pointed out that this failure to include other variables (such as per capita income) explicitly may introduce some bias in our estimate of the aggregate relationship.

Let us now proceed to make an estimate of the ratio in which the total tax burden may be distributed between the rural and urban sectors. In our estimated linear regression, if we assume the proportion of urban population to be zero, we get the rural tax rate as 0.178. This figure could be interpreted as the rural tax rate precisely because we assume that the ratio between the rural and urban tax rates is more or less constant for each state. Similarly, if we assume the proportion of urban population to be one, we get the urban per capita rate as 3.997. Thus we can estimate the rural and urban per capita tax rates

28 Using Fisher's "Z" transformation, the correlation coefficient was found to be significant at a confidence level of almost 100 per cent.

29 A linear fit is quite appropriate since the standard error of estimate is only 0.0518 which is 16.9 per cent of the standard deviation of Y.

for each state from the following formula:[30] $t = t_r + (t_u - t_r)p_u$

which can be rewritten[30] as $t_r = \dfrac{t}{(l - P_8) + Rp_u}$

where R refers to $\dfrac{t_u}{t_r}$, and $t_u = Rt_r$.

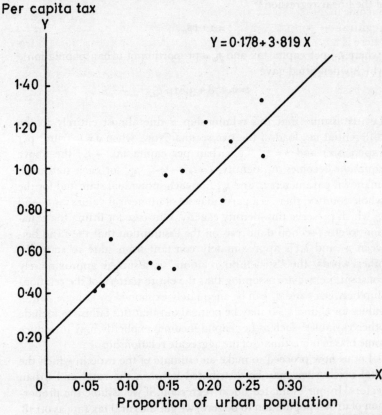

Per capita tax

$Y = 0\cdot178 + 3\cdot819\,X$

Fig. 1. Distribution of the Tax Burden of "Stamps and Registration," Model I

30 The steps are as follows:
$$t = t_r + t_u p_u - t_r p_u$$
$$= t_r - t_r p_u + t_r p_u$$
$$= t_r(l - p_u) + t_u p_u$$
$$= t_r(l - p_u) + Rt_r p_u$$

Therefore $\dfrac{t}{t_r} = (l - p_u) + R\,p_u;$ i.e. $t = [(l - p_u) + R\,p_u]\,t_r$

$$t_r = \dfrac{t}{[l - p_u + R\,p_u]}$$

Besides the above model, also a second model was constructed. It was found, from the revenue data, that states with a larger agricultural income relative to nonagricultural income showed a lower proportion of tax in total income. This observation suggested that there is a negative relationship between the proportion of agricultural income in the total income and the proportion of tax (from stamps and registration) in total income, in each state. Therefore, it was tested if there is any significant correlation between the two variables. It was found that there is a significant[31] negative correlation ($r=-0.718$) between the two. A linear relationship appeared to be adequate on the basis of Fig. 2. The linear regression $\dfrac{T}{Y} = a + b\,\dfrac{Y_a}{Y}$

(where T = total tax, Y = total income, and Y_a = income of the agri-

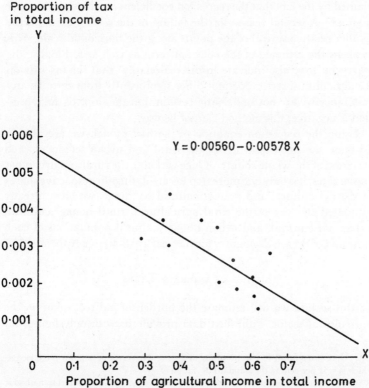

Fig. 2. Distribution of the Tax Burden of "Stamps and Registration," Model II

---

31 Using Fisher's Z-transformation, the correlation coefficient was found to be significant at a confidence level of almost 100 per cent.

cultural sector) when fitted[32] gave

$$\frac{T}{Y} = 0.00560 - 0.00578 \frac{Y_a}{Y}.$$

Now, when $a = \frac{T_{na}}{Y_{na}}$ (where T_{na} = tax of the nonagricultural sector and Y_{na} = income of the nonagricultural sector), and $b = \frac{T_a}{Y_a} - \frac{T_{na}}{Y_{na}}$ (where T_a = total tax of the agricultural sector, and Y_a = total income of the agricultural sector), the above equation becomes an identity,

$$\frac{T}{Y} = \frac{T_{na}}{Y_{na}} + \left(\frac{T_a}{Y_a} - \frac{T_{na}}{Y_{na}}\right) \frac{Y_a}{Y}$$

for each state. This model, however, could not be used for our purpose since the proportion $\frac{T_a}{Y_a}$ turned out to be negative. This result is explained by the fact that the regression coefficient b (with sign) is larger than a.[33] A second reason for the failure of the second model is the smaller relative spread of the points along the horizontal scale. This weakens the estimate of the constant term as well as b. Finally, the regression may also indicate (quite reasonably) that the tax rate on the agricultural sector does not differ significantly from zero. In any case, since we are not sufficiently certain that the slope of the regression is negative, this method cannot be used.

Using the regression equation of the first model, we are able to estimate the per capita tax of the rural and urban sectors of each state and of the whole country. Once we know the rural and urban per capita rates, it is only one more step to calculating the respective shares of the agricultural and nonagricultural sectors as we have already estimated the size of the rural agricultural, rural nonagricultural, urban agricultural, and urban nonagricultural populations of each state and of the whole country for the year 1958-59 (see Appendix II).

BURDEN OF INDIRECT TAXES

In this section we will estimate the burden of indirect taxes on the agricultural sector. Published data provide us with only figures for

---

32 Here also a linear fit is appropriate as the standard error of estimate is 0.0000520 which is 5.74 per cent of the standard deviation of $\frac{T}{Y}$.

33 The statistical failure of this method, however, does not mean that this method is unsound. But the standard error of the regression coefficient, b, was found to be 0.00409, which means that at 99 per cent confidence level the limits of b will be $+0.009966$ and -0.02152. Further, the slope can be considered to be negative only with a confidence level of 92.0 per cent.

TABLE 7
BURDEN OF "STAMPS AND REGISTRATION," 1958-59

Tax item	Total revenue (in million Rs)	Share of agricultural sector (in million Rs)	Per capita tax of agricultural sector (Rs)	Tax as per cent of agricultural income
Stamps and Registration:				
Central	34.1	7.652		
States	355.3	79.733		
TOTAL	389.4	87.385	0.299	0.14

NOTE: The regression was based on "revised budget estimate" figures for each state. The total revenue figure for the entire revenue from this source, however, is the actual or "accounts." Hence the "account figure" was split between the two sectors in the same ratio as we derive from the regression. The accounts figures are taken from Reserve Bank of India, *Report on Currency and Finance,* 1961-62, Statements 56 and 60.

the whole economy and not for each sector of the economy separately. We are, thus, again faced with the problem of apportioning the tax burden between the agricultural and the nonagricultural sector. However, we are in a much better position in respect of indirect taxes than we were in the preceding section where we dealt with direct taxes. Since the commodity taxes are assumed to fall on the consumers of the taxed commodities and services, we can apportion the tax burden between the two sectors in proportion to the expenditures of the two sectors. To do so we need data on the consumption expenditure pattern of the two sectors. They are furnished in the reports of the National Sample Survey (NSS). The National Sample Survey has conducted several rounds of study on consumer expenditure in India. For our purpose we will use the findings of the Fourth Round (April-September 1952).[34] The reasons for choosing the findings of the Fourth Round in preference to those of other rounds, as well as the nature and limitations of the National Sample Survey data, are given in Appendix I. How the National Sample Survey data have been used in this study to arrive at the proportions in which the burden of each commodity tax is distributed between the two sectors also is discussed in the same appendix.

We are estimating the burden of agricultural taxation for the year 1958-59 with the aid of consumer expenditure data relating to the

34 The National Sample Survey, Fourth Round: April-September 1952, No. 18, *Tables with Notes on Consumer Expenditure,* issued by the Cabinet Secretariat, Government of India (Calcutta: Eka Press, 1959).

period April-September 1952. In doing so, we assume that there was no significant change in the pattern of consumer expenditure between the two periods, i.e. we assume that the relative proportions in which the households distributed their consumption expenditure between various goods and services remained roughly the same between the two periods.

The National Sample Survey report deals with consumer expenditure pattern of the rural and the urban households. Using this information, we shall first apportion the total tax burden of each item between the rural and urban sectors. We shall then redistribute the total tax burden arising from commodity taxation between the agricultural and the nonagricultural sector on the basis of the information we already have relating to sectoral populations and incomes.

The principal indirect taxes, as we have seen in the previous chapter, consist of central excise duties, the general sales tax, and import duties, which together account for over 50 per cent of the combined tax revenue of the centre and the states. Central excise duties are levied on a large number of articles for which we have commoditywise data on the yield. We shall, therefore, distribute the excise revenue form each item between the two sectors individually. Wherever we are not in a position to use the National Sample Survey data to decide the proportion of the tax revenue coming from each sector, we will resort to other possible alternative methods. Table 8 presents our findings.

We observe that in 1958-59, according to our estimate, 64.3 per cent of the total revenue from indirect taxes came from the rural sector. The rural sector accounted for the largest proportion of the revenue in the case of state excise duties (74.90 per cent), and the lowest proportion in the case of entertainment tax (49.40 per cent).

Now that we have distributed the total burden of indirect taxation between the rural and urban sectors, we may go on to redistribute the burden between the agricultural and nonagricultural sectors. We have earlier assumed that 10 per cent of the urban population are agriculturists in the sense that they derive their main income from agriculture. Hence we may distribute 10 per cent of the urban share of the commodity taxes to the agricultural sector. Further, on the basis of the Reserve Bank of India's estimates of saving[35] in the Indian economy, we know that the rural sector had a disposable income of Rs 89762.9 million in 1958-59. Subtracting the urban disposable

35 *Reserve Bank of India Bulletin* (August 1961), pp. 1200-13.

TABLE 8

BURDEN OF INDIRECT TAXATION: SHARE OF RURAL SECTOR, 1958-59

Type of tax and tax item	Total revenue (in million Rs)	Rural proportion (percentage)	Rural share (in million Rs)
1. Central Excise Duties :			
Motor spirit	325.2	57.07	185.589
Kerosene	41.5	87.44	36.289
Sugar	522.7	70.32	367.574
Matches	192.1	80.06	154.150
Steel ingots	72.9	67.19	48.978
Tyres and tubes	71.6	57.07	40.862
Tobacco	490.9	71.58	351.396
Vegetable products	38.6	63.70	24.599
Coffee and tea	60.5	46.02	27.844
Cotton cloth	574.0	71.58	410.871
Artificial silk	19.6	67.19	13.168
Cement	139.1	67.19	93.454
Foot wear	10.5	70.38	7.390
Soap	22.3	61.75	13.770
Woollen fabrics	8.6	71.58	6.156
Electric fans	5.3	2.00	0.106
Electric bulbs	3.3	10.00	0.330
Electric batteries	9.8	25.00	2.375
Paper	67.8	43.73	29.651
Paints and varnishes	12.7	10.00	1.270
Vegetable nonessential oils	100.2	63.70	63.827
Refined diesel oils and vaporizing oils	96.0	60.26	57.853
Industrial fuel oils	47.7	67.19	32.047
Rayon and synthetic fibres	8.6	67.19	5.778
Motor cars	2.0	5.00	0.100
Coal cess	32.5	56.50	18.361
Cess on copra	1.3	63.70	0.828
Cess on oils and oil seeds	4.1	63.70	2.612
Miscellaneous	17.3	67.19	11.623
Total Gross Receipts	2998.6		2008.851
Refunds and drawbacks (1.02%)	30.5		20.480
Total Net Revenue	2968.1		1988.371
Additional Duties :			
Sugar	67.9	70.32	47.749
Textiles	52.2	71.58	37.365
Tobacco	41.1	71.58	29.420

TABLE 8 (Contd.)

Type of tax and tax item	Total revenue (in million Rs)	Rural proportion (percentage)	Rural share (in million Rs)
Total Additional Duties	161.2		114.534
Grand Total Net Revenue from Central Excise Duties	3129.3		2102.905
2. General Sales Tax	1116.8	55.39	618.575
3. Import Duties	1165.3	65.07	758.317
Refunds (3.14%)	36.6		23.811
Net Revenue from Import Duties	1128.7	65.07	734.506
4. State Excise Duties	469.4	74.90	351.585
5. Sales Tax on Motor Spirits	121.9	57.07	69.568
6. Motor Vehicles Tax	244.6	57.07	139.593
7. Tax on Railway Fares	108.8	60.26	65.566
8. Entertainment Tax	106.5	49.40	52.613
9. Electricity Duties	105.1	52.89	55.587
10. Other Taxes and Duties[a]	200.4	67.53	135.326
ALL INDIRECT TAXES	6731.5	64.26	4325.824

NOTE: (a) Other taxes and duties include sugarcane cess, tax on passengers and goods, tobacco duties, tax on prize competition and betting, inter-state transit duties, tax on raw jute, etc.

agricultural income from the total disposable agricultural income, we get the rural disposable agricultural income, which amounts to Rs 57742.688 million. Thus rural disposable agricultural income forms 64.33 per cent of the total rural disposable income. Assuming that the saving-income ratio is the same for the rural agriculturists and the rural nonagriculturists, we may distribute the rural share of the burden of commodity taxation between the rural agriculturists and the rural nonagriculturists in the ratio of their disposable incomes. On the basis of these calculations, we may redistribute the burden of commodity taxation between the agricultural and the nonagricultural sector as in Table 9.

As pointed out earlier, we are interested in the burden of taxation of not only the agricultural sector (as a whole), but also of the different groups within that sector. In other words, we are interested in intersectoral as well as intra-sectoral burden. However, we are faced with certain limitations of data. The National Sample Survey has furnished data on the consumer expenditure pattern of different rural expenditure groups. From this we could estimate the burden of commodity

TABLE 9

DISTRIBUTION OF THE BURDEN OF COMMODITY
TAXATION BETWEEN THE AGRICULTURAL
AND NONAGRICULTURAL SECTORS, 1958-59

	Amount (in million Rs)	Proportion (%)
1. Total revenue from taxes on commodities and services	6731.5000	
2. Share of the urban sector	2405.6760	35.7
3. Share of the urban agricultural sector	240.5676	3.6
4. Share of the rural sector	4325.8240	64.3
5. Share of the rural agricultural sector	2869.3191	42.6
6. Total burden of the agricultural sector	3109.8867	46.2
7. Total burden of the nonagricultural sector	3621.6133	53.8

taxation of each expenditure group. But we have no means of finding out how much of the tax in each expenditure group is accounted for by the rural agriculturists and how much by the rural nonagriculturists. Further, we are not in a position to have any estimates of the per capita, or household, income of each expenditure group. Thus, as far as groups within the rural sector are concerned, we are not able to relate per capita burden of commodity taxation to per capita income. Nevertheless, from an overall point of view, it may be useful to attempt to distribute the burden of commodity taxation among the various expenditure groups. Details regarding how the National Sample Survey data are used for this purpose are presented in Appendix I.

We observe that the per capita burden of indirect taxation varies greatly from one expenditure group to another. While the per capita burden of the lowest expenditure group is only Rs 4.39, it is Rs 50.80 for the highest. We are not in a position to draw any further inferences since we do not know the per capita income corresponding to each expenditure group. It is very likely that the higher expenditure groups have proportionately much higher incomes than the lower expenditure groups, and hence the burden of taxation, in the sense of tax as a percentage of income, is likely to be smaller in the case of the higher expenditure groups.

Our inquiry into the burden of indirect taxation within the rural sector has been in terms of expenditure groups and not occupational

TABLE 10

BURDEN OF COMMODITY TAXATION AMONG DIFFERENT RURAL EXPENDITURE GROUPS, 1958-59

Tax item	Total tax per expenditure group in million Rs					
	1-50	51-100	101-150	151-300	301-500	501-
I. Central Excise Duties:						
Motor spirit	10.314	30.678	34.603	52.789	28.334	28.880
Kerosene	0.644	13.734	9.583	9.056	2.492	0.781
Sugar	21.295	74.275	84.210	104.413	47.766	35.616
Matches	1.968	49.819	42.860	38.582	13.564	7.355
Steel ingots	2.458	9.964	9.662	14.042	6.861	5.991
Tyres and tubes	2.271	6.775	7.619	11.623	6.238	6.359
Tobacco	28.430	75.879	70.227	87.823	40.665	48.372
Vegetable products	—	—	2.460	3.690	7.380	11.070
Coffee and tea	1.678	5.896	5.778	8.279	3.531	2.682
Cotton cloth	35.528	89.588	80.027	115.111	52.341	38.277
Artificial silk	0.661	2.679	2.598	3.775	1.845	1.611
Cement	4.690	19.013	18.436	26.794	13.092	11.431
Footwear	0.334	1.241	1.615	2.221	1.164	0.816
Soap	1.107	2.831	2.680	3.687	1.793	1.672
Woollen fabrics	0.552	1.342	1.199	1.725	0.784	0.574
Electric fans	—	—	—	—	0.042	0.064
Electric bulbs	—	—	—	0.066	0.116	0.149
Electric batteries	0.119	0.483	0.469	0.681	0.333	0.291
Paper	0.461	2.145	4.763	8.873	5.516	7.894
Paints and varnishes	0.064	0.258	0.251	0.364	0.178	0.155

Vegetable nonessential oil	5.016	13.414	12.347	17.867	7.814	7.398
Refined diesel oils and vaporizing oils	3.293	9.815	11.154	17.031	9.180	7.469
Industrial fuel oils	1.608	6.520	6.322	9.188	4.490	3.920
Rayons and synthetic fibres	0.290	1.176	1.140	1.657	0.809	0.707
Motor cars	—	—	—	—	—	0.100
Coal cess	0.338	4.639	4.018	5.308	2.435	1.623
Cess on copra	0.065	0.174	0.160	0.232	0.101	0.096
Cess on oils and oil seeds	0.205	0.549	0.505	0.731	0.320	0.303
Miscellaneous	0.583	2.365	2.293	3.332	1.628	1.422
Total Gross Receipts	123.972	425.232	416.979	548.940	260.812	233.078
Refunds and drawbacks	1.264	4.335	4.251	5.596	2.659	2.376
Total Net Revenue	122.708	420.897	412.728	543.344	258.153	230.702
Additional Duties:						
Sugar	2.766	9.649	10.939	13.564	6.205	4.627
Textiles	3.231	8.147	7.278	10.468	4.760	3.481
Tobacco	2.380	6.353	5.880	7.353	3.405	4.050
Total Additional Duties	8.377	24.149	24.097	31.385	14.370	12.158
Grand Total Net Revenue	131.085	445.046	436.825	574.729	272.523	242.860

TABLE 10 (Contd.)

Tax item	Total tax per expenditure group in million Rs					
	1-50	51-100	101-150	151-300	301-500	501-
2. General Sales Tax	43.618	133.485	123.712	170.217	79.722	67.821
3. Import Duties	36.855	149.430	144.902	210.586	102.894	89.839
4. State Excise Duties	23.500	51.001	75.861	98.556	72.236	30.428
5. Sales Tax on Motor	3.866	11.450	12.971	19.788	10.621	10.826
6. Motor Vehicles Tax	7.758	23.075	26.027	39.706	21.312	21.722
7. Tax on Railway Fares	2.647	8.617	12.817	20.080	12.205	9.200
8. Entertainment Tax	1.567	7.288	7.083	22.038	7.422	7.215
9. Electricity Duties	2.092	8.481	8.919	14.037	10.009	12.048
10. Other Taxes and Duties	8.384	25.551	28.332	37.495	18.851	16.714
Total Tax (Commodity) Burden	261.372	863.424	877.449	1207.232	607.795	508.673
Estimated total population in each group (1958-59), in millions	59.527	106.452	70.573	75.356	22.236	10.013
Per capita burden of commodity taxation (in Rs)	4.39	8.11	12.43	16.02	27.33	50.80

NOTE: The expenditure groups such as 1-50, 51-100, etc. shown at the head of each column in the table refer to levels of monthly household consumer expenditure in rupees. Total as well as per capita tax burden of each group, however, refer to annual tax burden.

or social. We have no reliable data to pair each expenditure group with a certain occupational class. If we may venture to make a guess, we might say that the top two expenditure groups represent large landholders with substantial nonfarm incomes, and big merchants and moneylenders. The middle two groups should correspond to peasant proprietors with economic holdings, or prosperous tenant farmers with some land of their own. The lowest two groups must obviously consist of agricultural labourers with or without land of their own, small fulltime tenant farmers, and petty artisans or merchants.

We summarize in Table 11 our findings regarding the burden of agricultural taxation, direct and indirect.

TABLE 11
BURDEN OF AGRICULTURAL TAXATION IN INDIA, 1958-59

Tax item	Agricultural sector's share of burden (in million Rs)	Per capita tax (in Rs)	Per capita tax as per cent of per capita income
Land revenue	923.800	3.16	1.48
Agricultural income tax	84.200	0.29	0.13
Other direct taxes	126.583	0.43	0.20
Indirect taxes	3109.887	10.54	4.98
ALL TAXES	4244.470	14.52	6.80

NET BURDEN

Strictly speaking, what we have accomplished in the preceding paragraphs is a quantitative measure of the gross burden of agricultural taxation in India. In any realistic study of the burden of taxation, we should take into account both "positive" and "negative" taxes. The positive taxes constitute taxes in the ordinary sense. As far as the taxpayers are concerned, they form the debit side of the balance sheet. Negative taxes refer to the benefits enjoyed by the taxpayers. To arrive at the net burden, therefore, we have to subtract the negative taxes from the positive ones. What benefits we should subtract in order to get a quantitative measure of net burden and how much of the benefits (in terms of government expenditures) should be claimed for the agricultural and nonagricultural segments of the rural sector are, however, difficult problems. The budgets of the central and state governments consist of two parts—revenue account and capital account. Expenditures on the revenue account are supposed to be met from current revenue. Expenditures of an investment nature are not included in the revenue account. On the other hand, expenditures on the capital account are not usually met from current revenue. Expenditures on the revenue account benefit the recipients immediately whereas those on the capital account take time for fruition, and once it fructifies it may result in increased incomes for the people. For the purpose of this study, we may take into consideration only the relevant social and development expenditures on the revenue account, such as agriculture and rural development, irrigation, multipurpose river valley schemes, veterinary service, community projects, national extension service and local development works, education, and medical and public health service. Of these expenditures, almost the entire expenditure on agriculture and rural development goes to the agricultural sector, though a very small portion of this might benefit the nonagricultural segment of the rural sector. Since we do not have any data to show how much of this expenditure goes to the agricultural segment and how much to the nonagricultural, we make the assumption that roughly 95 per cent of the total expenditure on "agriculture and rural development" benefits the agricultural segment directly. We may ignore the indirect effects which spill over from one sector to another since there are no means of ascertaining them. As regards the expenditure on irrigation, we know that water rates are collected from the users in many states. So we may include only the net expenditure on this item. In the case of multipurpose river valley projects, part of the benefits goes to the urban people in the form of recreational facilities, electricity supply, etc. Again, since we have no way of ascertaining how much of these benefits go to the rural sector and how much to the urban, and within the rural sector how much to the agriculturists and how much to the nonagriculturists, we assume that 75 per cent of the total expenditure under this head benefits the agriculturists. This assumption seems to be quite reasonable in view of the fact that the major objectives of the river valley projects are irrigation and flood control both of which benefit the agriculturists directly. As far as expenditures on community development projects, national extension service, and local development works are concerned, most of it benefits the agriculturists. We assume that 90 per cent of the expenditure under this head benefits the agricultural sector. In the case of expenditure on education, data are available on the number of students from the rural parts attending schools and colleges and universities for the year

1957-58. We also have data on expenditure by the government for each type or stage of education for the same year. We may assume that this pattern continued in 1958-59, the year for which we are making the estimates. Further, assuming that government expenditures per student as between the rural and urban sectors are roughly the same, we may split the total expenditure on education between the rural and the urban sector in the ratio of students attending the educational institutions from the two sectors. The findings are summarized in Table 12.

TABLE 12

NUMBER OF STUDENTS IN RECOGNIZED EDUCATIONAL INSTITUTIONS, 1957-58

Type of school	*Total number of students*	*Students from rural areas*	*Proportion of students from rural parts*
Primary and pre-primary	27,513,655	19,166,237	0.69661
Secondary and middle schools	7,866,830	5,972,422	0.75919
Universities and colleges	859,646	293,212	0.34108
Schools for professional and special education	1,933,639	1,239,505	0.64102

SOURCE: Government of India (Central Statistical Organization Cabinet Secretariat), *Statistical Abstract of the Indian Union,* New Series, No. 9, Tables 38 and 42, pp. 93-9 and 108-12 respectively.

TABLE 13

DIRECT EXPENDITURE ON EDUCATION BY GOVERNMENT, 1957-58

Type of school	*Total expenditure (in Rs)*	*Proportion of rural sector in total expenditure*	*Amount spent on rural sector (in Rs)*
Primary and pre-primary	671,143,000	0.69661	467,524,925.23
Secondary and middle schools	671,297,000	0.75919	509,641,969.43
Universities and colleges	380,396,000	0.34108	129,745,467.68
Schools for professional and special education	101,937,000	0.64102	65,343,655.74
ALL SCHOOLS	1,824,773,000	0.64241	1,172,256,018.08

We find that 64 per cent of the expenditure on education benefits the rural sector. Once we know the rural share, it is easy to estimate the share of the agricultural segment since we know already the proportion of agricultural population in the rural and urban sectors.

In respect of expenditure on medical and public health services, there is no statistical information available on the sectorwise distribution of patients or expenditure. The most logical procedure, therefore, appears to be that of distributing the benefits between the rural and urban sectors in the ratio of their consumer expenditures on medicine. We have this information given in the National Sample Survey Report already referred to. It should be noted that this method of distributing the benefits is only a rough approximation to reality since as a matter of fact the poor people's medical care is subsidized to a greater extent than that of the rich. However, in the absence of any other data, we may accept this procedure as a rough approximation. On the basis of the National Sample Survey data on consumer expenditure pattern, we find that 61 per cent of the government expenditure on medical and public health care goes to the benefit of the rural sector. From this we could go on to estimate how much of the expenditure goes to benefit the agricultural sector. Our findings on the relative shares of public expenditure on social and development services accruing to the agricultural and nonagricultural sectors are summarized in Table 14.

TABLE 14

PUBLIC EXPENDITURES ON SOCIAL AND DEVELOPMENT
SERVICES: ALLOCATION BETWEEN AGRICULTURAL
AND NONAGRICULTURAL SECTORS, 1958-59

Item of expenditure	Total expenditure (in million Rs)	Share of rural sector (in million Rs)	Share of the agricultural sector (in million Rs)
Agriculture and rural development	412.900		358.480
Irrigation	171.600		171.600
Multipurpose river valley projects	79.100		59.325
Veterinary	107.700		107.700
Community projects, etc.	349.700		314.730
Education	1589.400	1021.031	922.763
Medical and public health	703.700	429.257	303.285
ALL ITEMS	3414.100		2237.883

SOURCE: (1) Government of India (Ministry of Information and Broadcasting) *India*, 1958, p. 233.
(2) Table 13 *supra*.

According to our estimate, out of a total of Rs 3414.100 million expenditure on social and development services in 1958-59, the share of the agricultural sector amounted to Rs 2237.883 million. On a per capita basis this works out to Rs 7.66.

TABLE 15
NET BURDEN OF AGRICULTURAL TAXATION IN INDIA, 1958-59

	Total (in million Rs)	Per capita (in Rs)	Per capita tax as percentage of per capita income
Gross burden	4244.470	14.52	6.80
Agricultural sector's share of public expenditure	2237.883	7.66	
NET BURDEN OF AGRICULTURAL TAXATION	2006.587	6.865	3.215

The net burden of agricultural taxation, according to our estimate, was Rs 2011.556 million in 1958-59. Per capita net burden amounted to Rs 6.88. This forms 3.22 per cent of the per capita income of an agriculturist in India.

CONCLUSION

1. We found that per capita burden of direct agricultural taxes—land revenue and agricultural income tax—amounted to Rs 3.45 in 1958-59. This formed 1.61 per cent of the per capita income of the agriculturists.

2. Per capita burden of other direct taxes such as expenditure tax, gift tax, wealth tax, etc. amounted to Rs 0.43, which formed 0.20 per cent of per capita income.

3. Indirect taxes (taxes on commodities and services) amounted to Rs 10.64 per capita. This constituted 4.98 per cent of income.

4. On the basis of the above findings, it was calculated that the total per capita gross burden of agricultural taxation was Rs 14.52, in 1958-59, which constituted 6.80 per cent of income.

5. It was further estimated that benefits from direct public expenditures on such items as education, medical and public health services, community development, etc. amounted to Rs 7.66 per capita during the same period.

6. Thus, the net burden of agricultural taxation in 1958-59 was found to be Rs 6.87 per capita. This constituted 3.21 per cent of the agriculturists' income.

CHAPTER IV

AGRICULTURAL TAXATION VERSUS NONAGRICULTURAL TAXATION

In connection with the role of taxation for economic development, many economists have, in recent times, expressed the opinion that agriculture in India is inadequately taxed. To quote a few such economists, Nicholas Kaldor referring to land revenue in his report on "Indian Tax Reform" held that "even if the yield were doubled (whether by revision of rates or by the long overdue reassessment of annual land values) it would clearly not represent an excessive burden."[1] Michael Kalecki, while discussing the financial problems of the Third Five Year Plan, has recommended a "properly scaled progressive land tax" in the case of relatively large holdings.[2] According to V.K.R.V. Rao, "the better-off among the agricultural classes are not making a proportionate contribution to the financing of public expenditure on social and economic overheads anywhere comparable to that which is being made by the corresponding income groups in the nonagricultural sector."[3] K.N.Raj has suggested an increase in the share of the rural sector in the total tax revenue.[4] Ursula K. Hicks in her recent book, *Development from Below*, refers to the "undoubted allergy of modern India to the effective taxation of the agricultural sector."[5] While all these economists hold the view that agriculture should be taxed more to meet the growing financial needs of an ever-expanding public sector in India, none of them has

1 Nicholas Kaldor, *Indian Tax Reform, Report of a Survey* (Issued by the Department of Economic Affairs, Ministry of Finance, Government of India, New Delhi, 1956), p. 4.

2 Michael Kalecki, "Financial Problems of the Third Plan, Some Observations," *Economic Weekly* (July 9, 1960), p. 1119.

3 V. K. R. V. Rao, "Public Finance, Economic Growth, and Redistribution of Income in India (1951-52 to 1960-61)," *Economic Weekly* (August 26, 1961), p. 1377.

4 K. N. Raj, "Approach to the Third Plan," *Yojana* (Vol. III, No. 1, January 26, 1959), p. 8, quoted in *Indian Journal of Agricultural Economics* (January-March 1960), p. 37.

5 Ursula K. Hicks, *Development from Below* (Oxford: Clarendon Press, 1961), p. 330.

tried to make any precise quantitative estimates of the tax contribution of the agricultural sector in relation to different income groups within itself or in relation to the rest of the economy. We will examine these questions in this chapter.

In the discussion that follows we assume that rapid economic development is an accepted goal of the Indian society. We further assume that, since the bulk of the investment in the Indian economy is undertaken by the government, every effort should be made to raise the maximum amount of internal resources for financing the Five Year Plans. Within the framework of these objectives, we shall examine to what extent agriculture is inadequately taxed.

When we say that a sector of the economy, or parts of it, is inadequately taxed, we imply that its "taxable capacity" has not been exhausted. The concept of taxable capacity, however, is highly controversial. Hugh Dalton has ridiculed it and has made a plea that "in the interests of clear thinking, it should be well that the phrase 'taxable capacity' should be banished from all serious discussions of public finance."[6] In spite of Dalton's opposition, however, several economists still use the term. In the absence of a better term, we are justified in making use of this already familiar phrase. Since the notion of "taxable capacity" underlies most discussions on the extent to which taxation could be pushed without leading to "undesirable effects," we may briefly examine the meaning of this term and its implications.

"Taxable Capacity"

According to Sir Josiah Stamp, taxable capacity is measured by the difference between the total quantity of production and the total quantity of consumption.[7] Though Stamp had the entire community or nation in mind, it is obvious that the concept could be applied to individuals and sectors within the community. Though Stamp did not spell it out, it would appear that he held that taxable capacity could be increased only through cutting down consumption. However, it is clear that it is the relative growth of production and consumption that is significant from the point of view of taxable capacity. Concluding his discussion of taxable capacity, Stamp points out that "the limit of taxable capacity is not an absolute or fixed figure." It depends

6 Hugh Dalton, *Principles of Public Finance* (New York: Frederick A. Praeger, Inc., 1955), p. 122.

7 Sir Josiah Stamp, *Wealth and Taxable Capacity* (London: P. S. King & Son, Ltd., 1922), p. 114.

upon (1) what the taxation is to be used for, (2) the spirit and national psychology of the people taxed, (3) the way the tax revenue is raised, and (4) on the distribution of wealth.

Dalton has distinguished two possible senses in which the phrase "taxable capacity" may be used: (1) the absolute taxable capacity of a single community, and (2) the relative taxable capacity of two or more communities.[8] In the first case, we may ask how much a particular community can be taxed without producing various "unpleasant" effects. (Dalton defines the unpleasant effects as a diminution of economic welfare.) In the second case, we may ask in what proportions two or more communities should contribute, by taxation, to a common expenditure. Dalton concludes that "relative taxable capacity is a reality, which can, however, be equally well expressed in other terms, while absolute taxable capacity is a myth."[9]

Both Stamp and Dalton have taken extreme stands in their approach to the concept of taxable capacity. They have not discussed the usefulness of the concept from the point of view of economic development. In recent times many economists have tried to give a new interpretation to the idea of taxable capacity and thus, in a way, rehabilitate the once discredited concept. Here we shall refer to two interpretations which seem to be typical, one formulated in terms of optimum resource allocation or resource transfer and the other in terms of economic surplus.

(1) *Taxable Capacity as Related to Optimum Allocation of Productive Resources.* Taxable capacity is defined by Haskell P. Wald as "that amount of purchasing power which might be diverted with economic advantage from private hands to the government."[10] From this definition, which is very different from the traditional definition, Wald derives the concept of an economically optimum level of taxation. The level of taxation most consistent with the optimum allocation of productive resources throughout the economy will be reached when taxation is expanded to the point where the available taxable capacity is all being absorbed. As applied to the land tax, the optimum level, according to Wald, is the one which, in conjunction with all other taxes and a given plan of government spending, would achieve the desired transfer of resources from private to public programmes.

8 Dalton, *op. cit.*, p. 118.

9 *Ibid.*, pp. 121-2.

10 Haskell P. Wald, *Taxation of Agricultural Land in Underdeveloped Economies* (Cambridge: Harvard University Press, 1959), pp. 138-9.

What is lacking in Wald's approach is that he does not spell out what he means by economic advantage in connection with the diversion of purchasing power (in real terms, physical resources) from private to public hands. Concepts like marginal productivity, marginal social advantage, etc. are absent in his analysis. In the field of government spending, considerations of social advantage are often as important, if not more, as economic advantage. The perspective, however, is development-oriented and as such useful for our purpose.

(2) *Taxable Capacity as Related to Economic Surplus.* According to this approach, the source of taxable capacity is to be found in economic surplus. Paul Baran makes a distinction between actual economic surplus and potential economic surplus.[11] The former is the difference between actual current output and actual current consumption. In familiar terminology it stands for saving. Potential economic surplus is the difference between the output that could be produced in a given natural and technological environment with the help of employable productive resources, and what might be regarded as essential consumption. Baran points out that, in an agrarian country like India, a great part of the surplus originates in the agricultural sector.

Kaldor has given a different version of the concept of economic surplus.[12] He agrees that taxes can only be paid out of the "economic surplus." But, for him, the economic surplus is not represented by the excess of production over the minimum subsistence needs of the population. "It would be more correct," says Kaldor, "to say that the taxation potential of a country depends on the excess of its actual consumption over the minimum essential consumption of the population."[13] Strangely enough, Kaldor has left out the difference between actual production and actual consumption, i.e. savings, from taxable capacity. If existing savings are already being directed into productive channels, then, it is true that further taxation potential depends on the excess of the country's actual consumption over the minimum essential consumption, but not until then.

Between these two versions of the economic surplus, I think,

11 Paul Baran, *The Political Economy* (New York: Monthly Review Press, 1957), pp. 22-3.

12 Nicholas Kaldor, "The Role of Taxation in Economic Development" (Unpublished paper read at the International Congress on Economic Development at Vienna, Austria, August 30-September 6, 1962), p. 2.

13 *Ibid.*

Paul Baran's approach is more in keeping with the requirements of economic development since he lays stress on the maximum output that could be produced in a given natural and technological environment with the help of employable productive resources. It is generally agreed that in most underdeveloped countries output, especially agricultural output, could be considerably increased with little or no additional investment. A fiscal policy based on a distinction between actual output and potential output is therefore very relevant for underdeveloped countries. Throughout our discussion in the following pages, we shall bear in mind these ideas relating to taxable capacity and see how far they are relevant in respect of agricultural taxation in India.

Level of Agricultural Taxation: Some Indices

The most important index we can think of is the total tax burden, inclusive of direct and indirect taxes, of the agricultural sector. We found, in the previous chapter, that the gross burden of agricultural taxation formed 6.81 per cent of the agriculturists' income in 1958-59. Further, taking into account the more direct public expenditure on the agricultural sector, we found that the net burden formed 3.22 per cent of the income in the same year. In the advanced countries like the United States, the United Kingdom, West Germany, France, etc. 25 to 40 per cent of the national income is collected in taxes by the national, state, and local governments. Figures for the proportion of taxes corresponding to the agricultural sectors of these countries are not available. In underdeveloped countries where the general level of income is pretty close to the subsistence level the proportion of income taken in taxes is bound to be much lower than in economically advanced countries. In the case of India we know the proportion of income taken in taxes is very low. But beyond stating that this proportion is low we have no means of showing, on the basis of this proportion alone, whether or not this proportion indicates a clear case of undertaxation of the agricultural sector.

Let us, therefore, turn next to the direct taxation of agriculture in India. The total tax burden of the agricultural sector includes the indirect (commodity) taxes which are common to the agricultural as well as the nonagricultural sector. Though the agricultural households have to pay both direct and indirect taxes, we cannot in a strict sense say that the indirect taxes fall on agriculture. Rather they fall on the agricultural households; in that respect the agricultural households are not different from the nonagricultural households. This distinction might look far-fetched, but in the interest of clear thinking this is a necessary distinction. To give a rather extreme example, if the tax on liquor is raised, we cannot say that agriculture is being increasingly taxed; if on the other hand the land tax is raised one could legitimately argue that agriculture is being increasingly taxed. Hence in judging whether agriculture is inadequately taxed or not we have to pay special attention to the direct levies on agriculture.

Direct taxation of agriculture in India includes land revenue and agricultural income tax. Table 16 presents the proportion of income taken in direct taxes during the decade 1950-51 to 1959-60. We observe that over the period 1950-51 to 1959-60 direct taxation of agriculture has remained almost static at a level of below two per cent of the income originating in agriculture. The rise in the proportion over this period is extremely negligible. It may be recalled that this stability in revenue yield was the result of land reforms and not the outcome of more intensive taxation. (The proportion of direct taxation increased from 1.1 per cent of the agricultural income in 1950-51 to 1.7 per cent in 1959-50.) Thus we got the impression that the agricultural sector in India is poorly taxed, but, again, we are not in a position to establish this point in any absolute sense. However, in so

TABLE 16
DIRECT TAXATION OF AGRICULTURE, 1950-51 to 1959-60

(At current prices in million rupees)

	1950-51	1951-52	1952-53	1953-54	1954-55
1. Direct taxes on agriculture	556.7	551.7	619.0	752.6	778.0
2. National income from agriculture	48900.0	50200.0	48100.0	53300.0	43500.0
3. Percentage of 1 to 2	1.1	1.1	1.3	1.4	1.8

	1955-56	1956-57	1957-58	1958-59	1959-60
1. Direct taxes on agriculture	869.5	989.3	958.7	1008.0	1046.7
2. National income from agriculture	45200.0	55200.0	52800.0	62400.0	62100.0
3. Percentage of 1 to 2	1.9	1.8	1.8	1.6	1.7

SOURCE: (1) Central Statistical Organization, Cabinet Secretariat, Government of India, *Estimates of National Income 1948-49 to 1959-60*, p. 2. (2) Reserve Bank of India, *Report on Currency and Finance*, 1957-58. (3) Reserve Bank of India, *Report on Currency and Finance*, 1960-61. (4) R. N. Tripathy, *Fiscal Policy and Economic Development in India* (Calcutta: The World Press Private Ltd., 1958), pp. 126-7.

far as there has been no substantial increase in the direct taxation of agriculture with increases in agricultural income, it would appear that this sector is rather lightly taxed.

We may further examine if agriculture is inadequately taxed or not by comparing the growth in agricultural income with the terms of trade of the agricultural sector (with the nonagricultural sector). Assuming that the bulk of the *cash* expenditures of the agricultural population is expended on the products of industry and commerce, we can judge whether the agricultural sector has become worse off or better off by examining its terms of trade with the nonagricultural sector. In Table 17 we present the terms of trade between the agricultural and nonagricultural sectors during the period 1948-49 to 1958-59.

TABLE 17

TERMS OF TRADE BETWEEN AGRICULTURAL AND NONAGRICUL-
TURAL SECTORS OF INDIAN ECONOMY, 1948-49 to 1958-59
(Wholesale prices 1952-53 = 100)

Year-end	Agricultural prices	Nonagricultural prices	Ratio of agricultural to nonagricultural prices	Index of revenue from direct taxation (1952-53 = 100)
1948-49	104.8	84.7	1.23	72
1949-50	108.7	86.1	1.26	81
1950-51	117.7	91.0	1.29	90
1951-52	121.3	100.0	1.21	89
1952-53	100.0	100.0	1.00	100
1953-54	94.2	106.3	0.88	122
1954-55	77.3	98.4	0.79	126
1955-56	95.0	102.7	0.93	140
1956-57	103.9	105.6	0.98	160
1957-58	100.4	110.1	0.91	155
1958-59	107.9	114.6	0.94	163

SOURCE: (1) A. M. Khusro, "Inter-Sectoral Terms of Trade and Price Policy," *Economic Weekly* (February 4, 1961), p. 290. (2) Table 16, *supra*. (3) Central Statistical Organization, *op. cit.*

The economic well-being of the agricultural sector depends partly on the consumption of agricultural products and partly on the consumption of nonagricultural products. The amount of food consumed depends on the output of food produced by the agricultural sector. The agriculturists can buy nonagricultural products only by selling their surplus agricultural produce. We might say that the amount of nonagricultural consumption is determined by the terms of trade between the agricultural and nonagricultural sectors, i.e. by the relative prices of agricultural and nonagricultural products. On the basis of the relative prices of agricultural and nonagricultural products, we may derive a "crude index of economic well-being" of the agricultural sector for each year in Table 17. This index will have two components, one relating to food (agricultural) consumption, and the other relating to nonfood consumption. The component of well-being relating to food consumption is derived from two factors: (1) the proportion of rural consumption expenditure on food,[14] and (2) an index of food output weighted by annual population increase. The component of welfare relating to nonagricultural consumption is derived from (1) the proportion of rural consumption expenditure on nonfood items, and (2) an index of terms of trade (relative prices of agricultural and nonagricultural products). Using the following notations, we may express the "formula" as:

$$W = P_f \cdot \frac{O_f}{PI} \quad + \quad \frac{O_f}{PI} \cdot P_{nf} \cdot T$$

where W = crude index of economic well-being of the agricultural sector; P_f is the proportion of rural consumption expenditure on food; O_f, the index of food output; PI, the index of population; P_{nf} proportion of rural consumption expenditure on nonfood items; and T, the terms of trade between the agricultural and nonagricultural sectors. On the basis of this formula, a crude index of economic well-being of the agricultural sector was calculated for each year during the period 1948-49 to 1958-59.

We may, next, relate changes in the revenue from direct taxation of agriculture to the index of well-being since. One would expect the agricultural sector to contribute more in taxes when its economic well-being is higher and vice versa. In order to relate changes in the yield of direct taxation of agriculture to the index of well-being, we need an index of changes in the yield of direct taxes. For this purpose, a trend line was fitted for the period 1948-49 to 1958-59. The equation to the

---

14 The proportion of food in rural consumption expenditure was taken as 65 per cent and nonfood consumption as 35 per cent on the basis of the findings of the National Sample Survey.

trend line was found to be

$$Y = 65.145 + 8.809\,X$$

where Y is an index of yield from direct taxation of agriculture and X, time measured in years. Further, for each year, the observed value of Y (i.e. Y_o) was expressed as a proportion of the theoretical value of Y (i.e. Y_c). This procedure brings out the magnitude of the year-to-year variations in the index of yield of direct taxation of agriculture. The results are presented in Table 18.

TABLE 18

INDEX OF ECONOMIC WELL-BEING AND INDEX OF VARIATIONS IN
THE YIELD FROM DIRECT TAXATION OF AGRICULTURE
IN INDIA, 1948-49 to 1958-59

Year	Index of well-being	Index of variation in direct taxes	$\dfrac{Y_o}{Y_c}$
1948-49	0.965	0.974	
1949-50	1.000	0.979	
1950-51	0.901	0.983	
1951-52	0.877	0.887	
1952-53	0.889	0.916	
1953-54	0.990	1.034	
1954-55	0.906	0.994	
1955-56	0.936	1.032	
1956-57	0.978	1.108	
1957-58	0.850	1.012	
1958-59	1.002	1.005	

Finally, let us see if there is any correlation between changes in the economic well-being of the agricultural sector and changes in its tax contribution (direct) Kendall's coefficient of rank correlation was applied because of its freedom from assumptions concerning the nature of population distribution. Moreover, as Mills points out, series ordered in time represent a promising area of use for such "nonparametric" measure.[15] Kendall's "*tau*" was found to be equal to + 0.309, which is not significant at a confidence level of 95 per cent. On the basis of this finding we could not conclude anything regarding whether agriculture is undertaxed or not. On the other hand, a significant positive or negative correlation would have

15 Frederick C. Mills, *Statistical Methods* (third edition) (New York: Henry Holt and Company, 1955), p. 317.

suggested more definitely whether agriculture is undertaxed or not. Before we conclude this section we may examine a familiar argument often put forth against raising taxation of the agricultural sector in India. The protagonists of this point of view, of whom there are many, argue that the per capita income of the agricultural sector is so close to the subsistence level that this sector cannot bear any more tax burden without detriment to the health and efficiency of the agricultural population. We have seen that taxes form a very low proportion of income in the agricultural sector. The supporters of the above view would say that this cannot be changed under the peculiar conditions of a low-income agricultural sector. We shall examine this argument, first, in terms of consumption and saving and, second, in terms of income distribution within the agricultural sector.

(a) *Savings in the Agricultural Sector.* It is well known that in spite of the low incomes the agriculturists in India do save. According to a study made by the Reserve Bank of India, the rural households saved 2.7 per cent of their disposable income in 1958-59. The findings of the Reserve Bank are presented in Table 19.

These estimates of savings do not include saving in the form of inventories in agriculture, nonmonetized investment, and consumers' durables. Hence, as the authors of the study admit, the above ratios reflect some underestimation.[16] As regards the pattern of rural savings we do not have any exact information. A reasonable guess is that much of the savings of the rural households goes into hoards of currency and gold which are unproductive. Any increased taxation of the agricultural households, therefore, need not affect the level of consumption. Further, the rural households spend a significant proportion of their income on nonsubsistence consumption. According to

16 According to an estimate made by P. G. Kesava Panikar for the year 1951, the net saving-income ratio of rural families in India is about 12 per cent [See P. G. Kesava Panikar, *An Essay on Rural Savings in India* (unpublished doctoral dissertation, Vanderbilt University, 1959), p. 182.]. This ratio is very much higher than that estimated by the Reserve Bank of India. For the purpose of our discussion, however, we may accept the Reserve Bank's estimates since *(a)* the Reserve Bank gives estimates of saving for both the rural and urban households, and also for other sectors of the economy which we could use for comparison; *(b)* the Bank has estimated the average saving-income ratios for different periods from 1950-51 to 1958-59, which give us more reliable results than an estimate for any single year; and *(c)* the Bank's estimates are the latest. It provides us with a saving-income ratio for the year 1958-59, the same period for which we have estimated the burden of taxation of the agricultural sector. It may be added that, as far as our findings in this section are concerned, Panikar's estimate only confirms them.

TABLE 19
SAVINGS OF THE RURAL SECTOR (HOUSEHOLDS)

(Rs million at current prices)

	1950-51	1951-52	1952-53	1953-54	1954-55	1955-56	1956-57	1957-58	1958-59
Savings	1899.3	1949.8	1868.2	2062.4	1689.5	1755.6	2144.0	2050.8	2423.6
Average saving	1950-51 to 1952-53			1953-54 to 1955-56			1956-57 to 1958-59		
Income ratio (%)	2.6			2.6			2.7		

SOURCE: *Reserve Bank of India Bulletin*, August 1961, pp. 1200-13.

TABLE 24
DIRECT TAXATION OF AGRICULTURAL AND NONAGRICULTURAL SECTORS

	1950-51	1951-52	1952-53	1953-54	1954-55	1955-56	1956-57	1957-58	1958-59	1959-60
Direct taxes as percentage income	1.14	1.10	1.29	1.42	1.79	1.92	1.79	1.82	1.62	1.69
Nonagricultural sector	3.73	3.91	3.72	3.18	3.04	3.09	3.51	3.60	3.56	3.84

SOURCE: (1) Table 23, *infra*.

the Fourth Round of the National Sample Survey,[17] 10.36 per cent of the consumption expenditure of the rural households went for non-subsistence expenditures (ceremonials 5.69 per cent, tobacco 1.91 per cent, intoxicants 0.61 per cent, *pan* 0.70 per cent, refreshments 1.03 per cent, and amusements 0.42 per cent). As Gustav F. Papanek very rightly points out, "While any definition of 'subsistence' has to be arbitrary, most of the above expenditures would not normally be classed in that category."[18] Increased taxation of agriculture could thus be met by reducing saving, or by cutting down consumption (of nonessentials if they choose), or partly by reducing saving and partly by reducing consumption. A fall in voluntary rural savings cannot have any serious effect on the economy since in any case the bulk of the savings is directed into unproductive channels. A reduction in consumption, again, would not necessarily mean undue hardship if the cut is applied to nonessentials.

(b) *Per Capita Income, Landless Agricultural Labourers, and Distribution of Landownership.* We have seen that, in spite of low per capita incomes, the rural households do save and also spend on nonsubsistence items of consumption. Let us, therefore, examine the per capita income aspect further. Per capita income is an arithmetic mean of the distribution. It is the result of a simple process of summation and division. The value of the arithmetic mean is, however, affected by the value of every item in the distribution. This elementary statistical principle is often lost sight of in discussions of the poverty of the agriculturists in India. Poverty there is, but more often than not it is exaggerated. The very practice of expressing the per capita income of underdeveloped economies in the United States dollars and comparing them with the per capita income of the United States and Western European countries is largely responsible for this exaggeration. To get back to the concept of per capita income, if distribution of income within the Indian rural sector was more or less equal, one could readily agree with the "poverty of the people" argument. But this is not so.

According to the Second All-India Labour Enquiry covering a twelve-month period ending August 1956, the per capita annual

17 National Sample Survey, Fourth Round: April-September 1952, No. 18, *Tables with Notes on Consumer Expenditure* (Delhi: Issued by the Cabinet Secretariat, Government of India, 1959), p. 4.

18 Gustav F. Papanek, "Development Problems Relevant to Agricultural Tax Policy," in Harvard Law School, *Papers and Proceedings of the Conference on Agricultural Taxation and Economic Development, January-February* 1954 (Cambridge, Mass: Harvard University Press, 1959), p. 206.

income of agricultural labour households in 1956-57 was Rs 99.40[19] (or Rs 437 per household consisting of on the average 4.4 members).[20] The average debt per agricultural labourer per annum was Rs 20 in the same year. No ardent enthusiast of increased agricultural taxation would advocate increased taxation of these people. Most of them are landless and hence do not pay any land revenue. Those of the agricultural labourers who own land own extremely small plots (often only a kitchen garden of their own) mostly less than an acre. If they pay any land revenue at all, the payment is very negligible. None of them pays agricultural income tax. Let us, therefore, leave out the agricultural labourers and focus our attention on the rest of the agricultural sector.

There were 15.8 million agricultural labour households in India in 1956-57. The average size of an agricultural labour household was 4.4. Of 15.8 million households, 6.6 million had land and 9.2 million were landless. The total agricultural labour population comes to 69.5 million. Subtracting 69.5 million from the agricultural population of 348.2 million we have an estimated nonlabour agricultural population of 278.7 million with a per capita agricultural income of Rs 173 for the year 1956-57, as against a per capita agricultural income of Rs 159 for the whole agricultural sector.

We, thus, find that as soon as we exclude agricultural labourers from the purview of our discussion, the per capita income figure changes by about 9 per cent. Now, we may go a step further and show that even this figure does not give a true account of the income position of the landowning nonlabour agriculturists. For that we have to examine the pattern of landownership. Since land is the major source of income for the agricultural sector, distribution of landownership may be taken as an approximate index of distribution of income. In doing so we assume that the fertility of the soil and the efficiency in cultivation are, roughly speaking, uniformly distributed over holdings of different sizes.

The latest authoritative information we have regarding the distribution of landownership in India is based on the census of land holdings and cultivation carried out in 1954-55. An analysis of the findings of this census shows that there is great inequality in the ownership of land in India, and therefore great inequality in income distribution. Herein lies the relevance of the undertaxation question. Since land revenue is a proportional tax, owners of tiny holdings in the

19 $ 1 = Rs 4.76 (at predevaluation rate).
20 *Reserve Bank of India Bulletin* (April 1961), p. 549.

range of 0-2.5 acres pay land revenue at the same rate per acre as owners of holdings above, say, 60 or 100 acres. Large landholders with an agricultural income of over Rs 3000 are required to pay agricultural income tax in most states of the Indian Union. But from the revenue statistics relating to this tax it is very clear that many landholders who ought to be paying agricultural income tax do not actually pay the tax. Agriculturists do not as a rule keep accounts and the general level of tax compliance is poor. Moreover, with the political, social, and economic influence and prestige which the rich landlords enjoy, it is easier for them to escape law enforcement. It is thus the upper agricultural income groups who are relatively undertaxed in relation to the lower agricultural income groups. The census of landholdings reveals the following pattern of landownership in India.

TABLE 20

DISTRIBUTION OF LANDOWNERSHIP IN INDIA, 1954-55

Percentage of owners	Size of holdings (acres)	Percentage of land owned
43.42	0-2.5	5.2
34.48	2.5-10	23.0
16.84	10-30	34.0
3.79	30-60	18.5
0.90	60-100	8.1
0.46	above 100	11.2

SOURCE: Government of India (Planning Commission), *Third Five Year Plan* (New Delhi, 1961), pp. 241-9.

While on the one hand 43.42 per cent of the landholders own only 5.2 per cent of the total agricultural land, on the other, less than one-half per cent of the holders have for themselves 11 per cent of the land. The extent of concentration of ownership of land is more strikingly brought out by a cumulative percentage distribution of holdings as presented in Table 21.

A Lorenz Curve, which follows, based on the above cumulative distribution of ownership of land distinctly shows a high degree of concentration.

Since 1954-55—the year to which the above distribution applies— land reforms of a vast magnitude have been introduced or implemented in all the states of the Indian Union. One of the key provisions of the nationwide land reform legislation, which militates against the

TABLE 21

CUMULATIVE DISTRIBUTION OF OWNERSHIP OF LAND
IN INDIA, 1954-55

Cumulative percentage	Size of holding (acres)	Percentage of agricultural land owned
43.42	below 2.5	5.2
77.90	— 10.0	28.2
94.74	— 30.0	62.2
98.53	— 60.0	80.7
99.43	— 100.0	88.8
100.00	all holdings	100.0

SOURCE : Table 20, *supra*.

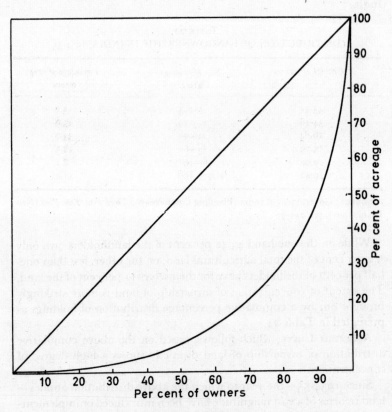

FIG. 3. Lorenz Curve Showing the Distribution of Ownership
of Land in India (1954-55)

concentration of ownership of land, is the ceiling on land holdings. The ceiling differs from state to state;[21] in most states the ceiling, in practice, applies to holdings above 60 acres. Several categories of holdings are exempt from the ceiling, plantations of rubber, tea and coffee being invariably one such exempt category. Allowances for size of household, extent of irrigation, etc. are also made in fixing the ceiling. Assuming that the legislation is scrupulously implemented,[22] its effect on distribution of ownership of land will be to reduce the size of holdings of the highest two classes (see Table 20) down to the ceiling and to distribute the surplus among the landless and those with tiny uneconomic holdings. Assuming that one-third of the lands owned by the top two groups are taken away from them and distributed among the bottom group, the resulting distribution would be as follows: 43.42 per cent of the holders (size range of holding 0-2.5 acres) would own 11.5 per cent of the agricultural land as against a 5.2 per cent before the implementation of the ceiling on holdings; at the other end of the scale, 1.36 per cent of the holders (the highest group) would own 12.86 per cent of the land instead of 19.30 per cent previously. Such a redistribution of holdings would reduce the concentration of holdings only by a small degree. Therefore, our contention, that the usual argument of low per capita income of the agricultural sector in connection with questions of additional taxation of agriculturists is meaningless, stands. Thus it appears that, while the entire agricultural sector may not be undertaxed, certain segments of the agricultural sector, namely, the upper-income groups, are certainly undertaxed. This point will be further explained later.

That there is considerable inequality in income distribution within the agricultural sector in spite of land reforms is confirmed by a recent study published by the Reserve Bank of India. The study indicates that there has been a slight decline in the per household income of the higher agricultural income groups. The relevant information from this study is presented in Table 22.

In this section we were not able to produce any conclusive evidence as to whether the agricultural sector in India is inadequately taxed or

21 See Government of India (Planning Commission), *Third Five Year Plan* (New Delhi: Government of India Press, 1961), pp. 236-8.

22 This is too much to assume. The Planning Commission itself has admitted that "frequently at the lower levels of administration, collusion and evasion have gone unchecked, and there has been failure also to enlist the support and sanction of the village community in favour of effective enforcement of legal provisions." (*Third Five Year Plan*, p. 221.)

not in any absolute sense. This should not cause us any surprise because there is no hard and fast criterion by which we can judge if any given sector of an economy is adequately taxed or not in an absolute sense. However, the data presented in this section strongly suggest that the agricultural sector is inadequately taxed.

TABLE 22

CHANGES IN INCOME DISTRIBUTION OF THE FARM HOUSEHOLD
GROUP BETWEEN PERIOD I (1953-54 to 1954-55) AND
PERIOD II (1955-56 to 1956-57)

	Period I Per household income		Period II Per household income	
	Personal	Disposable	Personal	Disposable
1. Low-Income Group	797	786	815 (+2.3)	803 (+2.2)
(a) Agriculture: labour households	399	399	401 (+0.5)	401 (+0.5)
(b) Nonlabour farm households	1007	898	995 (−1.2)	977 (−1.2)
2. High-Income Group	3543	3465	3402 (−4.0)	3308 (−4.5)
TOTAL	883	869	891 (+0.9)	876 (+0.8)

NOTE: (a) Incomes refer to annual household incomes in Rupees. (b) Low-income group refers to households with an annual income of Rs 3000 or less; high-income group refers to households with an annual income of more than Rs 3000. (c) The figures in brackets under Period II give percentage change in income in Period II over Period I.
SOURCE: *Reserve Bank of India Bulletin* (September 1962), pp. 1360-2.

COMPARISON OF THE TAX CONTRIBUTION OF THE AGRICULTURAL
AND NONAGRICULTURAL SECTORS

First, we will compare direct taxation of the two sectors and, then, the total tax burden. In comparing the total tax contribution of the two sectors we will compare both the gross and the net contribution. Also, we will compare the tax burden of income groups within each sector.

(1) *Direct Taxation of Agricultural and Nonagricultural Sectors.* Land revenue and agricultural income tax constitute direct taxation of the agricultural sector; personal income tax, profession tax[23] and corporation income tax form direct taxation of the nonagricultural sector. We leave out such direct taxes as wealth tax, expenditure tax, gift tax,

23 Profession tax is a very minor tax levied on professional people such as doctors, lawyers, professors, etc.

etc., because these taxes do not exclusively apply to any one sector as such. They are general taxes in the sense that they are to be paid by people regardless of whether they are agriculturists or nonagriculturists. An agriculturist might pay an expenditure tax but we cannot say it is a tax on agriculture. When we consider the total burden of taxation, however, we shall include all taxes.

TABLE 23

DIRECT TAXATION OF NONAGRICULTURAL SECTOR

(In million Rs at current prices)

	1950-51	1951-52	1952-53	1953-54	1954-55
Corporation income tax	404.9	414.1	438.0	415.4	373.3
Personal income tax	1327.3	1520.0	1414.3	1228.4	1222.6
Profession tax	00.7	0.7	0.7	0.8	1.1
TOTAL DIRECT TAX	1732.9	1934.8	1863.0	1644.6	1597.0
NATIONAL INCOME OF NONAGRICULTURAL SECTOR	46400.0	49500.0	50100.0	51700.0	52600.0
DIRECT TAXES AS PERCENTAGE OF INCOME	3.73	3.91	3.72	3.18	3.04

	1955-56	1956-57	1957-58	1958-59	1959-60
Corporation income tax	370.4	511.8	561.3	543.3	1065.6
Personal income tax	1313.5	1517.4	1637.0	1720.1	1488.5
Profession tax	1.1	0.9	2.4	3.3	3.8
TOTAL DIRECT TAX	1685.0	2030.1	2200.7	2266.7	2557.9
NATIONAL INCOME OF NONAGRICULTURAL SECTOR	54600.0	57900.0	61100.0	63600.0	66600.00*
DIRECT TAXES AS PERCENTAGE OF INCOME	3.09	3.51	3.60	3.56	3.84

*Preliminary estimate.

SOURCE: (a) Reserve Bank of India, *Report on Currency and Finance*, 1952-53, 1957-58, and 1960-61. (b) Central Statistical Organization, *op. cit.*, pp. 2, 11.

We find that the direct taxation of the nonagricultural sector constituted over 3 per cent of the national income originating in that sector for the decade 1950-51 to 1959-60. During the same period the level of direct taxation of the agricultural sector was much lower, almost less than half, as shown by Table 24 (p. 60).

(2) *Burden of Indirect Taxation of the Nonagricultural Sector.* We have already, in the previous chapter, estimated the burden of indirect

taxation of the agricultural sector. There we discussed the bases on which each indirect (commodity) tax was distributed between the agricultural and the nonagricultural sector of the economy. Hence we do not have to repeat here the reasoning and the detailed calculations by which we arrived at the proportions for apportioning the individual taxes between the two sectors. The nonagricultural sector's share of each indirect tax is presented in Table 25.

TABLE 25

BURDEN OF INDIRECT TAXATION OF NONAGRICULTURAL
SECTOR, 1958-59

Tax item	Total tax (million Rs)	Percentage share of urban sector	Share of urban sector (million Rs)
Central excises	3129.3	32.8	1026.395
General sales tax	1116.8	35.7	398.225
Import duties	1128.7	43.8	494.194
Sales tax on motor spirit	121.9	42.9	52.332
State excise duties	469.4	25.1	117.815
Motor vehicles tax	244.6	42.9	105.007
Tax on railway fares	108.8	39.7	43.234
Entertainment tax	106.5	50.6	53.887
Electricity duties	105.1	47.1	49.513
Other taxes and duties	200.4	32.5	65.074
ALL INDIRECT TAXES	6731.5	35.7	2405.676

All Indirect Taxes:
  (a) Share of the agricultural sector   3109.8867
  (b) Share of the nonagricultural sector   3621.6133

      TOTAL   6731.5000

So far we have left out the nonagricultural sector's share of direct taxes other than corporation and personal income taxes. As was pointed out in the previous chapter, there are a few relatively unimportant direct taxes such as expenditure tax, wealth tax, etc. We have already discussed in the previous chapter the criterion according to which the burden of these taxes may be distributed between the agricultural and nonagricultural sectors of the economy. The nonagricultural sector's burden arising from these taxes is given in Table 26.

Before we proceed to draw any conclusion from our study of the relative tax contributions of the two sectors, we may estimate the net burden of taxation of the nonagricultural sector.

Net Burden of Taxation of the Nonagricultural Sector. We worked out an estimate of net burden for the agricultural sector in the previous chapter. We may attempt a similar estimate for the nonagricultural sector in order to make the estimates comparable. As has been already noted in estimating the benefits of government expenditure accruing to each sector, we take into account only those public expenditures

TABLE 26

BURDEN OF "OTHER" DIRECT TAXES ON NONAGRICULTURAL SECTOR, 1958-59

(in million Rs)

Tax item	*Total revenue*	*Share of nonagri-cultural sector*
1. Expenditure tax	6.4	4.6071
2. Estate duty	27.0	19.4349
3. Wealth tax	96.7	69.6056
4. Gift tax	9.8	7.0541
TOTAL 1 TO 4	139.9	100.7017
5. Stamps and registration	389.4	302.0150
TOTAL 1 TO 5	529.3	402.7167

which directly benefit the sector concerned. Any category of public expenditure which cannot be clearly apportioned between the two sectors is excluded from the estimate. Public expenditures of an investment nature which benefit the sector concerned only in the long run also are excluded. Further, we do not take account of the spillover effects of public expenditures of one sector on another.

The relevant categories of public expenditure are the same as those for the agricultural sector—education, medical and public health, community development, rural development, etc. We have already discussed, in the previous chapter, how the expenditures on these items could be apportioned between the two sectors. According to these estimates, the nonagricultural sector's total share of public expenditure amounted to Rs 1176.217 million in 1958-59. We have estimated the gross burden of household sectors as two distinct categories. The exclusion of corporation taxes from the burden of taxation of the nonagricultural households, it should be noted, does not affect the validity of our conclusions regarding the relative inadequate taxation of the agricultural sector. On the other hand, their inclusion will only make the relative tax contribution of the nonagricultural sector greater.

The estimated gross burden of taxation of the nonagricultural sector is presented in Table 27. The estimate is for the year 1958-59, the same year for which we estimated the burden of the agricultural sector. The total burden of taxation of the nonagricultural sector was Rs.5747.730 million for the financial year 1958-59. In order to arrive at the net burden, we should subtract this sector's share of direct public expenditure which we have estimated at Rs 1176.217 million. Thus we get a net burden of Rs 4571.513 million for the nonagricultural sector.

TABLE 27

ESTIMATED GROSS BURDEN OF TAXATION OF NONAGRICULTURAL SECTOR, 1958-59

Type of tax	Share of nonagricultural sector (in million Rs)
Personal income tax	1720.1000
Professional tax	3.3000
Other direct taxes	402.7167
Indirect taxes	3621.6133
Total Burden of Taxation	5747.73
Total Personal Income	62762.42
Tax as Percentage of Personal Income	9.2

Comparison of Tax Contributions of the Two Sectors. We have now all the estimates we need to compare the tax contributions of the two sectors of the Indian economy. To make the comparison complete and comprehensive, we may compare both the gross and the net contributions of the two sectors.

TABLE 28

COMPARISON OF THE TAX CONTRIBUTION OF AGRICULTURAL AND NONAGRICULTURAL SECTORS OF THE INDIAN ECONOMY, 1958-59

Sector	Gross		Net	
	Amount (million Rs)	Tax as per cent of income	Amount (million Rs)	Tax as per cent of income
Agricultural sector	4244.5	6.8	2006.6	3.2
Nonagricultural sector	5747.7	9.2	4571.5	7.3

We have used the proportion of tax in income as a measure of the burden of taxation. Applying this measure to the relative contributions of the agricultural and the nonagricultural sector, we found that the nonagricultural sector paid a higher proportion of its income in taxes. Can it thus be said that the agricultural sector is relatively undertaxed? Undoubtedly, according to the most prevalent method of comparing tax burdens. This answer is, however, of questionable merit since a higher proportion of tax out of a markedly higher income does not necessarily mean a higher burden. To overcome this problem of comparison, Henry J. Frank has proposed another measure of tax burden according to which, in order to measure the burden (sacrifice of income) of taxation, we divide the per capita tax as a proportion of per capita personal income by per capita personal income.[24] He applied this technique to compare the tax burdens of different states in the United States. This technique too is not satisfactory for our purposes. First, there is an element of arbitrariness in the method since it divides per capita tax as a proportion of per capita personal income by per capita personal income once and once only. Secondly, we have under discussion the relative tax burdens of two sectors of an economy. This situation is not comparable to Frank's problem where he deals with a large array of states. The ordinal significance of the comparison of tax burdens loses much of its validity when we have only two observations.

We may, therefore, propose an alternative method which consists of deriving two linear tax functions, one for the agricultural sector and the other for the nonagricultural, based on thirteen observations corresponding to the thirteen states of the Indian Union.[25] The two variables used for deriving the regressions are per capita (personal) income and per capita (personal) tax. Both the variables had to be estimated on the basis of the available data for each state and for the agricultural and nonagricultural sectors separately. In many cases the available information was incomplete or inadequate and hence these estimates should be regarded as rough approximations. Every care was, nevertheless, taken to make the estimates of per capita tax burden as accurate as possible. Before we present our results, therefore, it would be appropriate to briefly indicate the procedure followed in deriving the variables required for the regressions.

24 Henry J. Frank, "Measuring State Tax Burdens," *National Tax Journal* (Vol. XII, No. 2, June 1959), pp. 179-85.

25 During 1958-59, the year for which we are making the estimates, there were 14 states in the Indian Union including Jammu and Kashmir. For the purpose of the regressions, however, we have excluded Jammu and Kashmir as we have very little information on its economy.

The statewise distribution of national income of the two sectors is based on K.N. Raj's estimates[26] of income from agriculture. These estimates, as he himself admits, are far from perfect since they are based on the output of a few dominant crops. However, for those states, like Kerala and Assam, where the crop pattern is very different from the rest of India, this method will result in an underestimation of the income from agriculture. Using the statewise distribution of population discussed in the last chapter, we derive the per capita agricultural income for each state. Since agriculture is conducted on an unincorporated basis, we do not have to make a distinction between per capita income and per capita personal income. Subtracting the income from agriculture from the total, we get the income of the nonagricultural sector. From this we subtract the retained earnings of the corporate sector and corporate taxes to get the personal income of the nonagricultural sector. Statewise data on retained earnings of the corporate sector are not available. Hence they were distributed among the states in proportion to their share in the income from factory and mining enterprises for which estimates are available.[27] Data on revenue from corporation taxes were not available for each state separately in all cases; in some cases the data related to two or more states together. In such cases the revenue was split in the all-India ratio of revenue from corporation tax to revenue from income tax.

Statewise figures of revenue from individual tax items were available in the case of land revenue, agricultural income tax, profession tax, personal income tax (ordinary), stamps and registration (state duty), tax on urban immovable property, and taxes on commodities and services, which consist of state excise duties, general sales tax, sales tax on motor spirit, motor vehicles tax, tax on railway fares, entertainment tax, electricity duties and "other taxes and duties." In respect of taxes such as personal income tax (central surcharge), wealth tax, gift tax, expenditure tax and estate duty, data are available for regions in the charge of each commissioner, which in certain cases consist of two states or one state and part of another state. In such cases the revenue had to be broken up and assigned to each state separately. These cases were very few and relatively unimportant

26 K. N. Raj, "Some Features of Economic Growth of the Last Decade in India," *Economic Weekly* (February 4, 1961), p. 265. Raj's estimates of income from agriculture were at constant (1948-49) prices and hence the figures were appropriately inflated to arrive at incomes at current prices.

27 *Ibid.*, p. 267.

from the point of view of revenue. First the revenue from wealth tax was estimated for each state; wherever the available figures were for more than one state, the revenue was split in the ratio of the revenue from income tax. The other taxes—personal income tax (central surcharge), gift tax, expenditure tax and estate duty—were split between the states in the same ratio as wealth tax since these taxes apply to similar categories of taxpayers. In the case of stamps and registration (central) the revenue was distributed among the states in the ratio of the revenue from stamps and registration (state), after making allowances for the share of the revenue on account of the central stamps and registration from territories under the direct administration of the Government of India. The revenue from central excise duties was apportioned among the states in the same ratio as the revenue from the state taxes on commodities and services. The only tax left out is the import duties levied by the central government. In this case there is practically no way of apportioning the revenue among the states. The problem here is that import duties are levied largely on luxury consumption goods. In this respect this tax is different from the sales tax or the excise duties which are levied on a wide variety of consumption goods. Assuming that the tax is eventually borne by the consumers according to the intention of the government, it is hard to locate the consumers on a statewise basis. Hence we are leaving out this tax. This, however, is not a serious omission since the revenue from import duties forms only about 10 per cent of the combined tax revenue of the state and central governments. This omission leads to a slight downward bias (relatively) in our estimates of the per capita tax burden of the nonagricultural sector since the import duties affect the nonagriculturists more than the agriculturists.

Once we have got the statewise distribution of revenue from individual taxes, we need to apportion them between the agricultural and nonagricultural sectors for each state. In the case of certain exclusive taxes this does not present any estimational problem. Land revenue and agricultural income tax are exclusively agricultural taxes; income tax and profession tax are exclusively nonagricultural. The rest are levied on both the agriculturists and the nonagriculturists. In the case of these general taxes, we had to adopt in each case a suitable criterion of distribution. In the case of stamps and registration, we saw (in the last chapter) that there is a strong correlation between per capita tax and the proportion of urban population. Using a linear regression we were able to split the revenue between the two sectors of the economy as a whole. We also found how the regression may be used to distribute

the burden of this tax between the agricultural and the nonagricultural sector of each state. The revenue from stamps and registration
(central) may be split in the same ratio as the state tax. In the case of
the wealth tax, expenditure tax, estate duty, and gift tax, we adopted,
in the last chapter, the criterion of distributing their burden between
the two sectors on the basis of the ratio of the incomes of the high-
income farm households and the high-income nonfarm households.
However, we do not have statewise data on income distribution.
Hence we may assume that the national ratio applies to each state.
Tax on urban immovable property was levied in 1958-59 only in two
states. We have already assumed that 10 per cent of the urban population derive their main income from agriculture. Hence 10 per cent
of the revenue from this tax is assigned to the agricultural sector.
Finally, we have the taxes on commodities and services to be distributed between the two sectors. The criterion adopted to derive a
sectoral breakdown is the ratio of consumption expenditure. In order
to arrive at the consumption expenditures, the following procedure
was adopted. From the total (personal) incomes of the two sectors
direct taxes were subtracted to get the disposable income. On the basis
of the estimates of saving in the Indian economy published by the
Reserve Bank of India for the year 1958-59,[28] it was estimated that
the agricultural sector saves 3.34 per cent of its disposable income and
the nonagricultural sector (households) 12.24 per cent.[29] Since we do
not have statewise data on savings, we may assume that these percent-
ages for the whole of India apply to each state as well. Subtracting
the savings from disposable income we get the consumption expenditures of the two sectors. Here we make an important distinction
between cash expenditures and noncash expenditures. The National
Sample Survey found that 56.3 per cent of the consumption expenditure of rural households and 89.7 per cent of that of urban households
was in cash.[30] Again, to make allowances for the cash expenditures of

28 *Reserve Bank of India Bulletin* (August 1961), pp. 1200-13.

29 The Reserve Bank estimated that rural households save 2.7 per cent and urban
households 16.9 per cent of their disposable incomes (1958-59). But, in order to make
allowance for the urban element in agriculture and the rural element in nonagriculture, the proportions are suitably altered.

30 The figures represent the averages of the findings of two surveys conducted by
the National Sample Survey, the Third and Fourth Rounds, in August-November
1951 and April-September 1952, respectively. See National Sample Survey, Report
No. 18, *Tables with Notes on Consumer Expenditure* (issued by the Cabinet Secretariat,
Government of India, 1959), p. 13.

rural nonagriculturists and urban agriculturists on the basis of population distribution, these proportions were suitably weighted. Thus it was estimated that 57.60 per cent of the consumption expenditure of the agricultural sector and 77.55 per cent of that of the nonagricultural sector were monetized. The revenues from taxes on commodities and services were accordingly divided between the two sectors in the ratio of the monetized consumption expenditures of the two sectors for each state. Detailed tables are given in Appendix IV.

Estimates of per capita tax on the basis of the above procedure are presented in Table 29.

TABLE 29

ESTIMATED PER CAPITA TAX BURDEN OF AGRICULTURAL AND NONAGRICULTURAL SECTORS OF THE INDIAN ECONOMY FOR 1958-59

(in Rs)

State	Agricultural sector		Nonagricultural sector	
	Per capita income	Per capita tax	Per capita income	Per capita tax
Andhra Pradesh	205.9	12.2	505.8	33.0
Assam	256.8	17.2	544.7	41.0
Bihar	177.9	9.5	471.6	24.6
Bombay	150.5	12.9	611.9	75.1
Kerala	125.8	10.0	601.4	45.3
Madhya Pradesh	273.4	10.6	452.5	17.4
Madras	175.4	11.8	510.5	41.4
Mysore	156.2	13.4	370.4	34.9
Orissa	151.0	6.1	364.1	15.4
Punjab	414.8	20.7	484.0	32.9
Rajasthan	179.7	11.8	428.5	24.0
Uttar Pradesh	233.0	9.8	512.6	20.3
West Bengal	210.0	16.1	667.2	98.5

Linear regressions were computed for both the sectors.[31] We got the equations $Y = 5.270 + 0.034X$ for the agricultural sector and $Y = -67.420 + 0.212X$ for the nonagricultural sector, where $Y =$ per capita tax and $X =$ per capita (personal) income. The scatter diagrams and the linear regressions are given in Figures 4 and 5.

What conclusions shall we draw from these regressions? Since

31 The standard error of estimate of the regression is 2.624 for the agricultural sector and 13.30 for the nonagricultural. The linear fit is good in both cases.

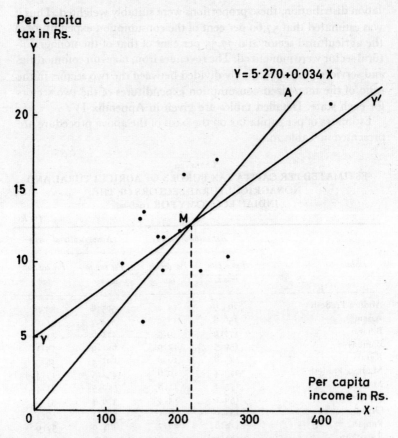

FIG. 4. Tax Burden of the Agricultural Sector, 1958-59

average incomes are markedly different in the agricultural and the nonagricultural sector, we cannot draw any valid conclusions about the relative tax burdens of the two sectors. These tax functions, however, provide us with some useful insights into the problem of intrasectoral burden of taxation in India, which in turn are relevant to the problem of mobilization of financial resources for the execution of the Five Year Plans.

Let us analyze the tax performance of the agricultural sector. From the estimates of per capita income and tax we have made for each state, we may derive the proportion of tax in income for the

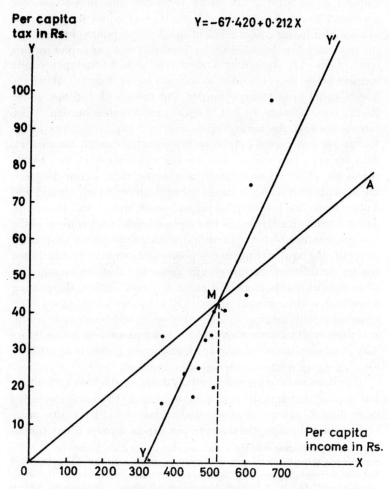

FIG. 5. Tax Burden of the Nonagricultural Sector, 1958-59

entire agricultural sector of the economy.[32] This proportion is found
to be 0.058. Draw a line *OA* passing through the origin of Figure 4
such that the slope of the line is equal to 0.058. This line may be called

32 Note that the estimates were made for thirteen states of the Indian Union. They
exclude Jammu and Kashmir as well as Union Territories.

the line of equal proportionate burden.[33]   If all taxpayers in the agricultural sector paid a tax which represents this proportion, the
regression line will coincide with the line of equal proportionate
burden. But in our case the line of equal proportionate burden cuts
the regression line from below (see Figure 4) at a per capita income
level of Rs 221. Agriculturist taxpayers with annual per capita
incomes below Rs 221 remain, as is shown by the diagram, above the
line of equal proportionate burden and those with incomes above
Rs 221 remain below the line of equal proportionate burden. Thus,
intra-sectorally, the agriculturists with per capita incomes above
Rs 221 are undertaxed in relation to agriculturists with incomes less
than Rs 221. This means that the tax structure is in fact highly
regressive. If the tax were made progressive, then, in our diagram,
the agriculturists with per capita incomes above Rs 221 should find
a place above the line of equal proportionate burden and those with
incomes below Rs 221 should find a place below. Our analysis of the
tax performance of the agricultural sector, thus, shows that intra-
sectorally the burden of taxation is poorly and inequitably distributed
among the different income groups. Assuming that the average size
of an agricultural household is about six, and, further, designating
households with an annual income of Rs 0-1500 as low-income group,
households with incomes of Rs 1501-3000 as middle-income group,
and those with incomes above Rs 3000 as high-income group,[34] we
may conclude that the middle- and high-income groups in agriculture
are undertaxed relative to the low-income group.

If incomes were pretty much equally distributed within agriculture,
our finding that agriculturists with an annual per capita income of
more than Rs 221 are relatively undertaxed would have little practical validity because the average per capita income of an Indian

33 Before proceeding with the model, we have to test if the Y-intercept, a, of the
regression for the agricultural sector is significantly greater than zero. The appropriate
test was, therefore, applied. [For formula, and discussion on the test, see Palmer O.
Johnson and Robert W. B. Jackson, *Modern Statistical Methods: Descriptive and Inductive*
(Chicago: Rand McNally and Company, 1959), pp. 324-7.] It was found that "a"
is significant at almost 95 per cent level of confidence. Also, the slope of the regression, b, was tested and found significant at 99 per cent level of confidence.

34 This classification of agricultural households into income groups roughly follows
the pattern set by the Reserve Bank of India in its study of income distribution in the
Indian economy [see *Reserve Bank of India Bulletin* (September 1962), pp. 1360-2].
The Reserve Bank gives only two income groups—low-income group (households
with annual incomes of less than Rs 3000) and high-income group (households with
income more than Rs 3000). We have added one more group, a middle-income group,
for greater clarity and completeness.

agriculturist is slightly less than this figure (in 1958-59). But our earlier analysis of landownership in India has revealed a high degree of inequality in the distribution of land. Assuming that agricultural incomes are distributed roughly in proportion to the amount of land owned, and also assuming that the pattern of land distribution in 1958-59—the year for which we have made the sectoral estimates of per capita tax—was substantially the same as in 1954-55—the period to which the census of landholdings relates—there were approximately 1.2 million agriculturists with an average per capita annual income of Rs 5635, 2.3 million agriculturists with per capita incomes of Rs 2083, 9.5 million with average incomes of Rs 1130, and 42.1 million agriculturists with per capita incomes of Rs 467. The next group of agriculturists numbering 86.2 million had, according to the same estimate, an average per capita income of Rs 154. This group corresponds to those agricultural households with landholdings in the range of 2.5 to 10 acres. A part of this group whose holdings are in the range of 5-10 acres are most likely to have average per capita incomes of over Rs 221. The remaining agriculturists consist of those with less than 2.5 acres and landless agricultural labourers. Thus as a very rough approximation, out of a total agricultural population of 292 million in 1958-59 as estimated earlier in Chapter III, about 100 million agriculturists had a per capita annual income of over Rs 221. Further, the income per acre of the net sown area of agricultural land in 1958-59 was Rs 193 for the whole of India. Assuming that the average size of an agricultural household is six, we find that, on an average, households with over seven acres of farm land are undertaxed relative to those with less than seven acres. All these estimates are admittedly rough but they tend to confirm that there is great inequality in the distribution of agricultural incomes and that the higher-income groups within the agricultural sector are undertaxed relative to the lower-income groups.

The tax performance of the nonagricultural sector gives altogether a completely different picture. Let us draw a line of equal proportionate burden for the nonagricultural sector similar to the one we drew for the agricultural sector.[35] The slope of this line is 0.083 which is the proportion of the total tax of the sector to its total income. The line of equal proportionate burdens cuts the regression line of the non-

---

35 The Y-intercept, a, of the regression for the nonagricultural sector was also tested for significance. It was found significant at 95 per cent level of confidence. Also, the slope of regression, b, was tested and found significant at 99 per cent level of confidence.

agricultural sector from above (see Figure 5) at a per capita income level of Rs 523. In the diagram, nonagriculturists with incomes below Rs 523 are shown below the line of equal proportionate burden and those with incomes above Rs 523 are shown above the line. One could argue that this is the situation one would expect under a system of progressive taxation and that, therefore, we cannot say that the high-income nonagriculturists are overtaxed in relation to the low-income nonagriculturists. But it should be noted that, before we started out on this inquiry, we had no information if the entire tax system governing the nonagricultural sector was progressive; we only knew that the direct taxes were progressive. We had no clear idea as to whether or not the inclusion of commodity taxes would make the entire tax system of the nonagricultural sector progressive. Our analysis has, however, revealed, in unmistakable terms, that the tax system pertaining to the nonagricultural sector of the Indian economy is progressive, whereas the tax system of the agricultural sector is regressive.

The major conclusion that emerges from the above analysis is that, while tax burdens are fairly well distributed among the different income groups within the nonagricultural sector, it is not so in the agricultural sector. In the case of the agricultural sector, the higher-income groups are clearly undertaxed relative to the lower-income groups. There is thus a strong case for increasing the tax-load of the higher-income groups within agriculture. The case is strengthened by the following considerations: (1) direct taxes are much less progressive in the agricultural sector than in the nonagricultural sector; (2) we may assume that, roughly speaking, indirect taxes affect equally the high-income groups in both the agricultural and non-agricultural sectors; and (3) there is considerable evasion of agricultural income tax.

The above analysis also strongly indicates that as between the high-income groups in the agricultural and nonagricultural sectors, the agricultural high-income groups pay less in taxes compared to nonagriculturists of similarly high incomes.

CHAPTER V

AGRICULTURAL TAXATION IN RELATION TO NATIONAL GOALS

IN the present chapter we will discuss the inadequacy of agricultural taxation in the context of achieving nationally accepted economic goals. We will show that, apart from considerations of intra-sectoral or inter-sectoral equity, it is an imperative necessity that more financial resources should be raised from agriculture which is by far the largest and the most important sector of the economy. Towards the latter part of the chapter we will discuss some of the likely effects of increased taxation of agriculture on the consumption, saving, output and marketed surplus of that sector. In particular, we will examine the relevance of a steadily increasing marketed agricultural (food) surplus in the early stages of economic development and how far increased taxation could be used as a tool for enlarging it.

AGRICULTURAL TAXATION AND NATIONAL GOALS

The Five Year Plans embody India's economic aspirations. The objective of the Five Year Plans ". . . is to provide sound foundations for sustained economic growth, for increasing opportunities for gainful employment, and improving living standards and working conditions for the masses."[1] Thus, achievement of rapid economic growth within the framework of a democratic society is the nationally accepted economic goal. In the words of the Planning Commission of India, ". . . it is imperative that over the next three plan periods all the possibilities of economic growth should be fully and effectively mobilized."[2]

Let us look at the saving behaviour of the Indian economy since the First Five Year Plan was launched in April 1951. Estimates of saving in the Indian economy are still in the rudimentary stage. Several estimates have been made in recent times, either for the entire economy or for individual sectors, the most comprehensive one being

1 Government of India (Planning Commission), *Third Five Year Plan* (New Delhi: Government of India Press, 1961), p. 6.

2 *Ibid.*, p. 22.

the study of the Reserve Bank of India for the period 1950-51 to 1958-59.[3] However, because of inadequate data, none of the estimates can be credited with any high degree of reliability. We shall not go into any detailed discussion of the problems involved in estimating saving but only refer briefly to a few issues.[4] As Dr K. N. Raj points out, there are two ways of estimating the increase in domestic saving: (1) directly estimating the saving of each of the three main sectors of the economy—government, corporations, and households—and (2) estimating the total investment in the economy and deducting from it the capital inflow from outside. For either method, fairly reliable sources of data are available for the government and corporate sectors; but for the household sector, which includes all the unincorporated enterprises, information is very scanty. The problem arises mainly from the fact that the household sector is predominantly agricultural. Household saving in the form of a net increase in asset holding (e.g. life insurance policies, savings bank deposits, etc.) can be estimated with a fair degree of precision. The difficulty is really in regard to the nonmonetary investment of the sector in the form of improvements in land and equipment which are created by the farmers' own labour. The data available regarding such investments by the household sector are extremely scanty, and this deficiency affects estimates of domestic saving computed either way.

Notwithstanding these limitations of saving estimates for the Indian economy, we may use the available estimates to get an overall picture of the relevant variables. The Reserve Bank of India estimates which are the latest available are presented in Tables 30 and 31. Though imperfect for reasons already mentioned, these estimates seem to be the most reliable in view of the fact the Bank commands excellent technical personnel and also because it has access to much data not available to private research workers. We note that for the entire economy the average saving-income ratio for the period 1951-52 to 1958-59 was 7.1 per cent, while the marginal saving-income ratio was 10.0 per cent. Sectorwise, the average saving-income ratio of the household sector during this period was only 5.8 per cent. It will be seen that the aggregate saving-income ratio is very much influenced by the ratio of the household sector since the latter accounts for 80 to

3 "Estimates of Saving and Investment in the Indian Economy: 1950-51 to 1958-59," *Reserve Bank of India Bulletin* (August 1961), pp. 1200-13.

4 For a detailed discussion, see *ibid.;* also see K. N. Raj, "The Marginal Rate of Saving in the Indian Economy," *Oxford Economic Papers* (Vol. 14, February 1962, No. 1), pp. 36-50.

86 per cent of the total saving in the economy. Thus the household sector consisting of rural and urban households is the key sector as far as the saving behaviour of the economy is concerned. Within the household sector we observe that the rural households, on the average, save only 2.6 per cent of their disposable income as against 14.1 per cent in the case of urban households. It is interesting to note that even with such a high percentage of saving by urban households, the aggregate average saving-income ratio for the household sector is only 5.8 per cent. We are led to the important conclusion that the average saving-income ratio of the Indian economy is very low because the ratio for the rural households is low. In other words, the saving behaviour of the rural household sector is the crucial element which influences the aggregate saving behaviour of the Indian economy. As regards the marginal rates of saving, the Reserve Bank has estimated only the aggregate marginal saving-income ratio of each period with reference to the previous period. No sectoral marginal saving-income ratios have been estimated by it. It may be noted that all these estimates are rough. As the authors of the estimates themselves admit, ". . . the data on which the saving estimates are based are inadequate and, under the circumstances, some errors are likely to be associated with the estimation procedures also. . . . Accordingly, no prevision can be claimed for the estimates; the estimates are likely to be much more reliable for a period of years than for any single year."[5]

According to the estimates of the Reserve Bank of India, the marginal saving-income ratio of the whole economy has varied from 14 per cent to 19 per cent from period to period. What can we say about the sectoral marginal saving-income ratios of the household sector? In the case of the average saving-income ratio, we found that the aggregate ratio was considerably pulled down by the ratio of the household sector, to be more specific, by the ratio of the rural household sector. Can we say the same thing about the marginal saving rate? Though there is no logical necessity that a low average saving-income ratio should be followed by a low marginal saving rate, one might suspect that this is true about the saving behaviour of the household sector. This suspicion is strengthened by certain findings relating to increases in food grains consumption between 1952-53 and 1960-61.[6] Between 1952-53 and 1960-61, estimated per capita income rose by about 14.3 per cent; the amount of food grains available for consumption increased during the same period by no less than 12.2

5 *Reserve Bank of India Bulletin* (August 1961), p. 1200.
6 K.N. Raj, *op. cit.*, pp. 47-9.

TABLE 30
SAVINGS IN INDIAN ECONOMY

(Rs million at current prices)

	1950-51	1951-52	1952-53	1953-54	1954-55	1955-56	1956-57	1957-58	1958-59
1. Government sector	938.4	1923.0	883.9	709.9	822.2	699.2	1289.2	1144.2	1030.0
2. Domestic corporate sector	321.6	564.9	42.9	228.7	388.8	543.3	536.9	172.0	342.7
3. Household sector	5098.8	2547.6	4926.1	5048.8	5616.4	7859.8	8103.6	6865.5	8375.7
(a) Rural household sector	1899.3	1949.8	1868.2	2062.4	1689.5	1755.6	2144.0	2050.8	2423.6
(b) Urban household sector	3199.5	597.8	3057.9	2986.4	3926.9	6104.2	5959.6	4814.7	5952.1
4. TOTAL SAVING (1+2+3)	6358.8	5035.5	5852.9	5987.4	6827.4	9102.3	9929.7	8181.7	9748.4

SOURCE: *Reserve Bank of India Bulletin* (August 1961), p. 1203.

TABLE 31
AVERAGE SAVING-INCOME RATIOS: AGGREGATE AND SECTORWISE (PER CENT)

	Period I 1950-51 to 1952-53	Period II 1953-54 to 1955-56	Period III 1956-57 to 1958-59	I Plan period 1951-52 to 1955-56	3 years of 2nd plan period 1956-57 to 1958-59	1950-51 to 1958-59
1. Government sector	13.5	7.4	8.2	10.3	8.2	9.7
2. Domestic corporate sector	34.2	41.0	32.4	37.0	32.4	35.8
3. Household sector	4.3	6.3	6.7	5.3	6.7	5.8
(a) Rural household sector	2.6	2.6	2.7	2.5	2.7	2.6
(b) Urban household sector	9.5	16.0	16.9	12.6	16.9	14.1
4. Aggregate saving	5.9	7.3	7.9	6.6	7.9	7.1
5. Aggregate marginal saving-income ratio	—	19.1	14.2	—	17.3*	—

1951-52 to 1958-59

Average saving-income ratio (%)
7.2
(at constant 1948-49 prices)

Marginal saving-income** ratio (%)
10.0
(at constant 1948-49 prices)

*Calculated with reference to the First Five Year Plan period (1951-52 to 1955-56).
**Marginal with reference to 1950-51.
SOURCE: *Reserve Bank of India Bulletin* (August 1961), pp. 1204, 1208.

per cent. Both 1952-53 and 1960-61 were normal agricultural years. Thus, over the period 1952-53 to 1960-61, the increase in per capita income by one per cent apparently raised per capita consumption of food grains by no less than 0.85 per cent. Thus we are inclined to agree with Dr Raj's statement that "it is not unlikely that the marginal propensity to consume among the higher-income groups in the rural areas is as high as among the lower-income groups."[7] He has concluded that "the problem of raising the marginal rate of saving in India to the levels required by the planned development programme has yet to be faced and solved."[8]

We have seen that the estimates of saving in the Indian economy indicate low levels of average and marginal rates of saving. We may next examine how insufficient these are in relation to the requirements of planned development as envisaged in the Five Year Plans. During the First Five Year Plan, the national income increased by 18 per cent; the target was merely 12 per cent. This was largely due to the increase recorded by agricultural production.[9] During the Second Plan, on the other hand, the increase in national income was 20 per cent though the target was 25 per cent. Thus, during the decade 1951-52 to 1960-61, the national income rose by 41.6 per cent, or at an average annual rate of 4.16 per cent. However, as the increase in population growth has been greater than had been anticipated, per capita income (at 1960-61 prices) increased only by about 16 per cent during the same period.[10] It is thus clear that in terms of growth of per capita income the results of one decade of planning in India are rather disappointing. This has prompted the Planning Commission to confess that "Experience of the past decade in India clearly shows that to make a significant impact on the level of living of the bulk of the people, the rate of economic development should be substantially stepped up."[11]

The Third Five Year Plan, which is in progress currently, aims at a 34 per cent increase in the national income over the five-year period 1960-61 to 1965-66. This works out to an average annual growth rate of nearly 7 per cent. Assuming that the population grows at an annual (average) rate of 2.1 per cent, which is the average growth rate during the last decade (this indeed is a conservative estimate), the

7 *Ibid.,* pp. 48-9.
8 *Ibid.,* p. 50.
9 *Third Five Year Plan,* p. 34.
10 *Ibid.,* p. 20.
11 *Ibid.*

above target would amount to about 5 per cent growth in per capita income annually. Compared to what was realized during the first decade of planned economic development, this appears a tremendously ambitious objective. Among other things, the realization of this target would require mobilization of domestic savings of the order of 11.5 per cent of the national income. It is estimated that during 1960-61, the last year of the Second Five Year Plan, domestic savings formed only 8.3 per cent of the national income. An increase in domestic savings from 8.3 per cent of the national income to 11.5 per cent would mean a 38.5 per cent increase in the level of savings. Such an increase will obviously call for a massive effort on the part of the planners to step up savings. Table 32 gives a summary view of the financial aspects of the Five Year Plans.

We have seen that domestic savings are inadequate to warrant a rapid rate of economic growth. Even with very modest growth objectives, domestic savings have fallen short of the targets. Now, domestic savings can be broadly divided into two parts, public savings and private savings. Public savings refer to the saving of the government through budget surplus, the sources being taxes and surplus of public enterprises. Private savings consist of retained earnings of corporations and the savings of the households. Since over 80 per cent of the domestic savings comes from the households, rural and urban, we can say that domestic savings are predominantly household savings. Any substantial increase in domestic savings, thus, has to come from the household sector. This is a matter of crucial importance for our analysis. The important question is: can domestic savings be substantially stepped up through voluntary savings?

Under the conditions prevailing in underdeveloped economies like India, it is too much to hope that voluntary savings will be forthcoming in sufficient quantities to finance rapid economic development. As Nurkse forcefully argues:

> To assume that if we only leave people alone they will save a sizable portion of their income, or even a sizable part of an increment in their income, may be unduly optimistic. In the poorer countries in the world today the propensity to consume is continually stimulated by the attraction of consumption patterns prevailing in advanced countries. This tends to limit the capacity for voluntary saving in the poorer countries.[12]

12 Ragnar Nurkse, *Problems of Capital Formation in Underdeveloped Countries* (Oxford: Basil Blackwell, 1960), p. 143.

TABLE 32
INDIA'S FIVE YEAR PLANS: TARGETS AND OUT-TURN
(current prices except where otherwise noted)

(In Rs millions)

	1 National income	2 Net Investment	3 Current foreign savings*	4 Domestic savings	% of 4 to 2	% of 2 to 1	% of 4 to 1
Plan I: Out-turn	498600	33600	1330	32270	96	6.7	6.4
Plan II: Targets (1955-56 prices)	572000	62000	11200	50800	82	10.8	8.9
Plan II: Out-turn	623000	67500	18870	48630	72	10.8	7.8
Plan III: Targets (1960-61 prices)	853000	104000	26500	77500	75	12.2	9.1
Last year, Plan I: Out-turn	99800	8500	330	8170	96	8.5	8.2
Last year, Plan II: Out-turn	145000	16000	3950	12050	75	11.0	8.3
Last year, Plan III: Target	190000	27000	5150	21850	81	14.2	11.5

*Balance of payments deficit on current account, excluding official donations. This neglects retained earnings of foreign-owned companies and is thus a somewhat low estimate of the inflow of foreign capital.

SOURCE: M. D. Little, "A Critical Examination of India's Third Five Year Plan," *Oxford Economic Papers* (New Series, Vol. 14, February 1962, No. 1), p. 6.

It is not known to what extent the demonstration effect is strong as an operative factor in stimulating increased consumption. Whether there is demonstration effect or not, one thing is certain: the masses of people in a newly independent country who always used to put the blame for low living standards on their foreign masters look to the national government to provide them with more of the necessaries of life, and thus seize every opportunity to enjoy increased consumption. We might call this phenomenon the "demonstration effect of freedom." On the negative side, however, there are factors like force of habit, lack of suitable financial institutions to channel savings, and lack of monetization, all preventing the growth of voluntary saving. These factors make it extremely difficult to increase voluntary saving.

What are the alternative sources of savings open to India? Assuming that India is not prepared to cut down the size of the Plan, i.e. to plan for a lower rate of growth, the alternatives are broadly two: (1) increased external assistance, and (2) increased involuntary or forced saving. First of all let us note that foreign aid is not something within the control of the receiving country. It largely depends on the economic and political climate in the aiding country. Secondly, India is already planning for the maximum external aid during the Third Plan period, and should feel fortunate if the expected aid is realized. Even if the entire amount of foreign aid envisaged in the Third Plan is realized, there will still exist a gap in domestic resources which has to be somehow filled if the planned rate of growth is to be achieved.

The other alternative to voluntary saving is forced saving. We may distinguish between two forms of forced saving. One is inflation, and the other taxation. Inflation or deficit financing has been resorted to in varying degrees by all underdeveloped countries in their effort to finance the developmental effort. During the Second Five Year Plan period deficit financing to the extent of Rs 9480 million was carried out. This was considered too high by economists like B. R. Shenoy. Over the five-year period the rise in the general index of wholesale prices has been about 30 per cent; prices of food went up by 27 per cent, industrial raw materials by 45 per cent, and manufactures by 25 per cent.[13] In view of the rise in prices that took place during the Second Plan period and in view of the fact that foreign exchange reserves of the Reserve Bank are not satisfactory, it is proposed to limit deficit financing in the Third Plan to a total of

13 *Third Five Year Plan*, p. 121.

Rs 5500 million over the five-year period. How far this constitutes a "safe" limit, even the Planning Commission is not able to say.[14] Broadly, one could say, the success of deficit financing will depend on how fast the production of food grains and other essential consumer goods increases. Whatever be the advantages of deficit financing during the early stages of development planning, it has serious limitations as an effective tool of economic development. According to B. M. Bernstein, it involves a shift in income to profit receivers caused by a shift in the ownership of investment from the general public to the profit receivers. Thus the ownership of wealth becomes more concentrated.[15] This is contrary to one of the basic objectives of the Five Year Plans and also against the Directive Principles of the Constitution of India. Further, continuous inflation induces the wrong kind of investment. Any investment in holding wealth rather than using it is likely to involve a high degree of "ownership" benefits and a low degree of "use" benefits.[16]

The other kind of forced savings is taxation. In the light of the analysis contained in the preceding paragraphs, it is clear that taxation is the most effective, and perhaps the most feasible, tool of increasing domestic savings in India. It is worth noting that the significance of taxation as a means of raising domestic resources for financing economic development is being increasingly realized by the Indian planners. During the Third Five Year Plan period the government proposes to raise Rs 17100 million through additional taxation including measures to increase the surpluses of public enterprises.[17] Additional taxation constitutes the most important single source of domestic resources for the implementation of the Third Plan. This is brought out in Table 33.

The additional taxation of Rs 17100 million envisaged in the Third Plan is about 70 per cent more than the additional taxation undertaken during the Second Plan. With the additional taxation of Rs 10520 million implemented during the Second Plan, the proportion of tax revenue to national income rose from 7.5 per cent at the beginning of the Second Plan to 8.9 per cent by the end of the Plan. It is estimated that, with the normal increase in tax yields as a result

14 *Ibid.*, p. 99.

15 B. M. Bernstein, "Financing Development in the Underdeveloped Countries," in Walter W. Heller, *Savings in the Modern Economy* (Minneapolis: University of Minnesota Press, 1952), pp. 287-9.

16 *Ibid.*, pp. 290-2.

17 *Third Five Year Plan*, p. 100.

TABLE 33
RESENCES FOR THE THIRD PLAN (PUBLIC SECTOR)

RESOURCES FOR THE THIRD PLAN (PUBLIC SECTOR)

(Rs million)

1. Balance from current revenues (excluding additional taxation)	5000
2. Contribution of railways	1000
3. Surpluses of other public enterprises	4500
4. Loans from the public (net)	8000
5. Small savings (net)	6000
6. Provident funds (net)	2650
7. Steel equalization fund (net)	1050
8. Balance of miscellaneous capital receipts over nonplan disbursements	1050
9. Additional taxation including measures to increase the surpluses of public enterprises	17100
10. Budgetary receipts corresponding to external assistance	22000
11. Deficit financing	5500
TOTAL	75000

SOURCE: *Third Five Year Plan*, p. 100.

of rising national income, and the additional taxation of Rs 17100 million proposed over the Third Plan period, the proportion of tax revenue to national income will go up to 11.4 per cent by the end of the Third Plan.[18] Thus, India needs to have additional tax revenue of the order of Rs 17100 million over the five-year period of the Third Plan to achieve an annual rate of growth of about 5 per cent. This objective cannot be achieved without taxing the agricultural sector more, for obviously the entire additional taxation of Rs 17100 million cannot be levied on the nonagricultural sector which is already taxed relatively heavily as has been shown in the last chapter. It is very curious that, in respect of such a vital question as this, the Third Plan has absolutely nothing specific to say. In the section entitled "Additional Taxation" in the Third Five Year Plan, the Planning Commission makes only broad statements, such as: "The details of tax measures to be adopted during the Third Plan will have to be decided upon in the light of the economic situation as it emerges from year to year."[19] "In the field of income tax, the scope for raising the rates generally is limited."[20] "The Third Plan will involve a substantial increase in indirect taxation."[21] But there is

18 *Ibid.*, p. 102.
19 *Ibid.*, p. 103.
20 *Ibid.*
21 *Ibid.*, p. 104.

not a single word about increased taxation of agriculture, the most dominant segment of the economy. In an economy where about 50 per cent of the national income originates in agriculture, taxation of agriculture has to play a key role in supplying the resources for economic development. This view is currently supported by many economists. In the words of Haskell P. Wald,[22]

> Generally speaking, in countries seeking to accelerate their economic growth, the optimum revenue goal is exceedingly large relative to any realistic appraisal of the amount of revenue that can in fact be raised. These countries must, therefore, seek to tap practically every available revenue source;... The very size of the agricultural sector in most countries creates a strong presumption that a substantial portion of the required revenue should be raised in that sector. Exactly how large that portion should be depends upon the level and distribution of agricultural income and upon agriculture's place in the overall developmental plan.

Instead of talking about the agricultural sector as a whole and suggesting that this sector should bear greater taxation, Kalecki divides the agricultural holdings into three classes:[23] (1) relatively large or medium holdings cultivated by peasants who own the land or have security of tenure with or without the assistance of hired labourers; (2) small holdings cultivated by peasants who own the land or have security of tenure; and (3) relatively large holdings leased by the owner to a number of small tenants without security of tenure either openly or by circumventing the existing laws providing for security, through shifting the tenants around at short intervals, leasing the land *de facto* to "servants" or "share-croppers," etc. In the case of the last class of landholders, Kalecki advocates a progressive land taxation.

Paul Baran agrees with many observers that India can invest 15 per cent of her national income without any reduction of mass consumption.[24] Walter W. Heller holds the view that the vicious circle

22 Haskell P. Wald, *Taxation of Agricultural Land in Underdeveloped Countries* (Cambridge, Mass.: Harvard University Press, 1959), pp. 181-2.

23 M. Kalecki, "Financial Problems of the Third Plan: Some Observations," *Economic Weekly* (July 9, 1960), p. 1119.

24 Paul Baran, *The Political Economy of Growth* (New York: Monthly Review Press, 1957), p. 225.

of extreme poverty can be broken, apart from foreign aid, by vigorous taxation and the government development programme.[25] It requires that fiscal policy should be assigned the central task of wresting from the pitifully low output of these countries sufficient savings to finance economic development programmes and to set the stage for more vigorous private investment activity.[26] Thus, in the light of our discussion in this chapter, we may conclude that the agricultural sector in India is inadequately taxed from the point of view of achieving rapid economic development.

So far we have tried to show that the agricultural sector in India is inadequately taxed from the point of view of achieving the national goals. If we were to stop here, we will not be able to offer much guidance to policy makers. For to locate areas of potential surplus is an important policy task. We have already seen in the previous chapter that the higher-income groups in agriculture are greatly undertaxed relative to the lower-income groups. This finding provides ample economic justification for taxing these groups more intensively. Although we were not able to draw any direct conclusions regarding inter-sectoral burden of taxation, our analysis strongly indicated that as between the high-income groups in the agricultural and nonagricultural sectors, the agricultural high-income groups pay less in taxes relative to nonagriculturists of similar incomes. This strengthens the case for raising more financial resources for economic development through increased taxation of the higher-income groups in agriculture. We may also add that a substantial portion of the income in agriculture consists of property income—rent and interest form about 28 per cent of agricultural income in India—which could be taxed further without detriment to productive efficiency.[27]

Some Economic Effects of Increased Taxation

We have found that, in order to achieve the economic goals set forth in the Five Year Plans, more financial resources need to be raised from the agricultural sector. Proposals for a suitable reform of the agricultural tax system will be made in Chapter VII. Meanwhile it

---

25 Walter W. Heller, "Fiscal Policies for Underdeveloped Economies," in *Agricultural Taxation and Economic Development* (Cambridge, Mass.: Harvard University Press, 1954), p. 63.

26 *Ibid.*

27 *Cf.* S. A. Shah, "Investment Potential in the Indian Agricultural Sector—An Exploratory Note," *Agricultural Situation in India* (August 1962), pp. 488-90.

may be in order to discuss briefly some of the likely economic effects of increased taxation of agriculture.

In a perfectly competitive (free enterprise) economy the optimum allocation of resources is achieved by the marginal principle. Equilibrium in the factor market is reached when each factor of production is priced according to its marginal (net) productivity. Equilibrium in the product market is reached when each product is priced according to its marginal cost. Perfect mobility of the factors of production enables them to move from fields where their marginal productivity is lower to fields where it is higher. Thus, under ideal conditions, factors of production are employed where their marginal productivity is the highest and hence also their remuneration. A similar process takes place in the product market also. Such a system results in the optimum allocation of resources.

In practice, however, the above type of system does not prevail even in the most advanced, free-enterprise, competitive economies like that of the United States. Welfare legislation, like minimum wages, collective bargaining, regional immobility of factors, various degrees of imperfect competition, all tend to make the economy move away from the optimum situation.

The situation is more different in underdeveloped countries. Even assuming perfect competition and free enterprise, the principle of marginal productivity does not automatically result in optimum allocation of resources and the maximum efficiency of the economy. In this context we shall confine our attention to overpopulated agricultural economies like India. How do conditions in an overpopulated agricultural economy differ from those existing in advanced capitalist economies? Does economic theory developed to explain capitalist systems apply to such agrarian backward economies? These questions have been discussed by N. Georgescu-Roegen in "Economic Theory and Agrarian Economies."[28] It is usually said that the marginal productivity of labour in overpopulated agricultural countries is zero. Georgescu-Roegen points out that "the statement that marginal productivity of labour is zero implies that the marginal productivity of skilled labour consists only of the marginal productivity of the capital invested in the production of skill."[29] An overpopulated peasant economy cannot function according to the principle of marginal productivity. Though the marginal

28 N. Georgescu-Roegen, "Economic Theory and Agrarian Economies," *Oxford Economic Papers* (Vol. 12, February 1960, No. 1), pp. 1-40.

29 *Ibid.*, p. 15.

productivity of labour is zero, the peasants have to have at least a minimum of subsistence. Production and distribution in such an economy cannot be regulated by capitalist principles. Feudalism takes better care of these problems than capitalism. In the feudal system of distribution there are workers who earn more than their specific contribution to output (e.g. the gleaners). This, as Georgescu-Roegen points out, is necessary for the efficient operation of an over-populated agricultural economy. In "strictly" overpopulated econo-mies leisure is not, properly speaking, an economic good, for it has no use except as leisure. In its development a strictly overpopulated economy has to pass through a phase where the working class has no leisure at all. This phase called the "Calvary of Capitalism" is not a basic feature of capitalism. It corresponds rather to the growing pains of capitalism. For capitalism could really exist only after the marginal productivity of labour had reached a sufficiently high level so that it could be equated with the wage rate. In the West, capitalism proper began only after this phase had come to an end. Increase in leisure, as different from unwanted leisure characteristic of the overpopulated peasant economy, for the working class consti-tutes its most distinctive feature. Georgescu-Roegen goes on to point out that "to regulate production by profit maximization is probably the worst thing that can happen to an overpopulated economy, for that would increase unwanted leisure while diminishing the national product."[30] He concludes by saying that in every overpopulated country there are numerous sectors which either by their nature or by their tradition permit the labour force to be used according to the feudal formula. Agriculture is almost everywhere in this category. In the agricultural sector labour may be used even to the point where its marginal productivity becomes zero.[31]

With these preliminary observations, let us see what the likely effects of increased agricultural taxation are from the point of view of economic development.

(1) *Consumption and Saving.* A marginal increase in agricultural taxation will reduce the real income of the agriculturists. How far a reduction in real income will reduce consumption depends on how their incomes were spent before the increase in the tax. (1) If

---

30 *Ibid.*, p. 33.
31 Also see Gustav Ranis and John C.H. Fei, "A Theory of Economic Develop-ment," *American Economic Review* (Vol. 51, September 1960), pp. 533-65; William H. Nicholls, "An Agricultural Surplus as a Factor in Economic Development," *Journal of Political Economy* (Vol. LXXXI, February 1963, No. 1), pp. 1-29.

previously their entire income was spent on consumption and nothing was saved, then the effect of increased taxation will be to reduce their consumption. Resources will, therefore, be released for use elsewhere. While the assumption of no saving is true about certain sections of the agricultural population, it is not true for the entire population. (2) Let us, therefore, assume merely that previously the agriculturists saved a portion of their income, however small it might have been. There are now three alternatives before the agriculturists: (*a*) They might pay the tax entirely out of reduced consumption and continue to save the same amount as before. (*b*) They might maintain the same consumption and pay the tax entirely out of saving. If the amount of the tax is less than the saving, this may not completely wipe out their savings. In such cases there will be only a fall in voluntary saving. In this case an increase in forced saving is exactly offset by a decrease in voluntary saving. In the peculiar conditions of India, however, this effect cannot be said to be entirely undesirable. For it is well known that much of the rural savings go into the purchase of gold and currency hoards. Assuming that the tax revenue goes into desirable development channels, the net effect of this alternative may not be unfavourable. While aggregate saving remains the same, its composition takes a favourable turn. (*c*) A third alternative is to pay the tax partly out of consumption and partly out of saving. In this case there is a decrease in voluntary savings, but the increase in forced saving more than offsets the decrease in voluntary saving. There is thus an increase in aggregate saving. From the point of view of mobilization of resources for economic development, this alternative is preferable to the second.

It is hard to say which of the above alternatives will, in practice, be followed and by which group of agriculturists. In the first place, depending on the type of tax, certain sections of agriculturists may be completely exempt from it and consequently their consumption and saving pattern will remain undisturbed. Further, the effect of increased taxation of agriculture on consumption and saving of different income groups are likely to vary as follows: (1) The upper-income groups—landlords and peasant proprietors of relatively large holdings—are more likely to maintain the same consumption and reduce saving in order to pay the increased tax. (2) The middle-income groups are likely to pay the increased taxes partly out of consumption and partly out of savings. (3) The lower-income groups are likely to pay the tax almost completely out of consumption. As far as India is concerned there has been no empirical study to show how taxes affect the relative positions of consumption and saving in the agricultural sector. One might reasonably argue that the lower the level of real income in an economy, the higher will be the proportion of tax increase coming out of consumption.

(2) *Output.* As the marginal tax rate is increased, the individual taxpayer suffers a diminution in his real income. This is called the "income effect" of the tax.[32] The tax increase has also a substitution effect in the sense that the individual taxpayer's disposition to work the last hour he was planning to work suffers a change, normally a diminution. In other words, the individual taxpayer might substitute leisure for work. While the income effect makes the taxpayer work more, the substitution effect makes him work less. A progressive tax involves a higher marginal rate than does the proportional tax; hence it involves a stronger substitution effect, adverse to work effort.[33] In the case of each individual the net effect will depend on the relative strength of the income and substitution effects. For the economy as a whole the net effect will depend on the relative positions of the different groups in the income scale. As Musgrave points out, the results that apply to the individual cannot be transferred mechanically to the group.[34]

This is the usual line of approach adopted in discussions on output effects of taxation. Such discussions have been made against the background of progressive income taxation in advanced Western countries. How far is this type of analysis applicable to overpopulated underdeveloped countries? Under the peculiar conditions prevailing in India the substitution effect of taxation is very likely to be zero for the bulk of the agriculturists. The only exception will be owners of highly commercialized farms whose net income from farming is far above the subsistence level. In such cases the smaller return from additional effort may act as a deterrent to increased output. Even in the case of such high-income groups, the negative substitution effect may not be very strong. In the case of high-income groups, the higher marginal rate of tax does not absorb the entire marginal increment in income and thus by reducing effort their total money income suffers a diminution. While this may be

32 Carl S. Shoup, "Taxation and Fiscal Policy," in Max F. Millikan (ed.), *Income Stabilization for a Developing Democracy* (New Haven: Yale University Press, 1953), p. 262.

33 Richard A. Musgrave, *The Theory of Public Finance* (New York: McGraw-Hill Book Co., 1959), p. 242.

34 *Ibid.*, p. 243.

a great sacrifice from the point of view of work-leisure choice, there may be noneconomic factors such as considerations of prestige, relative status in the income scale, etc. which counteract the substitution effect.[35] To conclude our discussion of output effects of increased agricultural taxation, we are inclined to believe that in an overpopulated agricultural sector as that of India, where the majority of farmers derive only a subsistence income from farming, the output effects of a marginal increase in taxation are not likely to be unfavourable. Past experience in India confirms that increased taxation of agriculture need not reduce agricultural output. One could also argue that an increase in taxation might help break the institutional and cultural rigidities and thus spur the agriculturists on to increased economic effort.

(3) *Marketed Surplus.* From the point of view of economic development, it is the marketed surplus of agricultural output that is of crucial importance. The marketed surplus of agricultural output constitutes the supply of "savings" for economic development. An increase in agricultural output by itself does not promote economic development unless it results in an increased marketed surplus. This is an especially difficult problem in underdeveloped economies where the existing levels of consumption are pitifully low. As a way out, Kaldor has suggested the "imposition of compulsory levies on the agricultural sector," which he thinks will "enlarge the supply of 'savings' for economic development."[36] Discussing the role of agriculture in economic development, Nicholls also arrives at similar conclusions.[37] Although he does not explicitly recommend taxation as a means of capturing the surplus, it is obvious from his analysis that an increased marketed surplus is a precondition of economic development.[38]

During the Second Five Year Plan, agricultural production increased by 16 per cent.[39] The Third Five Year Plan has set a

35 *Cf.* Musgrave, pp. 245-6.

36 Nicholas Kaldor, "The Role of Taxation in Economic Development" (Paper read at the International Congress on Economic Development at Vienna, Austria, August 30-September 6, 1962), p. 18.

37 William H. Nicholls, "The Place of Agriculture in Economic Development" (Paper presented at a Round Table on Economic Development, with Particular Reference to East Asia, sponsored by the International Economic Association, held at Gamagori, Japan, April 2-9, 1960).

38 *Ibid.*, p. 13.

39 *Third Five Year Plan*, p. 302.

target of 30 per cent increase in agricultural output.[40] Now, if this entire (planned) increase of 30 per cent goes into increased consumption by agriculturist families, it will not help the process of economic development except perhaps in an indirect and rather remote way by improving the productive efficiency of the people. Past experience has shown that, as the real income of the farmers increases, they sell a lower proportion of their output of food grains. To use Wicksteed's terminology, their "reservation demand" increases.[41] In this context we may refer to the interesting study of P. C. Bansil entitled "Problems of Marketable Surplus."[42] For the year 1958-59, he estimated that, out of a total production of 68.121 million tons of cereals and grain, the total "marketable surplus"[43] consisted of 19.117 million tons (i.e. 28.1 per cent). From the fact, that a bumper crop of 73.5 million tons of agricultural produce during 1958-59 and an all-time high import of 3.8 million tons of food in 1959 failed to have any appreciable effect on prices, Bansil concludes that the marketed surplus was much lower than the marketable surplus. Bansil attributes the fall in marketed surplus to (1) various land reform measures, (2) increased income of the cultivator, and (3) speculative tendencies due to uncertainty about prices.[44] In another study, Ram Saran shows that in the case of rice and wheat, the proportion of total produce marketed had declined from 40.5 per cent and 55 per cent in the pre-war period (undivided India) to 31.4 per cent (1956-57) and 32.7 per cent (1955-56) in the post-war period, respectively.[45] The decline in marketed surplus has been attributed by him to an increase in the retention of agricultural produce for various reasons.

---

40 *Ibid.*, p. 317. According to the estimates of increased production, the index of agricultural production (base 1949-50) should rise from 135 in 1960-61 to 176 in 1965-66, the total increase being about 30 per cent over the five-year period.

41 *Cf.* J.R. Hicks, *Value and Capital* (Oxford: Clarendon Press, 1957), p. 37.

42 P.C. Bansil, "Problems of Marketable Surplus," *Indian Journal of Agricultural Economics* (Vol. XVI, January-March 1961, No. 1), pp. 26-37.

43 Note that Bansil makes a distinction between "marketable surplus" and "marketed surplus." Marketable surplus represents "the theoretical surplus available for disposal with the producer, left after his genuine requirements of family consumption, payment of wages in kind, seed and wastage have been met." Marketed surplus represents "only that portion of the marketable surplus which is actually marketed and is placed at the disposal of the nonproducer." (See Bansil, *op. cit.*, p. 26.)

44 Bansil, *op. cit.*, p. 28.

45 Ram Saran, "Problem of Marketable Surplus of Food Grains in India," *Indian Journal of Agricultural Economics* (Vol. XVI, January-March 1961, No. 1), pp. 71-2.

For rice he has provided detailed estimates of retention for various purposes. This is shown in Table 34.

TABLE 34

RETENTION OF RICE PRODUCTION BY FARMERS

Purpose	Percentage of total produce	
	Pre-war	Post-war*
Household consumption	42.0	44.4
Payments in kind and use for barter	11.8	21.7
Seed	5.7	6.4
Total retention by farmers	59.5	72.5
Balance representing marketable surplus	40.5	27.5

*Average of 1946-47 to 1948-49.
SOURCE: Ram Saran, *op. cit.*, p. 73.

Clearly, in the above table, the marketed surplus must be smaller than the marketable surplus, which is estimated as 27.5 per cent for rice in the post-war period.

Inelastic Marketed Surplus: An Explanation. We have noted that a steadily increasing marketed surplus of agricultural produce is a precondition for rapid economic development in today's over-populated agricultural countries. In the case of India, however, we found that there has been a fall in marketed surplus. This pheno-menon can be explained in terms of the behaviour of agricultural producers in a nonmonetized subsistence sector of an underdevelop-ed economy. Under nonmonetized subsistence farming the indivi-dual producer is faced with a more or less fixed monetary commit-ment. That is to say, the agriculturist's need of money income is fixed. His limited monetary commitment may consist of purchases of manufactured articles, and direct taxes. The subsistence farmer's demand for manufactured articles, however, is meagre. One could limit it to three or four articles of essential consumption such as salt, certain types of clothing, kerosene, etc. Further, he pays very little tax, direct or indirect. Now, since the monetary commitments of these subsistence farmers are more or less fixed, they adjust their marketed surplus—sale of agricultural produce—to price in such a way that they get just enough money to meet their limited monetary commitments. From these premises it follows that, by increasing the monetary commitments of the subsistence farmer, he may be com-pelled to exchange more of his produce for money.

It may be pointed out in this context that, while several Indian economists[46] have attributed the decline in marketed surplus to limited monetary commitments, none of them has tried to work out the theoretical implications of the problem against the background of a predominantly nonmonetized subsistence agricultural economy. Such an attempt is made in the following pages.

Marketed Surplus Under Subsistence Farming: A Theoretical Model. For the purpose of this model, subsistence farming may be defined as a system of farming under which the farmer's output is so small that there is very little surplus left after the farm family's consumption of what it produces. If at all a small surplus is generated, it may be at the cost of meeting the nutritional requirements for physical fitness.

The unique case of the agricultural producer consuming most of his output himself and facing the market with only a small portion of his output presents very interesting conclusions. Figure 6 represents the indifference map of a typical subsistence farmer in an economy dominated by subsistence farmers, showing various combinations of food consumption on the one hand and consumption of all other goods and services including monetary payments on the other. Let OQ_1 be the output which represents the minimum required for the subsistence of the farming unit and OQ_2 the output which represents the maximum possible physical consumption of food the farming unit can undertake without incurring physical discomfort. Any output greater than OQ_9 will be marketed regardless of the price so long as the price is positive. Hence all indifference lines to the left of OQ_1 will be vertical in shape and all lines to the right of OQ_9 will be horizontal.

Let us assume that the farming unit has a fixed monetary commitment, i.e. a minimum which he has to spend in money. Let this fixed monetary commitment be represented by OM_2 and the price of this produce OM_4/OQ_4. If the farmer has no fixed monetary commitments, faced with an output of OQ_4 he will consume OQ_3 in food and sell Q_3Q_4 for OM_1 of money and purchase with that money nonfood products with it. But in order to meet his fixed monetary commitments, he has to sell Q_2Q_4 of his produce and

46 *Cf.* P.C. Bansil, *op. cit.,* p. 32; S.K. Bose, "Problems of Mobilization of the Marketable Surplus in India," *Indian Journal of Agricultural Economics* (Vol. XVI, January-March 1961, No. 1), p. 39; M. Srinivasan, "Problems of Marketable Surplus in Indian Agriculture," *Indian Journal of Agricultural Economics* (Vol. XVI, January-March 1961, No. 1), p. 110; A. M. Khusro, "Inter-sector Terms of Trade and Price Policy," *Economic Weekly* (February 4, 1961), p. 291.

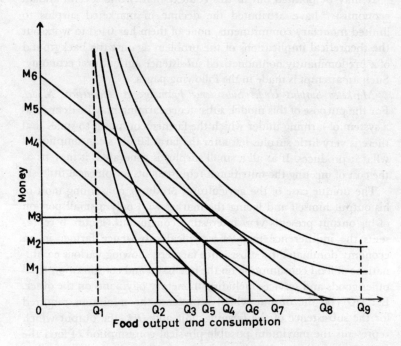

FIG. 6. Marketed Surplus under Subsistence Farming
(a) Constant Price and Varying Output

consume only OQ_2. At this level of consumption he is on a lower indifference curve. If, on the other hand, the gamble in the monsoons brings him an output greater than OQ_4 but less than or equal to OQ_7, the marketed surplus remains the same though he moves on to successively higher indifference curves (we assume here that prices remain the same). At the output of OQ_7, the marketed surplus remains at Q_5Q_7 ($= Q_2Q_4$), or, the quantity of food which produces a money income of OM_2. Thus any increase in output up to OQ_7 does not get reflected in the marketed surplus, though it improves the consumption level of the farming unit. But, beyond the output of OQ_7, any further increase in output will result in increased consumption of food as well as increased marketed surplus, until the consumption reached the limit OQ_9.

So far we have assumed constant price for the output of the farming unit. This assumption is not likely to be valid for any output greater

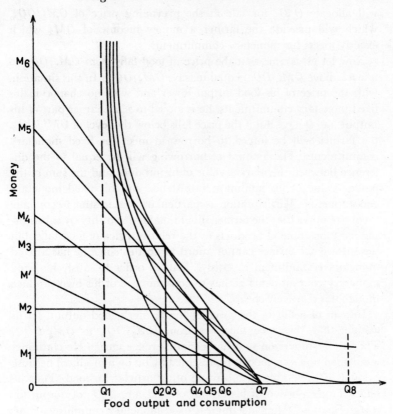

FIG. 7. Marketed Surplus under Subsistence Farming
(b) Varying Price and Constant Output

than OQ_7 because an increase in the marketed surplus is likely to result in a fall in prices in view of the fact that the nonagricultural sector is relatively very small and that their demand for food is rather inelastic. (The nonagricultural sector has much higher incomes than the agricultural sector and the higher the income level of a people the lower the elasticity of demand for food in the sense of farm products and not of services associated with food, as for example eating out in restaurants.) Therefore, in Figure 7 we assume the price to be varying and the output to be constant, so that we may study the effect of varying price on marketed surplus. OQ_1 and OQ_8 represent the minimum and maximum consumptions of the farm unit respectively. Let OQ_7 be an output similar to OQ_4 in Figure 6 such that, choosing the most preferred position, the farmer will allocate Q_4Q_7 for sale at the prevailing price of OM_5/OQ_7, which will provide the farmer a money income of OM_2 which exactly meets his monetary commitments.

Now let us assume that the price of food falls from OM_5/OQ_7 to a level above OM'/OQ_7, equal to, say, OM_4/OQ_7. In this situation, with the price of his food output lower and with no change in his fixed monetary commitments, he is forced to sell a larger part of his output, i.e. Q_2Q_7. But if the price falls below the level of OM'/OQ_7, the farmer will be forced to borrow to meet his fixed monetary commitments. The amount of borrowing will be equal to the difference between the market value of his produce and the sum of the money value of his minimum subsistence and his fixed monetary commitments. This situation is particularly interesting; economic theory requires that the farmer should maximize utility by substituting food for nonfood products as the relative price of food falls, but the subsistence farmer cannot afford to do this since he has a fixed monetary commitment to satisfy. Thus in order to satisfy his fixed monetary commitments he has to consume less of his own produce though it is relatively cheap.

Instead of a fall in the price of the farmer's food output, let us assume that the price increases from OM_5/OQ_7 to OM_6/OQ_7. The farmer moves on to a higher indifference curve. He consumes less of food now (i.e. food as represented by his own produce) because he finds it preferable to substitute other articles for food. Thus he sells a larger portion of his output of food, i.e. Q_3Q_7 of output for OM_3 of money. After meeting his fixed monetary commitments he has a net monetary income of M_2M_3. His food consumption falls to the level of OQ_3.

So far we have analyzed (1) the effect of changes in output, with prices held constant, and (2) the effect of changes in prices with output held constant—all with reference to the adjustments made by the subsistence farmer. Next we may study the effect of changes in both the variables, this time making certain reasonable assumptions about the elasticity of demand for food of the nonagriculturists. We assume that their demand for food is rather inelastic with regard to price changes. This would imply that an increase in supply which, in our model, is represented by the marketed surplus of the subsistence farmers will have a more than proportionate effect on prices of food output.

In Figure 8 let OQ_1 and OQ_8 represent the minimum and maximum of food consumption by the farming unit respectively. Let

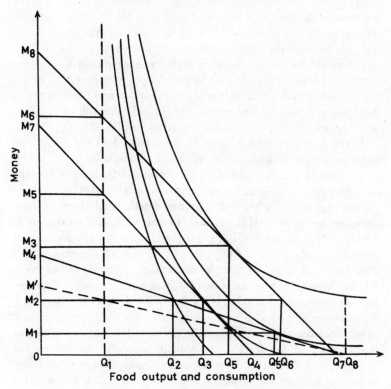

Fig. 8. Marketed Surplus under Subsistence Farming
(c) Both Price and Output Varying

us start with an initial output of OQ_4. Given the preferences of the farming unit as represented by the indifference curves, the farming unit will sell Q_3Q_4 of his output at the current price of OM_7/OQ_4 for a monetary return of OM_2 of money which will exactly meet his monetary commitments. We might as well start with any output between OQ_1 and OQ_4, the only difference in the situation being that at any output lower than OQ_4 the farming unit will be able to move on to a higher indifference curve in the absence of fixed monetary commitments.

Now suppose the next harvest brings in an output of OQ_7 instead of OQ_4. With the increased output, had the price remained the same, the farmer would have had the choice between consuming OQ_5 of food and exchanging Q_5Q_7 for OM_2 of money, or consuming OQ_5' of food and selling $Q_5'Q_7$ for OM' of money. He will naturally prefer the first since it represents a higher standard of living. But the increase in the marketed surplus results in a fall in prices and thus reduces his money income. With a fall in money income the farmer is not able to meet his fixed monetary commitments. Therefore he is forced to sell more of his output to realize enough money to meet his monetary commitments. It may be noted that, with every fall in the price of his output, the farmer will have to sell more of his output to meet his monetary commitments. The equilibrium will be reached with a price of OM_4/OQ_7 and a marketed surplus of Q_2Q_7.[47]

At the new equilibrium price of OM_4/OQ_7, had the farmer no fixed monetary commitments, he would have sold Q_6Q_7 of his output and be satisfied with a consumption of OQ_2 units of his output. His standard of living has not improved as a result of the increase in output; on the other hand, it has deteriorated since he now consumes less of food. If the farmer, to start with, had an output to the left of OQ_4 at the prevailing price of OM_7/OQ_4, any increase in output up to the point of OQ_4 will not lead to a fall in prices since it does not result in an increase in the marketed surplus. Thus every increase in output up to the point of OQ_4 causes a successive improvement in the standard of living of the farming unit. On the other hand, if the farmer started with an output greater than OQ_4, any increase in output, from the start, causes the prices to fall because of the inelastic demand for food from nonagriculturists. An interesting special case of the model is the one of monetary commitments being so high as to force the farmer to sell all the output in excess of his minimum consumption.

This brings us to the question of the relevance of the above model for our purpose. We started with a formulation of the supreme importance of a steadily increasing marketed surplus in economic development. This led us to an analysis of the behaviour of the marketed surplus in a predominantly subsistence agricultural sector. We found, among other things, that it is the existence of a more or less fixed

---

47 It can be shown that the point of equilibrium is fixed once we know the elasticity of demand for food of the nonagriculturists. Assuming that we know their elasticity of demand for food, the equilibrium may be found as follows:

$$E = \frac{(Q_2Q_7 - Q_3Q_4)/Q_3Q_4}{(OM_7 - OM_2)/OM_7} \ldots (1); \quad (Q_2Q_7/OQ_7) = (OM_2/OM_4) \ldots (2)$$

Using the value of Q_2Q_7 obtained in equation (2) in terms of OM_4 we get

$$E = \frac{(OM_2 \cdot OQ_7 - OM_4 \cdot Q_3Q_4)/OM_4 \cdot Q_3Q_4}{(OM_7 - OM_4)/OM_7}$$

Since all variables other than OM_4 are known, it can be calculated; the value of OM_4 thus found out can be used to find the value of Q_2Q_7 in equation (2).

monetary commitment that compels the subsistence farmer to sell a portion of his meagre output for money. Any fall in the price of his output, which may be due to an increase in production, forces the farmer to sell more of his output to realize the same amount of money needed to fulfil his monetary commitments. By the same token any increase in his monetary commitments, the price of his output remaining the same, forces the farmer to sell more of his output. Thus to make the subsistence farmer sell more of his produce, i.e. increase the marketed surplus, either the monetary commitments should be increased (his output remaining the same), or prices of his output should fall (the fixed monetary commitments remaining the same). Direct taxes, as we have noted, form part of the fixed monetary commitment. By increasing taxes we could increase the monetary commitment of the farmer and thus compel him to sell more of his produce at any given price. Our conclusion, therefore, is that increased taxation of the agricultural sector will affect the marketed surplus of agricultural produce favourably. Besides increased taxation of the agricultural sector, there are, of course, other methods of increasing the monetary commitments of the subsistence farmers. One method is to keep agricultural prices deliberately low relative to nonagricultural. prices. This may run into administrative difficulties (and also probably political opposition) and also may not be desirable from the economic point of view. Another alternative is to bring some demonstration effect into play by exposing the agriculturists to modern fanciful manufactured consumer goods, and thus tempting them into selling more of their produce for money. From the strictly limited point of view of marketed surplus this alternative may deliver the goods. But it encourages consumption and thus reduces savings. Compared to these alternatives of increasing the monetary commitments of the farmers, taxation has the advantage of increasing the forced saving of the community and at the same time increasing the marketed surplus, which is of crucial significance for economic development.

CONCLUSION

In this chapter we examined if the agricultural sector in India is inadequately taxed from the point of view of the nationally accepted goal of rapid economic development. We found that, in order to achieve even the modest targets of growth laid down in the Third Five Year Plan,.additional taxation of the order of Rs 17100 million is needed. A considerable portion of this has necessarily to come from the agricultural sector. Nonagricultural incomes, both corporate and personal, are already pretty highly taxed and hence there is not much scope for further taxation of those incomes, though probably as part of an all-out financial drive even those incomes could be taxed further. But before doing so we have to explore all the possibilities of raising more financial resources from the agricultural sector. And we have shown that such possibilities do exist. We then went on to analyze the possible effects of a marginal increase in taxation of agriculture on the consumption, saving, output and marketed surplus of that sector. We concluded that, in the case of low-income farmers, increased taxes are likely to come almost entirely from consumption whereas, in the case of the higher-income groups, increased taxes may be met partly from consumption and partly from saving, or entirely from saving depending on the level of income. The latter may not be altogether undesirable in view of the fact that a considerable part of rural savings go into unproductive channels. As far as output effects are concerned, we concluded that the output effects of a marginal increase in taxation will not be unfavourable. Finally, we discussed the importance of a steadily increasing marketed surplus of agricultural produce in economic development. We analyzed the behaviour of the subsistence farmer vis-a-vis marketed surplus and found that fixed monetary commitments play a crucial role in determining his marketed surplus. Increased taxation is one way of increasing the monetary commitments of the farmers and thereby raising the marketed surplus of agricultural produce. Though there are other ways of increasing the monetary commitments of the farmer than taxation, taxation is preferable since it encourages forced saving.

CHAPTER VI

TOWARDS AN IMPROVED SYSTEM OF AGRICULTURAL TAXATION IN INDIA
(I) A CRITICAL REVIEW OF THE EXISTING SYSTEM

OUR discussion in the two preceding chapters raises the pertinent question: what modifications and improvements are called for in the present system of agricultural taxation to make agriculture play a significant role in the process of economic development? We shall be concerned with this question in the present chapter and the next.

It may be in order to refer briefly to the role of fiscal policy in underdeveloped economies and how it differs from that in developed economies. The difference is only a matter of degree and not of kind. In developed economies fiscal policy is mainly used as a tool of stabilizing the economy, and only secondarily as a tool of growth. Maintenance of full employment is accepted as a goal of economic policy by many of the developed capitalist economies.[1] In order to achieve full employment, these economies resort to compensatory fiscal policy via built-in-stabilizers and discretionary fiscal measures. In the less developed economies, on the other hand, the primary cause of unemployment is the absence of complementary resources to work with and also the scarcity of skilled labour. This can be remedied only by capital formation, both material and human.[2] Thus the main emphasis in underdeveloped economies is on fiscal measures to promote capital formation, which in turn will promote employment and growth. This does not, of course, mean that fiscal policy is not used as a tool of growth in the developed countries, or as an instrument of stabilization in the underdeveloped countries.

The organization of this chapter will be as follows: First, we shall discuss the objectives of agricultural taxation in the context of economic development. Secondly, we shall undertake a critical exami-

[1] Arthur Lewis, *The Theory of Economic Growth* (London: George Allen and Unwin, Ltd., 1957), pp. 380-1.

[2] For detailed discussion, see *ibid.*, pp. 376-83; also, Ragnar Nurkse, *Problems of Capital Formation in Underdeveloped Countries* (Oxford: Basil Blackwell, 1960), p. 148.

nation of the existing system of agricultural taxation and see how far it conforms to the objectives and criteria set forth earlier. Finally, we shall examine and evaluate the proposals of reform suggested by the Taxation Enquiry Commission (1953-54) and other experts, Indian and foreign. In the next chapter we shall present our own recommendations.

I

The primary overall objective which agricultural taxation may be asked to serve in the context of India's economic development should, of course, be to accelerate the rate of growth of the economy.[3] Our task is to analyze what aspects of agricultural taxation need special emphasis in the Indian context and how well the different, often conflicting, objectives could be reconciled so that capital formation is encouraged and economic growth accelerated. For the convenience of discussion, the objectives of agricultural taxation are grouped under two heads: (1) the "external" purposes which economic, social, and political policy may call upon taxation to serve, and (2) the conventional "internal" tests or criteria of taxation such as equity, ease of compliance, etc.

External Objectives

(1) *To Alter the Distribution of Income, Wealth and Landownership.* Taxes and related measures are used in almost all the countries to alter the distribution of income and wealth as between the different sections of the population. In India, "reduction of disparities in income and wealth" and the "prevention of concentration of economic power" are accepted as basic goals of "development along socialist lines."[4] In respect of landownership which is a major source of income, the government, by imposing ceilings on land-holdings, is trying to reduce disparities in income and wealth in the agricultural sector of the economy. According to some observers,[5]

3 For the discussion in this section, I have relied heavily on Walter W. Heller, "A Survey of Agricultural Taxation and Economic Development," in Harvard Law School, *Agricultural Taxation and Economic Development* (Cambridge, Mass.: Harvard University Press, 1954), pp. 117-71; also, Heller, "The Use of Agricultural Taxation for Incentive Purposes," *ibid.,* pp. 222-44.

4 Government of India (Planning Commission), *Third Five Year Plan* (New Delhi: Government of India Press, 1961), p. 9.

5 See, for example, P.C. Bansil, "Problems of Marketable Surplus," *Indian Journal of Agricultural Economics* (Vol. XVI, January-March 1961), p. 28.

the ceiling on landholdings and other related land reform measures have appreciably reduced the marketed surplus of food grains which is of crucial importance in a developing economy. Apart from the ceiling on landholdings, no measure, fiscal or otherwise, has been adopted in India to alter the distribution of income within the agricultural sector. Progressive agricultural income tax does exist in many states of the Indian Union but it is primarily meant as a revenue-raising, and not as a redistributive, measure. Even if agricultural income tax has a redistributive purpose, it is doubtful if that intent is realized. Since most agriculturists do not keep records of their incomes and expenditures, and since it is easy to conceal and to under-report agricultural incomes, the effect of agricultural income tax as a redistributive measure has been very limited.[6] In the opinion of this writer the best way to reduce disparities in the distribution of agricultural income and wealth without harming economic development would be the inclusion of agricultural land within the purview of the wealth tax and the estate duty. At present agricultural land is subject to neither estate duty nor wealth tax, whereas almost all other forms of wealth are subject to these taxes. There is no economic reason why agricultural land should be singled out for such favourable treatment.

(2) *To Promote Economic Stability.* Economic stabilization is one of the important objectives of fiscal policy in which agriculture has a large stake and to which taxation of agricultural crops—especially at the point of export—can often make a special contribution.[7] India, though a predominantly agricultural country, cannot be considered "an exposed economy." Hence much of the stabilization policy necessitated in the case of export-oriented economies is not applicable to India. In 1959-60 the total value of foreign trade constituted only 11.7 per cent of the national income of the country and the value of exports only 5 per cent.[8]

(3) *To Stimulate Desired Changes in the Private Allocation and Use of Agricultural Resources.* We may consider here various possible incentive effects of taxation. Taxation may reward desirable, and penalize

6 Iqbal S. Gulati, *Resource Prospects of the Third Five Year Plan* (Bombay: Orient Longmans Private, Ltd., 1960), pp. 69-73.

7 Harvard Law School, *op. cit.*, p. 133; also see *ibid.*, pp. 72-8.

8 Government of India (Ministry of Information and Broadcasting), *India, A Reference Annual* (Delhi: Government of India Press, 1961), p. 333; Government of India (Central Statistical Organization, Cabinet Secretariat), *Estimates of National Income, 1948-49 to 1959-60* (New Delhi: Government of India Press, 1961), p. 2.

undesirable, economic activity in agriculture. The existing system of agricultural taxation in India lays stress primarily on the revenue aspect; incentive effects are merely incidental. We may note in this connection that there is no unanimity among economists as to how much emphasis should be given to the incentive, and how much to the fiscal, aspects of agricultural taxation. Kaldor, for example, holds that a great deal of the prevailing concern with incentives is misplaced: "It is limitation of resources and not inadequate incentives which limits the pace of economic development. Indeed the importance of public revenue from the point of view of accelerated economic development could hardly be exaggerated."[9] Between the two objectives of incentives and resources, if we were to choose one to the exclusion of the other, then certainly we have to opt for the fiscal objective of raising tax revenue. However, as a matter of fact, we do not have to make such a choice; it is possible to build some incentive provisions into the tax laws so that we may raise more revenue as well as achieve certain incentive purposes. With these observations as a background, we may examine some of the incentive purposes of taxation.

(a) To increase incentives to work. This type of incentive may take the form of reductions of high marginal rates of tax or, more often, of replacing taxes which respond directly to output with taxes which are either fixed in amount or only indirectly responsive to changes in output. The goal of such policies is to levy taxes in a manner that leaves the rewards for additional effort undiminished, i.e. to minimize the "substitution effect" of taxes.[10] Apparently the land revenue system as it functions in India at present provides for this type of incentive since the land revenue is, in practice, a fixed payment. Any increase in output due to increased effort need not be shared with the government. But this incentive is more apparent than real. As Heller points out, incentive taxation seeks to influence economic activity primarily through the structure of the tax system rather than through the level of taxation.[11] For example, if the level of taxes is low—as it is in the case of land revenue in India— the incentive impact of variations in structure is likely to be weak.

9 Nicholas Kaldor, "The Role of Taxation in Economic Development" (unpublished paper read at the International Congress on Economic Development, Vienna, Austria, August 30-September 6, 1962, under the auspices of the International Economic Association), p. 1.

10 Harvard Law School, *op. cit.,* p. 223.

11 *Ibid.*

A quite different approach to stimulate additional effort is to tax agriculturists so heavily that their disposable income is pushed below the levels which they regard as customary or otherwise worth striving to attain. This use of the "income effect" is occasionally advocated in areas where land is abundant relative to labour and additional labour is the chief source of increases in output. However, in the Indian conditions under which land is not abundant in relation to labour, this use of the income effect is not generally applicable.

(b) To increase incentives to invest. While the preceding section mainly deals with short-run incentives of the cultivator, the present section deals with stimuli to longer-run improvements of land, mainly by the landowner.[12] The general approach is to grant exemption or preferential treatment in regard to land, property, and income taxes to improvements in and structures on the land. In recent times Australia and New Zealand have adopted such incentive measures. To provide a stimulus to the development of land, the International Bank Mission to Jamaica recommended the use of unimproved land value as the basis of taxation.[13]

In contrast to the above measures which attempt to protect the rewards for investment in agriculture from discouraging taxes, it is occasionally suggested that landlords be taxed so heavily that they are driven to increase their income through capital improvements in their land.[14] However, it is important to note that, where leeway remains for further exploitation of debtors and tenants through raising interest and rental charges, the income effect of heavier land taxes may not lead to additional investment. Legal rates of agricultural rent have been fixed in all the states of India. In some states, as in Gujarat, Maharashtra, and Rajasthan, the maximum rent is one-sixth of the produce. In Assam, Kerala, Orissa, and the Union Territories, the rent payable is about one-fourth of the produce or less.[15] We do not, however, know how far these laws are enforced. As the Government of India admits, "where there is pressure on land and the social and economic position of tenants in the village is weak, it becomes difficult for them to seek the protection of law."[16] Thus we may conclude that any step to tax the landlords more

12 *Ibid.,* p. 225.

13 Report of a Mission of the International Bank for Reconstruction and Development, *The Economic Development of Jamaica* (1953), p. 19.

14 Harvard Law School, *op. cit.,* p. 225.

15 Government of India (Planning Commission), *op. cit.,* p. 222.

16 *Ibid.,* p. 223.

heavily in order to make them undertake improvements in land should be followed by enforcement of legislative measures limiting agricultural rents.

(c) To discourage undercultivation. The use of taxes to get idle land into cultivation or to stimulate an "upgrading" of its utilization is widely advocated. Such taxation is largely used in countries where land is held for prestige or speculative purposes. The most outstanding example of this type of incentive taxation is provided by several Latin American countries such as Brazil, Colombia, Panama, and Chile.[17] Though in India there is still considerable scope for increasing the intensity of land use through labour-intensive methods, the problem of undercultivation in the above sense of the term is not serious. By framing a land tax based on potential income and not on actual income, however, we shall be able to provide incentives for more intensive utilization of land in India.

(d) To channel agricultural resources into particular crops. Although the incentive measures under this head involve a change in land utilization, they are not designed to penalize nonuse or below-capacity use of land. Rather, by taxing or subsidizing particular crops, they seek to redirect agricultural effort into channels which serve aims of national policy.[18] Some of the Brazilian states, for example, have rather detailed provisions for special exemptions or reductions for land planted to such specified crops as fruit, wheat, and forage crops, for land to be reforested and for land used for raising high-grade livestock.[19] As far as India is concerned, the present practice is to encourage the cultivation of certain crops through subsidies or exemption from taxes. For example, to encourage the production of commercial crops such as cotton, jute and oil seeds, and plantation crops such as tea, coffee and rubber, the government proposes to provide an elaborate system of subsidies.[20] At present India does not produce enough food for her vast population and, hence, penalty taxes on food crops are unwarranted. As a matter of fact the government is trying to increase the production of all crops, commercial as well as food.

17 *Cf.* Harvard Law School, *op. cit.*, pp. 226-7; Haskell P. Wald, *Taxation of Agricultural Land in Underdeveloped Economies* (Cambridge, Mass.: Harvard University Press, 1959), pp. 38, 217, and 220; United Nations, Technical Assistance Administration, *Taxes and Fiscal Policy in Underdeveloped Countries* (New York, 1954), pp. 43-110.

18 Harvard Law School, *op. cit.*, p. 227.

19 *Ibid.*

20 Cf. *Third Five Year Plan*, pp. 301-23, especially, pp. 318-21.

(e) To improve conditions of land tenure. In most underdeveloped countries agricultural taxation has not been used as an incentive measure to improve conditions of land tenure. Instead, other legislative steps are being resorted to. In India this objective is being achieved through land reform legislation relating to the size of holdings, fair rent, and security of tenure.

(f) To discourage land speculation. Tax measures to prevent speculation in land have been used in a number of countries to encourage active rather than passive use of land, to help discourage large accumulations of land, and for the ethical purpose of preventing unwarranted gains derived either from economic development or from inflation. For example, Denmark and Portugal levy highly progressive land value increment taxes at the time of transfer.[21] In the case of India, speculation in agricultural land is negligible. Hence there does not seem to be any need for incentive taxation to prevent land speculation.

(g) To alter the relationship between agricultural and other sectors. Although the influence of taxation on the relation between the agricultural and nonagricultural sectors of the economy is mainly a function of the relative levels of taxation and flows of government expenditures as between the two, incentive effects of taxation also will affect the relationship.[22] It is frequently argued that the existing redundant labour on farms, or labour which is made redundant by technological and capital improvement, constitutes the primary source of capital formation from domestic sources in underdeveloped countries.[23] The problem, here, is not only to provide work opportunities for such surplus labour outside of the farm economy but also to wrest from the agricultural producer the food they formerly consumed as members of the farm community.

The problem of redundant labour, however, cannot be solved entirely through fiscal measures. Notwithstanding the general immobility of labour in India—inter-sectoral as well as inter-regional—the main problem is one of inadequate openings in the nonfarm sector. Any transfer of redundant labour on a sufficiently large scale can come only as the result of adequate industrialization. In the short run, therefore, India should concentrate on getting a larger marketed surplus of agricultural produce from the existing farm households.

21 Harvard Law School, *op. cit.*, p. 229.
22 *Ibid.*
23 *Cf.* Nurkse, *op. cit.*, pp. 36-47.

In concluding our discussion of incentive taxation, a word may be added about the prerequisites for the successful operation of tax incentive measures. Among the barriers to effective operation of incentive tax devices in underdeveloped economies are: weakness of the profit motive; failure of the reward for productive effort to flow to those who make the effort; ignorance of techniques and tools with which to take advantage of the financial rewards offered; such low levels of taxation that tax penalties or rewards do not enter significantly into the farmers' economic calculations; and lack of credit and marketing facilities. All these barriers exist in varying degrees in India. The removal of these barriers is both a cause and effect of economic development.

(4) *To Mobilize and Redirect Resources via Government.* This is perhaps the most obvious and the most important objective of agricultural taxation in underdeveloped economies. Nurkse cites the example of Japan having provided capital for public works and industrial expansion, especially in the 1870's and 1880's, by stiff taxation of the agricultural population.[24] That the Indian government is well aware of the need for mobilizing domestic resources is clear from the following statement:[25]

A measure of strain is implicit in any development plan, for, by definition, a plan is an attempt to raise the rate of investment above what it would otherwise have been. It follows that correspondingly larger effort is necessary to secure the resources needed. It is from this point of view and in the light of the continuing requirements of the economy over a number of years that the task of mobilizing resources has to be approached. Domestic savings have to be stepped up continuously and progressively in order to secure the objective of rapidly rising investment and national income.

Mobilization of resources is accompanied by redirection of resources. Redirection of resources by the government may take several forms: (1) from private to public hands, (2) intra-sectoral transfers, and (3) inter-sectoral transfers.

(a) Change between private and public control of resources. In the early stages of development the government is called upon to provide many

24 Nurkse, *op. cit.*, p. 148.

25 Government of India (Planning Commission), *Second Five Year Plan* (New Delhi: Government of India Press, 1956), pp. 81-2.

of the requisites for greater private participation later on. These requisites can be broadly grouped under social overhead capital. In the case of such requisites the necessary financial resources are raised by the government and also directly invested by it. As Nurkse points out, "If there is a place for government activity on the investment side, it is by almost general consent in the field of essential public works and services, ranging from roads and railways to telegraph and telephone systems, power plants, water works and—last but not least—schools and hospitals."[26] In addition to social overhead capital, the government in India participates also in direct investment in steel mills, heavy chemicals, aircraft, and mining.[27] There is a second (intermediate) zone of redirection of resources in which the actual investment projects are in private hands but the funds are made available through government finance.[28] In India much of the investment in agriculture, barring river valley projects and other major irrigation projects, falls under this category. Also private industrial enterprises receive considerable financial assistance from specialized government institutions like the Investment Credit Corporation as well as from the government directly, in the form of interest-free loans, deferred payments, etc.[29]

Another problem intimately linked with the change in the balance between private and public control of resources is that of increasing the ratio of savings to consumption. The objective should actually be twofold: (1) to capture for development purposes the savings that would otherwise be misdirected, and (2) to increase the proportion of savings to national income at the initial stages of development (the nation's average propensity to save) as well as the proportion of increments in national income that are saved (its marginal propensity to save).

(b) Inter-sectoral transfers of resources. Development policy may have a decided interest in inter-sectoral transfers of resources in agriculture. One facet of this is upper-to-lower income groups shifts. Another type of resource transfer may be in the form of nonmonetary investment, i.e. utilization by the cultivators of their labour in capital-forming ways, not just current-output-increasing ways.

26 Nurkse, *op. cit.,* p. 152.

27 *Cf.* "Industrial Policy Resolution," in Government of India (Planning Commission), *Second Five Year Plan* (New Delhi, 1956), pp. 43-50.

28 United Nations, *Taxes and Fiscal Policy in Underdeveloped Countries* (New York, 1954), p. 3.

29 *Cf. Third Five Year Plan,* pp. 455-7.

To accomplish this, the government may have to provide all the incentives needed as, for example, security of tenure to tenants.

As far as transfers of resources from upper- to lower-income groups in agriculture is concerned, the Indian government has done practically nothing through agricultural taxation. Whatever relative income-shifts there have been are almost entirely the result of the splitting up of large estates due to the ceiling on holdings.[30] Actually all the taxes paid by the agriculturists with the exception of the agricultural income tax are mainly proportional and thus the upper-income groups in agriculture are relatively lightly taxed. Agricultural income tax is somewhat progressive but the extent of compliance is extremely unsatisfactory.

We may recommend progressive taxation of the upper-income groups in agriculture, not as a means of transferring resources from one group to another within the same sector, but as a process of diverting surpluses originating in the higher-income groups into the hands of the government (so that the government can use the savings for investment in the agricultural or the nonagricultural sector). On the other hand, if resources were transferred from one group, say landlords, to help another group, say landless agricultural labourers, through taxation, it would not constitute sound economic policy, for inefficient use of resources and unproductive investment of savings are features widespread in Indian agriculture. Under such conditions as those prevailing in Indian agriculture it is more appropriate to think in terms of individual cultivators rather than groups based on status (e.g. landlords, tenants, etc.). The efficient cultivator should be encouraged and the inefficient penalized, regardless of their occupational status.

(c) Inter-sectoral transfers. Inter-sectoral transfers of resources—transfers from the urban sector to the government for investment in the rural sector and vice-versa—involves some of the most basic issues that have to be faced in setting up the structure of taxation for economic development.[31] It appears that much of the controversy over "agriculture versus industry" arises from a lack of clear thinking on the short-run and long-run objectives, and also from

---

30 Cf. *Reserve Bank of India Bulletin* (September 1962), pp. 1348-63.

31 See discussion in William H. Nicholls, "The Place of Agriculture in Economic Development" (paper read at a Round Table on Economic Development at Gamagori, Japan, April 2-9, 1960, sponsored by the International Economic Association); also see Gustav F. Papanek, "Development Problems Relevant to Agricultural Policy" in Harvard Law School, *op. cit.*, pp. 189-221.

not making a distinction between agricultural economies that are overpopulated and those that are not. The short-run objective of development planning in an overpopulated agricultural economy should be to increase agricultural production so that a steadily increasing agricultural surplus will be available for supporting the industrial base.[32] In the case of India this seems to be the most appropriate policy and as far as the Third Five Year Plan goes the Government of India has accepted this position. To quote from the Third Plan:[33]

> In the scheme of the development during the Third Plan, the first priority necessarily belongs to agriculture. Experience in the first two plans, and especially in the second, has shown that the rate of of growth in agricultural production is one of the main limiting factors in the progress of the Indian economy. Agricultural production has, therefore, to be increased to the largest extent feasible, and adequate resources have to be provided under the Third Plan for realizing the agricultural targets.

It may be appropriate at this point to mention that there is a growing group of economists (among them Higgins, Leibenstein, and Hirschman) who, while recognizing the need for raising agricultural output, hold that it can be accomplished only by giving top priority to an all-out, "big-push" industrialization programme. Higgins, for example, maintains that "cumulative improvement in agricultural productivity" is possible only through "an initial jump to a more highly mechanized and larger-scale agriculture" which can be brought about only through government policy.[34] Thus whatever agricultural progress he foresees in underdeveloped economies is conditional to a rapid rate of industrialization. Higgins, in fact, is highly sceptical about the advisability of putting too much reliance on agricultural improvement. He points out that "while India may never have a highly efficient agriculture, some observers maintain that it already has the most efficient iron and steel industry in the world. On the basis of comparative advantages, India should probably be an importer of food stuffs, and an exporter of products of heavy industry."[35]

32 Kaldor, p. 7; also Nicholls, pp. 25-6.
33 *Third Five Year Plan*, p. 49.
34 Benjamin Higgins, *Economic Development, Principles, Problems and Policies* (New York: W.W. Norton and Company, Inc., 1959), p. 461.
35 *Ibid.*, pp. 42-3 (quoted from a previous publication of the author).

The fallacy in the argument of Higgins and other economists of his persuasion, as Nicholls rightly points out—and we agree with him—is that they overlook the *short-run* potentialities of raising agricultural output with given supplies of land and labour, and existing small-scale farming units.[36]

In the Third Five Year Plan, out of a total investment of Rs 75000 million in the public sector, Rs 17180 million (i.e. 23 per cent) is to be invested in the agricultural sector. Sectorwise, this is the largest investment. In addition to this direct investment in agricultural development and irrigation, Rs 14860 million is to be invested in transport and communications (i.e. 20 per cent), and Rs 10120 million (i.e. 13 per cent) in power. These investments, undoubtedly, will considerably benefit the agricultural sector. These investments add up to a total investment far in excess of the taxes collected from the agricultural sector. There will be, thus, a net inflow of resources for investment into the agricultural sector. This is as it should be in view of the grave food situation in India. With a rapidly increasing population which already has reached the size of 432 million it is almost impossible to depend for long on grants of food surpluses from the United States or imports of food from the United States and elsewhere. According to the Ford Foundation Agricultural Production Team, unless India triples its present rate of increase in food production, it will face an annual food deficit of 28 million tons in 1965-66.[37] It is pointed out that a deficit of 28 million tons would approach the United States annual wheat production and would completely exhaust even America's huge storage stocks of wheat within a year and a half.[38] The very fact that there is going to be considerable net inflow of financial resources for investment in the agricultural sector makes it all the more imperative that the agricultural sector should raise internally, through savings and taxation, the maximum domestic resources it can. Hence the rationale of increased taxation of agriculture. The emphasis, as Nurkse points out, should be on capturing as large a share of the increment in output as possible.[39]

36 Nicholls, p. 5.

37 Ford Foundation Agricultural Production Team, *Report on India's Food Crisis and Steps to Meet It* (Government of India, Ministry of Food and Agriculture, 1959), pp. 3-15.

38 Nicholls, p. 24.

39 Nurkse, p. 142.

Though there is a net inflow of financial resources for investment in agriculture over the Third Five Year Plan period, it is useful to distinguish between specific items of physical resources. There is already a redundance of labour, and a scarcity of land suitable for cultivation and capital equipment in Indian agriculture. It is reasonable to assume that there will be a net outflow of labour from agriculture into other sectors and a net inflow of capital into agriculture.

We have discussed the external objectives of agricultural taxation at such great length in order to show that there is a wide range of objectives different countries may want to pursue in initiating and implementing a scheme of taxation of agriculture. For any given economy it is better to focus attention on a limited set of objectives; too many objectives may result in achieving none. For India the important objective of agricultural taxation should be to mobilize and redirect resources in a manner consistent with providing incentives for the maximum productive efficiency and for the time being all other possible objectives have to be relegated to the background.

Internal Objectives of Agricultural Taxation

Internal objectives of agricultural taxation refer to the conventional internal tests or criteria of taxation, namely, administrative efficiency and effectiveness, ease of compliance, and impartiality of treatment. These internal tests were originally presented by Adam Smith and have since then become famous as Adam Smith's "canons of taxation." As Walter W. Heller points out, in many of the underdeveloped countries, especially in their rural sectors, Adam Smith's famous canons enjoy a validity as goals still to be achieved which they have long since lost in the most advanced economies.[40] India is, however, in a better situation as far as tax administration is concerned than many other underdeveloped countries.

(1) *Equity or Impartiality.* In Adam Smith's words, "The subjects of every state ought to contribute towards the support of the government as nearly as possible, in proportion to their respective abilities; that is, in proportion to the revenue which they respectively enjoy under the protection of the state."[41]

40 Harvard Law School, p. 148.

41 Adam Smith, *The Wealth of Nations* (London: J.M. Dent and Sons, Ltd., 1954), Vol. II, Book V, p. 307.

The interpretation of "equity" depends considerably on general value preferences. Adam Smith apparently conceived of equity in terms of proportionality. Other economists have followed this lead.[42] For Pigou the principle of equity implied "equal sacrifice among similar and similarly situated persons."[43]

In many underdeveloped economies, supervening economic objectives are permitted to intrude on impartiality or neutrality. Taxpayers who are otherwise in identical circumstances with respect to income or wealth and family status may nonetheless be treated differently either (a) by penalty taxes, if they hold the land idle or reap speculative gains from it, or (b) by special concessions, if they pursue favoured land uses or make improvements and investments in their land.[44] Impartiality, of course, can still govern within the structure of any one of these intrusions.[45]

It is not difficult to understand that, owing to widespread illiteracy, lack of reliable taxpayer accounts, etc., the governments of the underdeveloped countries have not found it feasible to introduce, especially in agriculture, the "advanced" taxes which conform to the equity criterion. However, in a setting of underdevelopment, such modifications as personalizing their less advanced taxes by building into them allowances for the family size and deductions for liabilities may be the preferred way of moving closer to equity or impartiality in taxation. In India the chief agricultural taxes—land revenue and agricultural income tax—operate in a glaringly inequitable manner, not only in the inter-sectoral sense, but also intra-sectorally.

(2) *Administrative and Compliance Considerations.* Under this head we may include the remaining three canons of Adam Smith, namely, certainty, convenience, and economy.[46] It is important to note that Adam Smith conceived of economy strictly in terms of cost of collec-

---

42 Note the classic statement of J.R. McCulloch: "The moment you abandon in the framing of such taxes, the cardinal principle of exacting from all individuals the same proportion of their income or of their property, you are at sea without rudder or compass, and there is no amount of injustice and folly you may not commit" [*A Treatise on the Principles and Practical Influence of Taxation and the Funding System*, 2nd Ed., 1865, quoted in footnote in John F. Due, *Government Finance* (Homewood, Ill.: Richard D. Irwin, Inc., 1959), p. 117].

43 A.C. Pigou, *A Study in Public Finance* (London: Macmillan and Co., Ltd., 1928), p. 61.

44 Harvard Law School, *op. cit.*, p. 150.

45 *Ibid.*

46 Adam Smith, pp. 307-8.

tion which, while important, is only part of the whole question of administrative efficiency. An efficient tax administration cannot remain content with minimizing the cost of collection alone. It has to set for itself other goals as well, such as raising the maximum revenue consistent with maintaining at least the productive efficiency of agriculture, introducing the most advanced techniques adaptable to the agricultural sector, and seeing to it that those who ought to be paying taxes, according to the criterion already adopted, do not evade payment.

Though India is in a better position in respect of administrative and compliance criteria compared to other underdeveloped countries, there remains much to be accomplished. The greatest need for administrative action is in the field of revision of land cadastres and assessments. The anomaly of having two taxes on income from land, namely, land revenue and agricultural income tax, is another problem calling for reform. Further, agricultural taxes being state taxes, there exist wide disparities in the practices prevailing in different states of the Indian Union. Finally, the lower-level officials of the revenue department are so poorly paid that they do not take their responsibilities seriously.

II

Let us now examine how far the existing system of agricultural taxation conforms to the objectives and criteria discussed in the preceding section. We may start with a few general observations. The most conspicuous characteristic of the Indian agricultural tax system is its inflexibility. Land revenue, for example, has ceased to have any correspondence with current incomes and prices. It has become a fixed payment on land. According to one estimate, taxes took 25 per cent of the increase in income in current prices gained from 1950-51 to 1959-60 in the nonagricultural sector, but in the agricultural sector taxes took only 6 per cent of that increase.[47] According to another estimate, in the urban sector 40 per cent of this increase in income was taxed away compared to only 15 per cent in the rural sector.[48] An inflexible tax system which does not respond automatically to changes in the economy is not a useful instrument,

47 Pranab Kumar Bardhan, "Agriculture Inadequately Taxed," *Economic Weekly* (December 9, 1961), p. 1831.

48 P.K. Mukherjee, "Surplus in Agriculture," *Agricultural Situation in India* (August 1959), p. 433.

whether for developed or for underdeveloped economies. In the case of underdeveloped economies, however, it presents a bigger problem because "a sustained, rapid pace of development will be difficult to achieve ... unless part of the increase in agricultural income is captured by appropriately flexible revenue instruments...." Another defect with the Indian agricultural tax system is that taxes are not "personalized" by introducing allowances for the taxpayer's marital and dependency status and for other personal circumstances that bear upon his taxpaying capacity. This stands out in sharp contrast to the practice followed in India in the case of personal income taxation, and thus violates the canon of impartiality as between the agricultural and nonagricultural sectors. As Wald emphasizes[49] the administrative burdens of a plan for personal deductions or credits should not be underestimated. Nevertheless, a start could be made and, instead of reducing revenue yield as often suspected, it may pave the way for a broadening of the tax base and for rate increases. Finally, under the present system, several categories of persons and incomes are not taxed. An enterprising tenant cultivator, for example, may be cultivating the lands of several landlords in the same vicinity, in many cases fields adjacent to each other. His income in the aggregate may be several times higher than that of a single landlord and yet, since the income from his own holding is below the exemption limit of the agricultural income tax, he escapes paying any income tax. Since leases of land are seldom registered legally, such "capitalist" tenant farmers are able to conceal their incomes. Another related problem is the taxation of the nonagricultural incomes of the farmers. A farmer, for example, may be running a small business in his neighbourhood. The only direct tax he pays is land revenue on his holding of land while his combined income may be much higher than that of a salaried person who pays an income tax on his salary income. The example of the farm-cum-shopkeeper may be easily extended to farmer-cum-school teachers, farmer-cum-clerks, etc. The crux of the problem posed by these examples is that these persons escape paying taxes on their incomes not necessarily because their incomes are concealed but because the incomes from different sources, treated separately, fall below the exemption limits of agricultural income tax and personal income tax (though when combined they fall well within the limits of taxability).[50]

49 Wald, p. 153.

50 *Cf.* R. Balakrishna, *Recent Trends in Indian Finance* (University of Madras, 1955), p. 100.

With these general observations on the Indian agricultural tax system as a background, we may now turn to a critical appraisal of individual taxes.

Land Revenue

(a) The greatest defect of the land revenue system is its inflexibility. The same rates have remained in force for decades, although agricultural prices and incomes have increased considerably, with the result that the land revenue has become just a nominal tax on land. Though originally conceived as a tax related to current income, it has been, through the failure of the governments to revise the assessments according to changes in prices, reduced to the status of a crude acreage tax. As Ursula K. Hicks rightly points out, "Exactly as in the case of the flat-sum poll tax, a crude acreage tax will always be poor, both in yield and equity."[51] It was the shortage of the necessary technical staff, the huge costs involved in resettlement operations, and the fear of provoking the political opposition of peasants that appear to have prevented the utilization of land revenue as an effective tax on agricultural income.[52] If land revenue could be made more responsive to price and production changes, its effects will be beneficial not only from the point of view of equity but also from the point of view of economic effects. To quote Wald, "Increased responsiveness will ordinarily increase the equitableness of the tax, but its main advantage lies in its economic effects. A flexible tax contributes to the goal of economic stability and it also serves the important function of diverting part of the increase in income, as a country's development programme bears fruit, to the financing of new development projects."[53]

(b) The tax base is not clearly defined and is not uniform as between different states and even between different parts of the same state. This defect, however, has no operational significance since the tax base, whatever it may have been originally, has long since ceased to function. Any reform of land revenue in India should certainly include the rationalization of the tax base. As Wald points out, ". . . land tax has been relatively untouched by the twentieth-century trend toward taxes based upon income as best fitted to promote justice in taxation and maximum economic growth."[54]

---

51 Ursula K. Hicks, *Development from Below* (Oxford: Clarendon Press, 1961), p. 335.
52 *Cf.* R.N. Tripathy, *Fiscal Policy and Economic Development in India* (Calcutta: The World Press Private, Ltd., 1958), p. 132.
53 Wald, pp. 202-3.
54 *Ibid.*, p. 185.

(c) As far as incentive provisions are concerned, they are almost completely lacking in the land revenue system. If they exist at all in some measure, they are lopsided. For example, while partial or full remission of land revenue is allowed when crops are damaged due to natural calamities, no credits are allowed for improvements on land or other useful investments, and no penalty imposed for improper use of land. One might argue that, since land revenue is in effect a crude acreage tax, increases in output do not have to be shared with the government and thus this constitutes an incentive element in the land revenue system. This is based on a wrong view of incentive taxation. As Walter Heller points out, ". . . incentive taxation seeks to influence economic activity primarily through the *structure* of the tax system and particular taxes—through variations in the tax liabilities of particular taxpayers, i.e., in the *distribution* of burdens— rather than through the *level* of taxation, i.e., through variations in the *total burden*."⁵⁵ In other words, incentive taxation works through differential taxation and not by keeping the general level of taxation low, as in the case with land revenue.

(d) The land revenue is a proportional tax based (as it obtains today) on the size of holding. This violates the principle of ability to pay. With a proportional land revenue and a large marketed surplus, the bigger landowners do not make a contribution to economic development corresponding to their ability. The state governments in recent years have been levying progressive rates of surcharges on the land revenue. We do not have separate data on the yield of the surcharge. From the available statistics on total revenue it is evident that the surcharge has not altered the situation substantially.

The proportional system of land revenue violates intra-sectoral as well as inter-sectoral equity. While nonagriculturists earning less than Rs 3000 annually do not have to pay any tax on their income (at 1958-59 rates), agriculturists who own land have to pay a certain amount of land revenue whatever their income from land. At present there are no exemptions from this tax. While it is impracticable, and probably unwise, to exempt all small farmers from paying any land revenue, a basic minimum exemption should be allowed for all holdings. As the Fiscal Division of the United Nations points out, "The taxation of subsistence levels ultimately depletes the human capital which is simultaneously the end and means of economic

---

55 Walter W. Heller, "The Use of Agricultural Taxation for Incentive Purposes," Harvard Law School, *op. cit.*, p. 223.

development."[56]

(e) Finally, while land revenue is a tax on land, tenant cultivators do not have to pay this tax. This is due to the inappropriate tax base. It is paradoxical that, under the Indian system of agricultural taxation, the subsistence owner-cultivator has to pay a land revenue whereas the tenant farmer whose income from farming is often higher than that of the subsistence owner-cultivator does not have to pay it.

Agricultural Income Tax

(a) The agricultural income tax was introduced for the first time in the 1930's. There is no economic rationale for this duplication in the system of agricultural taxation by introducing another tax which is essentially on land. This tax has grown out of the financial expediency and the administrative lethargy of the state government. As a financial expediency the agricultural income tax has been a gross failure in the majority of the states. The most appropriate step would have been to reshape and revitalize the land revenue as a flexible fiscal tool. This, of course, would have cost the state governments a good deal of administrative effort and financial expenditure. As an escape, they resorted to the short-cut of an additional tax which has proved to be a failure. Both land revenue and agricultural income tax are meant as taxes on income from land, though in the case of the former, through the neglect of the state governments, it has been reduced for all practical purposes to a crude acreage tax. Under the conditions existing in underdeveloped countries, a land tax is more appropriate than an agricultural income tax. Many of the attributes of an income tax could be built into the land tax without at the same time getting involved in the intricate problems associated with an agricultural income tax. This still leaves unsolved the problem of taxing the agriculturists' nonagricultural incomes.

(b) The agricultural income tax is levied, collected, and administered by the state governments. It is a graduated progressive tax with exemption limits varying from Rs 3000 to Rs 6000. The progression is not so steep as in the case of personal income tax. We may observe the following aspects of the tax: (1) Since the exemption limit is not less than Rs 3000, the vast majority of agriculturists

56 United Nations (Fiscal Division, Department of Economic Affairs), "Taxation and Economic Development in Asian Countries," *Economic Bulletin for Asia and the Far East* (Vol. IV, No. 3, November 1953), p. 13.

are left out. To realize an annual net income of Rs 3000 from farming, a farming household should have at least ten acres of good farm land (wet or adequately irrigated). On the average, it takes from ten to thirty acres to have an income of Rs 3000. We have seen that, according to the Census of Holdings carried out in 1954-55, 78 per cent of the owners have holdings below ten acres, and they own 28 per cent of the agricultural land. Seventeen per cent of the owners have holdings from ten to thirty acres and five per cent of the owners above thirty acres. As a broad generalization we could say at least 75 per cent of the landowners are outside the purview of the agricultural income tax. To have an exemption so high as to keep out 78 per cent of the landowners is not a wise policy. It may be noted that Rs 3000 is about ten times the national per capita income. As the Fiscal Division of the United Nations points out, "...if economic development is to be secured through domestic financial resources in a poor country, the standard of minimum taxable capacity might have to be placed at a lower absolute level."[57] (2) The remaining five per cent of the landowners hold about 38 per cent of the agricultural land. From the available information it is clear that many of them do not pay any agricultural income tax. The causes of this state of affairs are not far to seek. Most agriculturists do not keep any accounts of their receipts and disbursements. The tax officials, thus, have no records to check. If the agriculturists under-report their incomes it is hard to "prove" that they are false.

The extent of noncompliance in the case of the agricultural income tax cannot be accurately estimated since the only information we have is the distribution of holdings, which is partly based on enumeration of sample holdings. However, there are some rough estimates of the extent of noncompliance. Kaldor estimated that in 1953-54, out of a total assessable income of Rs 3350 million, the income actually assessed to agricultural income tax was only Rs 500 million.[58] We can thus say the degree of compliance is only about 17 per cent of the potential. Pointing out that any quantitative "estimate" can be anything but "the wildest guess," Kaldor concludes that "it certainly is not reasonable that the total yield of agricultural income tax—with an exemption limit of only Rs 3000—should amount to somewhat over Rs 30 million in an area accounting for over one-

57 United Nations, *op. cit.*, p. 8.

58 *Cf.* Nicholas Kaldor, *Indian Tax Reform, Report of a Survey* (issued by the Department of Economic Affairs, Ministry of Finance, Government of India, New Delhi, 1956), pp. 104-6.

half of the agricultural output of the country, valued at Rs 5000 crores."[59] I.S. Gulati has made an estimate for 1952-53 according to which the realized revenue from agricultural income tax (Rs 40 million) was only one-fifth of what should have been realized.[60] Gulati's estimate of noncompliance comes very close to that of Kaldor. Referring to the performance of agricultural income tax in 1952-53, Gulati concludes that "the agricultural income tax was being applied most ineffectively" and that "its higher rates existed on paper only."[61] He holds that it was unnecessary to have ever instituted a separate tax on agricultural income. A.M. Khusro has expressed the same view in an article.[62]

III

We have seen that the existing system of agricultural taxation in India is inadequate to serve the purpose of economic development. Several authorities have in recent times made suggestions as to how the system could be improved. Some of the proposals have been made specifically for India; others have been in the nature of general principles applicable to any economy. In all cases, of course, the context is economic development. The only official body that has inquired into the matter is the Indian Taxation Enquiry Commission, 1953-54 (which was concerned with the entire field of taxation, and not agricultural taxation only). We will present the views of the Commission and then the views of experts, Indian and foreign.

The Taxation Enquiry Commission proposed the following scheme of land revenue reform. Assuming that there already has been a land revenue settlement in a given state which at present faces the need for revision, the Commission's recommendations run in two steps: first, standardization of assessment over the state as a whole, and, second, revision of the standardized assessment at reasonable intervals. As regards the first step, subject to a maximum increase of 25 per cent in the present assessment, lands may be reassessed on the basis of the rise in the price level since the last assessment. The price level of the base period is given by the average of the prices prevailing during

59 *Ibid.,* p. 106.

60 I.S. Gulati, *Resource Prospects of the Third Five Year Plan* (Bombay: Orient Longmans, 1960), p. 69n.

61 *Ibid.,* p. 69.

62 A.M. Khusro, "Taxation of Agricultural Land," *Economic Weekly* (Annual Number, February 1963), p. 275.

ten to twenty years preceding the date of the last assessment. The earlier the date of the last assessment, the higher the percentage increase in the present standardized assessment, but not more than 25 per cent in any case. The most recently settled areas will have to bear no increase at all. Once the assessments are standardized in this manner, henceforth the land revenue will be revised once in ten years with reference to changes in the price level during the current period. For the future revision of land revenue, the Commission has recommended different rates of adjustment for rise and fall in prices. For any upward or downward change in the price level, not exceeding 25 per cent, there will be no adjustment in land revenue assessment. Beyond the 25 per cent change in the price level, the adjustment in the assessment will be at a higher rate in the case of a fall in the price level than in the case of a rise in the price level. The maximum upward revision in the case of a rise in the price level will be 12.5 per cent and the maximum downward revision in the case of a fall in the price level 25 per cent. Apart from these adjustments, in the case of lands which undergo drastic changes in their character such as from dry land to irrigated land or vice versa, ad hoc measures may be adopted by the government.

The recommendations of the Taxation Enquiry Commission in respect of land revenue are extremely conservative and do not show sufficient awareness of the importance of mobilization of domestic resources for capital accumulation and economic development. In the first place, the Commission's recommendations are quite unsatisfactory as a long-run solution for the problem of inadequate domestic resources for growth. It does not contain any provisions which will encourage the efficient use of land and penalize the inefficient use. Further, the Commission does not permit any progression in land revenue rates: proportionality would remain a permanent feature.

Secondly, even as short-run measures, the Commission's recommendations are not satisfactory. For one thing, standardization of rates by raising them on the basis of the previous settlement (or resettlement) is suggested. Thus, if the previous settlement was faulty, the new rates also will be faulty. Furthermore, quite apart from the issue of previous settlement, the increases in land revenue rates recommended are inadequate. The maximum increase proposed is 25 per cent in the case of holdings settled at the earliest date in the past. It should be noted that this increase does not take into consideration the size of the holding. On the average, however, the increase in assessment will not amount to more than 12.5 per cent. Ignoring all considerations of equity, incentives, etc., a 12.5 per cent increase in land revenue rates will not improve the domestic resources situation to any appreciable extent. The reason the Commission gives for keeping the new assessment so low is that the local governments should have some margin available for their own taxation. This stand taken by the Commission, it may be noted, is not sound. Local governments are still in their infancy in India. Most of them do not undertake any development projects. Most likely many local governments will not avail themselves of this available margin. Moreover, the local governments which undertake projects that are specifically beneficial to the locality will not find it difficult to raise the resources needed through other levies. In any case, to give the local governments a blank cheque is not a wise policy. The most appropriate policy seems to be for the state governments to levy and collect the maximum land revenue possible under given conditions, and to let the local governments have a share of it for financing their own investment expenditures. This would ensure better financial administration as well as better evaluation of projects in the light of the overall targets of the Five Year Plans.

With regard to agricultural income tax, the Taxation Enquiry Commission recommended its extension to all the states of the Union and to all agricultural incomes above Rs 3000 annually. Such an extension, it feels, is justified because large agricultural incomes now escape taxation since they are not taxed under the central income tax. The Commission thinks that no revision of the land revenue rates will be adequate enough to tax away a due share of the higher agricultural incomes. It believes that the extension of the agricultural income tax will make the land revenue systems in India more equitable and also help to reduce the major anomaly that the higher incomes from agriculture contribute much less to the treasury than the corresponding nonagricultural incomes.[63] The Commission hopes that eventually both agricultural and nonagricultural incomes will be brought under the same income tax. As a first step in this direction it recommends a surcharge on agricultural income tax on the basis of the assessee's nonagricultural income, if any. It is surprising that the Commission recommends a surcharge on agricultural income tax on the basis of the assessee's nonagricultural income when, in practice, the assessee does not pay even the regular tax on his agricultural income.

63 Commission, *Report*, Vol. III, *op. cit.*, p. 223.

The Taxation Enquiry Commission's recommendations regarding agricultural income tax are highly unrealistic. At a time (the Commission reported in 1953-54) when the agricultural income tax functioned most ineffectively in the majority of the states where it had been introduced, the Commission nevertheless recommended its extension to other states. And, to confound the confusion, it recommended a surcharge on agricultural income tax as if the solution consisted in raising the rates of taxation. Of course, one can easily agree with the Commission that the rate-schedule including the exemption limits of the agricultural income tax is faulty. But we have seen that even at the existing low rates, and in some cases with high exemption limits, the extent of compliance is only about one-sixth. The real problem, therefore, is not one of faulty rate structure, but of lack of enforcement. Under the present conditions it is almost impossible to get accurate returns of agricultural incomes from the agricultural income-earners. "Eventually," as the Commission hopes, the situation might improve. But "eventually" in this context may mean a few decades. Obviously, the government cannot wait for that long to augment its revenue resources. The plain fact is that for a considerable time to come land revenue has to remain the major land tax. Therefore the most practicable thing to do is to make the land tax take on as many features of the income tax as possible. Land revenue has several advantages over agricultural income tax. "A tax on land is difficult to evade since land is visibly and unalterably there for everyone to see and further land revenue encourages improvements on land since all the increase in produce obtained through harder and more efficient work accrues to the holder himself."[64]

Among other proposals for reform, we may briefly examine those put forth by I. S. Gulati and A. M. Khusro specifically for India, and those proposed by Kaldor, Ursula Hicks, and Haskell P. Wald in the form of guiding principles.

According to Gulati's proposals,[65] household holdings up to a size of twenty acres will pay a land revenue of Rs 2.5 (or whatever be the present rate on such holdings) per acre. For holdings above twenty acres Gulati recommends progressive rates as follows: first twenty acres at Rs 2.50 per acre; next ten acres at Rs 5 per acre; next ten acres at Rs 7.50 per acre; next ten acres at Rs 10 per acre; next fifty acres at Rs 15 per acre; and for any higher class interval the

64 Khusro, p. 275.
65 Gulati, pp. 73-7.

marginal rate will be Rs 25 per acre.

Gulati has committed the same mistake as the Taxation Enquiry Commission, namely, the failure to distinguish between an immediate and a long-run solution. Since his scheme is not based on any scientific evaluation of the yield potential of each holding, or category of holdings, based on such considerations as soil, climate, availability of water, etc., it is not satisfactory as a long-run solution. As a short-run solution, his proposals leave much to be desired. Nevertheless, his recommendations could be the basis of a broad pattern of reform. However, even as a short-run measure, his proposals are too crude. They could be refined considerably with distinctions between wet and dry lands, newly reclaimed and old farm lands, and similar classifications. For the first twenty acres, Gulati has suggested the existing rate of land revenue (roughly Rs 2.50 per acre). This is not a sound proposal. Holdings up to the size of twenty acres form about 40 per cent of the total agricultural land in India. To leave out such a large proportion of agricultural land does not seem reasonable, especially since 43 per cent of the landowners in India have holdings below 2.5 acres. Finally, instead of introducing progressive rates for each higher class interval in the size of the same holding, it may be much simpler to introduce progression by having higher rates for larger holdings and lower rates for smaller holdings.

Khusro's proposals for land revenue reform are based on much more detailed information regarding farm incomes than those of Gulati.[66] They also show more sound economic reasoning. Khusro makes three basic proposals: (1) Holdings up to the size of five acres may continue to pay the present assessment, i.e. Rs 3 per acre on the average. According to him, "... an enhancement of rates per acre in these land brackets is not desirable, for holdings below five acres do not fulfil the norms of efficiency and surplus generation."[67] (2) In the size groups above five acres but below ten acres the rate of land revenue can be enhanced to no more than Rs 5 per acre. Khusro points out that this relatively small increase is warranted by some important characteristics of Indian farming in terms of efficiency, employment, and surplus generation. The minimum acreage for the full absorption of the manpower of an average family works out to be well above five acres and in many cases above ten acres. (3) Above the ten-acre size, land revenue could take a jump from Rs 5 to Rs 10 per acre and thereafter, for all higher size groups, stay constant at

66 Khusro, *op. cit.*, pp. 275-82.
67 *Ibid.*, p. 279.

this rate. According to him, there are strong reasons why a doubling of tax per acre must be suggested as land size increases above ten acres. "In holdings above this size, bullock wastage is eliminated, family labour fully absorbed, and norm incomes of Rs 1200 and above reached. Aggregate production and consumption is substantial and marketed surplus of a considerable order arise."[68] If these reforms are implemented, he estimates, there will be an increase of about Rs 2000 million in land revenue collection. According to Khusro, the ratio of tax to income rises from about 3 per cent in the lowest size groups to no more than 23 per cent in the highest size groups. "The main attraction of the proposals," he points out, "obviously is the simplicity in the grading of land into three slabs and no more. The grading, of course, will have to be in terms of standard and not simple acreage."[69] Khusro's proposals are, on the whole, more acceptable than those made by Gulati. However, he also has made no distinction between the immediate and eventual solutions for the land revenue problem. As an immediate solution, his proposals with some slight modifications (e.g. making the rate schedule a little more elaborate to take into account variations in conditions from state to state and from region to region within the state) are acceptable. The implementation of his proposals may relieve the government considerably of its present financial strain. But, as an eventual solution, the system recommended by him is too simple. The only desirable feature is the element of progression. That alone, however, does not make a tax system ideal from the point of view of economic development.

Besides the above proposals, there have been a few others to which we shall make only a passing reference since they are either totally unacceptable or impracticable, or differ in details only. Harold M. Groves and Murugappa C. Madhavan[70] have suggested a "blanket increase" of 10 to 30 per cent in the existing land revenue rates and the doubling of the existing land revenue on acreage under commercial crops. They also recommended a surcharge at the rate of Rs 0.50 per acre on big landowners whose holdings exceed ten acres. They are not in favour of continuing the agricultural income tax since its usefulness "as a revenue producer in the present Indian

68 *Ibid.*, p. 281.

69 *Ibid.*

70 Harold M. Groves and Murugappa C. Madhavan, "Agricultural Taxation and India's Third Five Year Plan," *Land Economics* (Vol. XXXVIII, No. 1, February 1962), pp. 56-64.

situation is limited."[71] It may be noted that Groves and Madhavan do not offer any permanent solution to the problem. As immediate expedients, the proposals may have some merit, but even then they are a bit too arbitrary and too crude. Most objectionable, however, is the discriminatory treatment of land under commercial crops. Such a measure will distort the crop pattern of the country. The criterion of taxation should be income from land under its *best use*, whatever be the crops cultivated, unless, of course, the government wants to discourage the raising of commercial crops. I.M.D. Little has put forth some proposals the purpose of which appears to be the use of land revenue as an instrument of enforcing a ceiling on land holdings.[72] He has suggested a steeply progressive scale of land revenue with as many as twenty-seven size intervals. The lowest of these, ranging from 0 to 5 acres, was to be exempted from land revenue while the highest sized holdings of thirty acres and above were to pay such penalty rates that they would constitute a disincentive for holding more than thirty acres. Little's proposals are clearly unrealistic. We have already emphasized earlier that agricultural taxation should not be used as an instrument of land redistribution in the Indian context. Apart from this, his proposals are unacceptable since the base of taxation is acreage and not income derived or derivable from the holding. (In Chapter IV we referred to the unequal distribution of landownership in India in order to show that there is considerable inequality in income distribution. We resorted to this procedure only because we did not have detailed data on income distribution.) For holdings above thirty acres, Little has suggested between 350 and 700 per cent increases in the land revenue rates. This is certainly inequitable, inter-sectorally as well as intra-sectorally. K. N. Raj has made three proposals:[73] (1) doubling of land tax on holdings above five acres, (2) imposing a tax on agricultural rent, and (3) levying a surcharge on holdings above five acres under commercial crops. The first suggestion is broadly acceptable. The second one is impracticable since under Indian conditions it is hard to identify the rent payer and also to get exact information from him regarding the amount of rent. (According to Raj's proposals, the tax on agricultural rent is to be deducted at the source from the

---

71 *Ibid.*, p. 61.

72 I.M.D. Little, "Tax Policy and the Third Plan" (Institute of Economic Growth, Delhi, 1959, mimeographed). Quoted in Khusro, *op. cit.*, p. 279.

73 K.N. Raj, "Resources for the Third Plan: An Approach," *Economic Weekly* (Annual Number, January 1959). Quoted in Khusro, *op. cit.*, p. 279.

tenants.) The third proposal is unacceptable since it involves un-warranted discrimination against commercial crops. Also it is impracticable since it involves a continuous check-up of the nature of the crops grown from season to season and necessitates much larger administrative machinery.

Finally, let us examine the guiding principles of agricultural tax reform put forth by such authorities as Kaldor, Ursula Hicks, and Haskell P. Wald. As noted earlier, they have discussed the problem in general and not with particular reference to the needs of any one economy. Nicholas Kaldor would favour a system of land tax which is progressive and which is based on the potential output from land.[74] Potential output, according to him, is the "... output which the land would yield if it were managed with average effici-ency."[75] In his view a land tax based on potential output will have a certain built-in incentive. The inefficient farmer whose production is less than the average for the region and for the type of land con-cerned would be penalized, whereas the efficient farmer would be correspondingly encouraged. Under this scheme, once we have the basic data relating to the holdings, we do not need frequent reassessment of each holding. We need, however, a thorough survey of landholdings to introduce the system for the first time. The pur-pose of this survey is to "... assess the potential fertility of individual pieces of land in relation to the national or regional average on the basis of more or less permanent criteria such as annual rainfall, irrigation, slope and inclination of land, porousness or other qualities of the soil, etc., and once this work of evaluation of 'potential relative fertility' is accomplished, it need not be repeated at frequent inter-vals."[76] On the other hand, the actual tax liability could be changed year by year by estimating the average value of output per acre for the country or region as a whole and multiplying this by the coeffi-cient which relates the fertility of any particular acre to the national average.

Kaldor's proposals, it may be noted, include only the agricul-turist's income from farming and it is imposed, implicitly, on land-owners and not on tenant farmers or other non-landowning parti-cipants in agricultural production. Thus his scheme is very similar to the tax system which Lord Lugard introduced in Northern Nigeria

---

74 Kaldor, "The Role of Taxation in Economic Development," *op. cit.*, pp. 7-10.
75 *Ibid.*, p. 9.
76 Hicks, pp. 330-2.

during his regime which started in 1894.[77] Lugard's Nigerian tax was to be levied in principle on the income and profit of each individual. But in practice the income in question was that derived from land. The assessment was not to be based on the actual incomes but on the yield of the land "if cultivated up to a good average standard"; thus in intention somewhat penalizing bad farming and encouraging good farming.[78] However, since the Lugard system did not include any principle of automatic revision of assessment on the basis of certain indices, it retrograded to the level of the Indian tax system. As Ursula Hicks points out, during the long inflation of the 1950's the base of the North Nigerian direct tax became little better than a lump-sum poll tax.[79] Kaldor's proposals avoid this pitfall.

Ursula Hicks would go a step further than both Kaldor and Lord Lugard, and include in the land tax the potential income of the family, whether the income is derived from farming or not. In this she is guided by the Uganda system under which "... the taxation of farmers and rural communities in Uganda is being carried out successfully and with increasing efficiency."[80] Since Mrs Hicks has been very articulate in her admiration for the Uganda system, we may quote from her work the following passage describing it:[81]

A list is first drawn up of the main categories of sources of income in the area, not only the various types of farming (and fishing, if relevant), but also trading occupations, salaries, and service incomes. Against each is then marked estimated potential unit receipt (e.g., 4s. per coffee tree)—this standard return is estimated on a fairly generous scale (leaving incentive for better farming), and broadly corresponds to Lugard's Northern Nigerian "fair average cultivation"; but it can be made more flexible according to the season as well as to the type of land. For shops, an estimate of stock in trade is made (so far as possible with the cooperation of the owner), and a net income, e.g., of 60s. assumed for a unit stock value of 100 x. Land under general cultivation is counted at so much an acre. Finally, a general "catch all" takes up any other sources of income not included already. Total (expected potential) income is then found by adding up standard income from all

77 *Ibid.*
78 *Ibid.*, p. 331.
79 *Ibid.*
80 *Ibid.*, p. 343.
81 *Ibid.*, p. 340.

sources. Assessment can then be made in blocks, incomes below
1200s. per annum paying at one rate, incomes between 1200s.
and 1650s. at a higher rate, and so on up to any desired figure,
so far as the central government permits.

This method of assessment, Mrs Hicks points out, leans heavily
on the reliability of local assessment committees. The Uganda
system requires the tax assessment form to be made out in triplicate,
of which one copy is kept by the taxpayer. It is signed (or marked)
by the taxpayer, and separately by the village chief and the councillor
who have accompanied him in making the assessment.

The graduated land tax, Uganda style, is the "ideal" tax we can
recommend for any developing country which wants to tax farmers
and rural communities most effectively. The introduction of such a
land tax in a country like India, however, can remain only a distant
possibility. One probable reason why this system has succeeded in
Uganda is that farming conditions are fairly uniform throughout
the nation. In contrast, a high degree of diversity exists in India.
The vast bulk of the rural population is illiterate. It would take a long
time before these people could be familiarized with the notion of tax
returns or assessment forms. It will be extremely difficult to get reliable information from each and every agriculturist about his nonagricultural income. Under these conditions it will not be easy to
implement a land tax which will include the entire income of the
household. But for the fact that all incomes are included in the
Uganda tax, Mrs Hicks' proposals are broadly similar to those of
Kaldor.

Haskell P. Wald has made certain proposals which are in substance similar to those put forth by Kaldor. According to him, "The
most valuable and efficient tool for a successful reconstruction of
land taxation, giving particular emphasis to rationalizing the tax
base, is a system of soil classification and rating according to indices
of productive capacity and relative income potential."[82] He presents
a detailed account of how the soil classification according to productive capacity could be carried out.[83]

82 Wald, p. 186.
83 *Ibid.*, pp. 188-99

CONCLUSION

In the first part of this chapter we briefly pointed out the difference between the role of fiscal policy in the developed and the under-developed economies of the world. While stabilization is the major objective in the former case, capital formation is the chief purpose in the latter. This difference, it should be clearly understood, is only a matter of degree and not of kind.

We next considered the different objectives—external as well as internal—which agricultural taxation may be called upon to accomplish in underdeveloped economies. Though all possible objectives were outlined, the discussion was with special reference to India. We found that mobilization and redirection of resources, above all, are the most important objectives for India. The net inflow of resources into the agricultural sector as proposed under the Third Five Year Plan was considered legitimate in view of the grave food situation in the country.

Our examination of the existing taxes on agriculture revealed several serious deficiencies. In respect of land revenue it was found that the land revenue is, in effect, a crude acreage tax. We also noted its inflexibility, lack of properly defined tax base, inadequate incentives, and proportionality in rates. As regards agricultural income tax, we reached the conclusion that its role is insignificant. The exemption limits are too high and the progressivity of the rates too low. The greatest defect of the agricultural income tax, however, is noncompliance. The extent of compliance is estimated at one-sixth. This, we found, is inevitable under Indian conditions, with widespread illiteracy, lack of business accounting on the part of the farmers, and low tax morality.

Following the evaluation of the existing system of agricultural taxation, we discussed critically some of the more important proposals for reform. The Taxation Enquiry Commission's recommendations were found to be very unsatisfactory. The increases in tax rates proposed by the Commission are nominal and thus inadequate to meet the fast-growing financial needs of the government. The Commission favours the continuance of agricultural income tax which has already proved a gross failure in most states. According to Gulati's proposals there will be no increase in land revenue rates on holdings below twenty acres. This would mean that about 40 per cent of the agricultural land will be unaffected by the tax reform. In his opinion the agricultural income tax serves no useful purpose and should, therefore, be abolished. Khusro's suggestions are more realistic than those of Gulati. He would exclude holdings below five acres from any upward revision of land revenue rates and the highest increase he proposes is 200 per cent. I.M.D. Little's recommendations are drastic and impracticable. He has suggested a steeply progressive scale of land revenue with twenty-seven size intervals. On holdings above thirty acres he recommends between 350 and 750 per cent increases in the land revenue rates. Raj's recommendation to tax agricultural rent at source does not seem to be practicable since it is hard to identify the rent payer and to get exact information from him. Harold Groves and Murugappa Madhavan focus their attention only on the immediate financial needs of the government and have not, therefore, suggested any permanent reform.

A defect common to all these proposals is that they do not distinguish between what could be done immediately and what is desirable in the long run. If raising more revenue resources were the only purpose of tax reform, this would not matter much. But in the Indian context we need an integrated tax system which is mutually consistent between its various objectives. Hence raising the land revenue rates alone is not a sufficient, though a necessary, condition of tax reform.

Finally, we examined the salient features of the reforms suggested by Kaldor, Mrs Hicks, and Haskell P. Wald, which are not tailored to suit the needs of any one particular country, but which could be applied with suitable modifications to India or any other country looking for ways of effective taxation of the rural community.

CHAPTER VII

TOWARDS AN IMPROVED SYSTEM OF AGRICULTURAL TAXATION IN INDIA
(II) RECOMMENDATIONS FOR REFORM

In the light of the discussion in the preceding chapter, we present below our own recommendations for the reform of the agricultural tax system in India. The recommendations are divided into two parts, one consisting of immediate measures and the other of eventual measures. The immediate steps are designed specifically to raise more domestic resources in the short run (i.e. during the next three to five years) for the financing of economic development. Such measures are required because it takes time to frame a comprehensive tax system and implement it. In the interim period, therefore, the government should introduce certain expedient measures to augment its meagre domestic resources.

IMMEDIATE MEASURES

(1) The present rates of land revenue are extremely low and their burden quite nominal. The most obvious step which could, therefore, be adopted immediately is to raise the land revenue rates. The increase of the rates should be carried out in as equitable a manner as possible, though some inequities are likely to remain in any case. This would mean that, even in the short run, land revenue rates should be raised with due attention to known differences in soil, climate, crops, and, above all, size of holdings. There can be no all-India pattern for land revenue since conditions vary substantially from state to state. Variations in these conditions among states, however, do not present any serious administrative or legislative difficulties because land revenue is levied, collected and retained by the state governments. Each state could, therefore, work out the details of the scheme in the best manner possible, given the peculiar situation in each region. The question of inter-state equity will be taken care of largely if each state does its best in the matter of raising the rates of land revenue. Within each state, conditions vary greatly

between different regions. This is especially true of states within which very distinct geographical regions exist. In such states, soil conditions differ from region to region and hence also the crops. For the purpose of the revision of land revenue rates, each state may be divided into a few geographical regions or zones. Within each zone a distinction may be made between dry and wet lands on the basis of the availability of water for irrigation. Further, for each zone, the size of a given holding may be expressed in standard acres. For example, one acre of wet land cultivated to crop A may be treated as equivalent to 2.5 acres of dry land cultivated to crop B. While these classifications are deemed necessary to insure some degree of fairness in the revision of land revenue rates, care should be taken not to make these classifications too elaborate and complicated lest it may take too long an interval to introduce the scheme. Once we have divided each state into a limited number of zones and within each zone worked out an equivalence between dry and wet lands and also other categories, the revision of land revenue rates could be finalized with one more step, namely, fixation of rates for different holdings on the basis of size (the size is expressed in some kind of "standard acres"). The rates could be revised in terms of percentage increase in the existing rate. The percentage increase in rates should, of course, be progressive with the size of the holding. Holdings below the size of 2.5 acres may be exempted from any upward revision of rates; they will continue to pay at the present rate. Holdings between 2.5 and 5 acres may be subject to a nominal increase of 25 per cent. The maximum increase may be limited to 200 per cent in the case of the largest holdings. The revision of rates may be along the following lines:

Size of holding (acres)	Percentage increase in land revenue per acre
0— 2.5	0
2.5— 5.0	25
5.0—10.0	50
10.0—15.0	75
15.0—30.0	100
30.0—60.0	150
Above 60	200

This rate schedule is meant as a rough pattern only; minor modifications could be introduced to suit the special circumstances prevailing in each state or region. Much of the information required for this reform already exists. In fixing ceiling on landholdings most state governments have worked out certain rations of equivalence between different types of land. What is needed for the implementation of this scheme of reform is just a consolidation, and systematic use, of the relevant information already available. Specific proposals for reform for each state along these lines could be finalized over a period of six months to one year since most of the required information already exists and since it does not require any additional personnel. No fresh surveying, registration, and classification of lands is involved. The proposals could be finalized during a year's time at the most and could come into effect for the next fiscal or agricultural year. This plan should remain in force until a permanent solution is worked out over a period of, say, three to seven years.

It may be pointed out, in passing, that our proposals for immediate action are very similar to those suggested by Khusro[1] (note that he did not make a distinction, as we have done, between the immediate and the eventual solutions). Khusro exempts all holdings below 5 acres from any enhancement of land revenue rates. According to our proposals only holdings below the size of 2.5 acres will be exempted from enhanced rates. Holdings between 2.5 and 5 acres are liable to pay 25 per cent more than their present assessment. In terms of revenue yield this may not make much difference but in terms of equity it does. For holdings between five acres and ten acres, the two proposals are very similar. Further, Khusro has grouped all holdings above ten acres together in one category and prescribed a 200 per cent increase in their land revenue rates. We have, instead, introduced four groups of holdings and prescribed increases ranging from 75 per cent for holdings between ten and fifteen acres to 200 per cent in the case of holdings above sixty acres. In terms of administrative convenience our proposals are simple enough while in terms of equity they are more acceptable than those recommended by Khusro.

The implementation of these measures will result in greater burdens of land revenue for the higher groups of landholders. The burden, however, will not exceed 10 per cent of income in the case

---

[1] See Chapter VI.

of the largest-sized holdings.[2] It is difficult to give any exact indication of the potential gain, in terms of revenue, of these immediate steps since (1) the size intervals of holdings are expressed in "standard" acres and (2) the pattern of landownership is undergoing a steady change. As a rough estimate, we might say the revenue will increase by at least 75-125 per cent.

(2) What shall be the status of the agricultural income tax in the immediate future? In the case of holdings which yield net incomes below the exemption limit of the agricultural income tax (roughly, holdings below twenty acres), our proposals regarding land revenue do not introduce any new complication. In the case of holdings which come within the purview of the agricultural income tax, the tax which would yield the highest revenue may be applied. Thus if the average rate of agricultural income tax on a certain holding (note that we mean the actual, realized agricultural income tax) is higher than the land tax for similar holdings, the existing agricultural income tax may continue on such holdings. And whatever amount is paid as land revenue at the old rates may be deducted from the agricultural income tax liability. This will avoid the double taxation of such holdings. If, on the other hand, the new land tax is higher than the existing agricultural income tax, then the latter may be done away with and the land taxed on the basis of the new rates of land revenue.

(3) Needless to say, if, in any state, there has been during the last one or two years an adequate revision of land revenue rates, either for the whole state or for particular regions, the new rates will not apply in such cases.

(4) There has been, in the recent past, a continuous upward revision of commodity taxes. With the implementation of the short-run measures of agricultural tax reform there should be no further enhancement of the rates of taxation of essential consumer goods like kerosene, inferior textiles, matches, etc. which figure prominently in the budgets of low-income groups, the bulk of which consists of agriculturists.

---

2 Though at present land revenue is a proportional tax (i.e. proportional to the size of the holding), a certain amount of progressivity is already implicit in the system since larger holdings generally yield a lower average income per acre. See Khusro, "Taxation of Agricultural Land," *Economic Weekly* (Annual Number, February 1963), p. 276.

LONG-RUN MEASURES

Since land revenue is the oldest and the most important of the agricultural taxes, we may start with this tax in the presentation of our proposals for the eventual pattern of agricultural tax system. It is actually land revenue which stands in need of the most thorough overhauling.

(1) *Land Revenue Reform.* Land revenue in its present form is nothing but a crude acreage tax. It poorly reflects the ability to pay of the landholders and meets the revenue needs of the government inadequately. It thus hampers the "smooth process of development." In order to make land revenue reflect truly the ability to pay of the cultivators, it is necessary that it should be based on income from land and not on acreage. Further, to insure intra-sectoral equity, i.e. to make tax payments truly reflect the relative ability to pay of the agriculturists belonging to different income groups, the rates should be made progressive. There cannot be much debate on the validity of these propositions. As we have seen in the last chapter, differences of opinion are likely to crop up regarding only the operational aspects of such a tax. In presenting the following proposals, only the principal lines along which the reform should be carried out are indicated. Needless to say, it is hard to present concrete details of each proposal for a country as diverse as India within the scope of a work of this nature.

(a) The potential income from each holding under average conditions of production should be the tax base of land revenue. The potential output of each holding should be estimated on the basis of a soil classification according to productive capacity. It may be expressed as a proportion of the average per acre output of the region concerned. (This may be in the form of an index number or coefficient.) The average potential output per acre for each region in the nation should be updated occasionally to allow for changes in the drainage situation, sedimentation, erosion, and land improvement programmes. Once these steps are adopted, annual revision of the assessment on each holding could be made on the basis of changes in the agricultural price level in each region. In years of extreme distress due to drought or flood, or other calamities, complete remission of land revenue should be granted for the regions affected.

(b) The assessment should be applied to the entire holding of the household. This will avoid the artificial partitioning of land among

members of the same household to escape higher marginal rates of taxation.

(c) Nonfarm incomes should be added to the farm income and the total income taxed at the appropriate rate.

(d) Under the new system, tenant farmers also should be subject to the land tax. In assessing the tenant cultivators, they should be allowed a tax credit in recognition of their rental obligations. The landlords, however, should be taxed according to the full potential income from the land making due allowance for the share of the produce that goes to the tenants.

(e) The appropriate marginal rates of tax should be applied to the potential income from the entire landholding of the household whether they are located in one block or scattered in different places. In other words, holdings are to be treated on a consolidated basis.

(f) A basic minimum exemption should be allowed in all cases irrespective of the size of the household or the status of the agriculturists (tenant, owner-cultivator, etc.). This exemption limit should be fixed at a certain level of income and not at a certain size of holding of land. It should be placed at a much lower level than the existing levels applied in the case of the agricultural income tax and personal income tax. (A corresponding lowering of the exemption limit is called for in the case of the personal income tax also.) The exemption limit may be fixed at a multiple of the national per capita annual income, the multiple depending on the average size of the family for the nation. Thus, under present conditions, Rs 1500 seems to be a proper exemption limit (per capita national income is roughly Rs 300 a year and the average size of the family is taken as five). It may be noted that this exemption limit is half the present level applied in the case of agricultural income tax and personal income tax.

(g) Besides the basic exemption, each taxpayer may be allowed a personal deduction for additional dependents over and above the number taken into account in fixing the basic exemption. Instead of granting a deduction for each additional dependent, it will be better to establish a few dependency classes (e.g. one to two persons, three to five persons, and six or more persons).

(h) Land revenue rates should be made progressive with increases in income. The rates should be comparable with those for nonagricultural incomes as required under the personal income tax.

(i) As a measure to promote economic development, certain

approved categories of savings and investment may be given credit in calculating the taxable income of the farm household. For example, savings in the form of life insurance policies, government bonds, post office bank savings, provident funds, etc. could be exempted. Similarly, investment in the form of tractors, irrigation equipment, other farm equipment, farm buildings, etc. could be exempted.

(2) Ownership of land confers greater security on the agriculturist compared to salary earners and labourers. This security enables (or could enable) him to maintain higher levels of consumption, for he does not have to worry so much about saving for the future. In other words, current income is only one measure of the ability to pay taxes; wealth is another. According to our proposals relating to land revenue, landowning agriculturists will be taxed at the same rates as non-landowners such as salary earners, labourers, etc. Therefore, in order to make the total tax burden of the landowning agriculturists more equitable, a property tax may be levied on all landholdings.

(3) Special levies on land such as irrigation or betterment duties may be dropped in the context of the present proposals. For, so long as irrigation or other public works improve the productivity of agricultural land, it will be reflected in the current output (or potential output if farmers do not make use of the improved irrigation or other facilities—this should not make any difference since land revenue will be based on potential yield) and will be subject to a larger assessment. On the other hand, in so far as irrigation or other public facilities enhance land values, the increased value will be subject to the new property tax suggested under proposal (2). Increased land values will also be subject to a capital gains tax in the case of sales, as explained in the following paragraph. At present, irrigation duties and betterment levies are collected by the state government, though the revenue from these levies is quite nominal. These levies are justifiable in the existing context since the land tax is very light. However, under the new system proposed, land revenue will be based on the potential output from land under average conditions. If, in addition to such a land tax, we also impose an irrigation levy, it will amount to double taxation.

(4) A capital gains tax may be levied on all land sales. Such a levy will more than compensate for the loss of revenue caused by the abolition of irrigation and betterment levies. The property tax suggested under proposal (2) will be proportional to the current value of the property and will be paid by the owner so long as the property is in his possession. However, the burden of the property

tax will be negligible compared to the increment in the value of the property which he may receive in the case of a sale, assuming, of course, that, as a result of irrigation and other public works, land values have risen considerably. The capital gains tax suggested will close this loophole.

(5) Visible public expenditures, the benefits of which have no direct effect on agricultural productivity, such as hospitals, roads and bridges, schools, etc., should be financed, as far as possible, through separate local levies. It may be pointed out that though the benefits of these public expenditures are not really localized, the villagers tend to think of the benefits as local and are, thus, more enthusiastic in supporting such projects than those physically remote from them. One method will be to make the villagers bear the entire cost or a considerable portion thereof of the initial cost of plant and equipment. Those among the villagers who are unable to pay the levies in money may be given the option to make their contribution in the form of labour services. The running expenses of these works could be met partly from fees charged for services and partly from the general revenue of the state or central government, or both. As Ursula Hicks rightly points out, willing tax compliance on the part of farmers can more easily be achieved "if it is apparent to the taxpayers that a substantial part of the revenue is being spent on things that will benefit the rural community especially on those things they themselves have chosen."[3]

(6) With the implementation of the proposed land revenue reform, a separate agricultural income tax has no place in the tax system of India. As a matter of fact the new land revenue will be, in a meaningful sense, an income tax, the salient features of an income tax being incorporated into the land tax. The new land tax, as we have seen, will be based on the potential incomes from land under average conditions and these incomes will be taxed at rates comparable to those applicable to nonagricultural incomes under the personal income tax. The new land tax is different from the existing agricultural income tax in that the former will not rely on any kind of faulty reporting of agricultural incomes by individual farmers. It will be a true land tax for it is not based on the acreage of the holding, but on the income from it. Thus, the new land tax will combine in one tax the twin taxes (existing) on agriculture, namely, agricultural income tax and land revenue. In Assam and Kerala, however,

3 Ursula K. Hicks, *Development from Below* (Oxford: Clarendon Press, 1961), p. 332.

where a considerable portion of the nonsubsistence agricultural sector is organized along plantation lines, there may be some logic in letting the present agricultural income tax continue. In these states, it may be noted, agricultural income tax has been operating rather effectively. Agricultural income tax may, therefore, be allowed to function side by side with land revenue in these individual cases.

(7) At present agricultural land is exempted from taxation under estate duty and wealth tax. There is no reason why there should be a discriminatory treatment in favour of agricultural land as a form of wealth and against other forms of assets such as nonagricultural land, buildings, jewelry, stock, etc. These taxes, therefore, should be extended to include agricultural land also.

(8) Finally, since it is hoped that adequate revenue will be raised as a result of the above proposals, it is desirable that taxes on essential commodities of mass consumption should be reduced to a bare minimum lest the lower strata of the society should be put to extreme hardship. On the other hand, taxes on commodities of luxury consumption could be raised further. At present taxes on luxury articles are quite low compared to those on essential consumption. (This is not true in the case of imported luxury items which are subject to highly prohibitive taxes, but such imports are very restricted.)

It is difficult to say exactly what would be the potential gain, in terms of tax revenue, of the long-run measures outlined above. Broadly, what we have proposed is a land tax comparable, in its essential features, to personal income tax which at present is confined to the nonagricultural sector. The implementation of such a land tax would mean that direct taxation of agriculture will be raised to the level of the nonagricultural sector. At present the proportion of income paid in direct taxes by the agricultural sector is less than half the proportion paid by the nonagricultural sector. Thus, as a very rough estimate, we might say that revenue from direct taxation of agriculture will increase by about 100 per cent as a result of the long-run measures of reform.

CONCLUSION

Our proposals for the reform of the agricultural tax system in India were presented under two groups: immediate and long-run measures. The immediate measures focus attention mainly on the upward revision of land revenue rates for all holdings except those below the size of 2.5 acres. The maximum increase proposed was 200 per cent in the case of the largest class of holdings. The total burden of land revenue on such holdings will still amount to only slightly less than 10 per cent of the income from such holdings. The eventual measures proposed are more detailed and include several reforms. These include (1) reform of the tax base of land revenue; (2) proposals for making land revenue a progressive tax; (3) suggestions for "personalizing" land revenue; (4) exemption of certain categories of savings and investment from taxation; (5) levying a property tax on all holdings; (6) imposing a capital gains tax on land sales; (7) abolishing irrigation and betterment levies; (8) financing of local (development) public works such as schools and hospitals through special levies as far as possible; (9) abolition of the present agricultural income tax; (10) inclusion of agricultural land within the purview of the wealth tax and estate duty; and (11) reduction of commodity taxes on articles of essential mass consumption.

CHAPTER VIII

SUMMARY AND CONCLUSIONS

THIS study was undertaken to investigate the role of agricultural taxation in financing India's economic development. The study addressed itself to (1) an estimation of the burden of taxation of the agricultural sector, (2) a comparison of the agricultural sector's contribution to governmental revenue with that of the nonagricultural sector, (3) an examination of agricultural taxation in relation to national goals, (4) an appraisal of the existing system of agricultural taxation from the point of view of financing economic development, and (5) policy recommendations in the light of the findings under (1) to (4).

As pointed out in the Introduction, according to the programme of planned economic development accepted by the Government of India, the public sector is expected to grow faster, both absolutely and relatively, than the private sector. This implies that more and more investment will be directly undertaken by the government. Every effort, thus, needs to be made to increase the financial resources of the government. In our study we discussed this problem in relation to the agricultural sector. Agriculture is the largest sector of the Indian economy, as in all underdeveloped countries, both in terms of the labour force employed and the national output produced. The agricultural sector, being the largest segment of the economy, must, therefore, bear a substantial portion of the cost of economic development.

For the purpose of this study, we included under agricultural taxation all the relevant central (federal) and state taxes. Local taxation was not taken into account since we did not have enough data on local taxes. This, however, is not a serious omission as local taxation within the rural sector is negligible.

PRESENT STATUS OF AGRICULTURAL TAXATION IN INDIA

Among the major taxes affecting the agricultural sector, we may mention land revenue, stamps and registration, general sales tax, excise duties, and import duties. Of these, land revenue is the only tax levied exclusively on agriculture. The other taxes are borne by the agriculturists in their capacity as consumers or property owners. Land revenue is levied and collected by the state governments. Land revenue, though its relative importance has greatly declined in recent times as a result of inflation and also due to the introduction and extension of many new levies, is still the most important tax on agriculture. It accounted for 8.5 per cent of the combined tax revenue of the central and state governments in 1958-59. Different states have, in the past, adopted different bases in assessing the land revenue. But, because there has been no regular revision of the assessment during the last few decades, these have fallen into disuse and thus lost their practical validity. The land revenue has, as a matter of fact, become a crude acreage tax. The revenue from "stamps and registration" has been rather significant. The receipts come from three sources mainly: the sale of judicial stamps, court fee stamps, and registration of documents. These taxes are levied and collected by the central as well as the state governments. In 1958-59, stamps and registration accounted for 3.6 per cent of the combined tax revenue of the central and state governments. Sales tax is a comparatively new levy, though an increasingly important one. It is levied and collected by the state governments. Since 1957-58 the revenue from the general sales tax has exceeded the receipts from land revenue. Generally, food grains are either totally exempt from sales taxation or taxed only under certain special circumstances. The receipts from general sales tax constituted 10.2 per cent of the combined tax revenue of the central and state governments in 1958-59.

Of all the taxes levied in India, excise duties are the most important from the point of view of revenue. Excise duties are levied and collected by the central and state governments. By far the major portion of the revenue from excise duties is, however, accounted for by the central taxes. Twenty per cent of the net proceeds of the central excise duties is distributed among the states. Excise duties, central and state, accounted for 33 per cent (central excises 28.7 per cent and state excises 4.3 per cent) of the combined tax revenue of the central and state governments in 1958-59. During the financial year 1962-63, forty-seven categories of commodities were subject to central excise duties, the most important of which, from the point of view of revenue, were tobacco, sugar, motor spirit, cotton cloth, matches, refined diesel oils and vaporizing oils, industrial fuel oils, and cement. The relative importance of import duties has markedly fallen since in the recent years greater reliance has been placed on central excise duties. Import duties are levied on several items of goods including both consumption and capital goods. Luxury consumption goods are taxed at penalty rates. In 1958-59, import duties contributed about 11 per cent of the combined tax revenue of the central and state governments. Import duties are levied and collected by the central government.

Among the minor taxes we may note agricultural income tax, expenditure tax, estate duty, wealth tax, gift tax, sales tax on motor spirit, motor vehicles tax, entertainment tax, and electricity duties. Agricultural income tax, sales tax on motor spirit, motor vehicles tax, entertainment tax, and electricity duties are levied and collected by the state governments. The remaining ones are central taxes. Of the minor taxes, agricultural income tax is levied exclusively on agriculture; others apply to both agricultural and nonagricultural sectors. Expenditure tax, estate duty, wealth tax, and gift tax are new levies. These taxes were introduced in India on the recommendation of Nicholas Kaldor who submitted his report in 1956. These new levies play a very minor role in the tax system. They contributed only 1.3 per cent of the combined tax revenue of the central and state governments in 1958-59. Among the other minor taxes, the tax on motor vehicles is the most important. It accounted for 2.2 per cent of the combined tax revenue of the central and state governments in 1958-59. All the minor taxes together contributed 8.4 per cent.

As regards the trend in the relative yields of the various taxes, we found that the relative contributions of agricultural income tax, expenditure tax, estate duty, wealth tax, gift tax, stamps and registration, land revenue, general sales tax, entertainment tax, and electricity duties remained more or less the same over the period 1950-51 to 1961-62. The relative importance of import duties and state excise duties considerably declined during the same period. And central excise duties, sales tax on motor spirit, and motor vehicles tax recorded considerable growth in their relative contribution during this period.

BURDEN OF AGRICULTURAL TAXATION

An attempt was made to measure the gross as well as the net burden of agricultural taxation in India for the year 1958-59. This particular period was chosen because it was found the most suitable from the point of view of availability of data. The term "burden" was used to mean "the social accounting calculation of the proportion of people's income paid over to taxing authorities in a defined period." The term "incidence" was not used, as far as possible, to avoid any confusion between "formal" and "effective" incidence. Although effective incidence is a valid and important concept, no quantitative estimate of it is possible. Gross burden of taxation takes into account only the "positive" taxes whereas net burden takes into consideration also the benefits arising from government spending.

We estimated that, among direct taxes, the per capita gross burden of land revenue amounted to Rs 3.16 which constituted 1.4 per cent of the per capita agricultural income. Per capita burden of land revenue was highest in Rajasthan (Rs 4.88) and lowest in Kerala (Rs 1.41). In terms of percentage of per capita income, the burden varied from 0.7 in Punjab to 2.7 in Rajasthan. The per acre (of net sown area) burden of land revenue was also estimated. It varied from Rs 1.73 in the case of Orissa to Rs 5.82 in Bihar. The national average was found to be Rs 2.85 per acre. The burden of agricultural income tax, which is the only other direct tax on agriculture, was found to be nominal. The per capita burden, for the whole country, was only Rs 0.29 in 1958-59, which formed 0.13 per cent of per capita agricultural income. Among individual states, it varied from Rs 0.01 in Madhya Pradesh to Rs 2.00 in Kerala. We found that the yield of agricultural income tax was markedly higher in those states where plantations are a dominant feature. The reason for the low yield of this tax, however, is to be found in the fact that the enforcement of this tax is poor.

The burden of nonagricultural direct taxes was examined next. These consist of expenditure tax, estate duty, wealth tax, gift tax, and stamps and registration. Since these taxes are not levied exclusively on any one sector of the economy, their burden had to be distributed between the agricultural and nonagricultural sectors according to the most appropriate criterion available. All such criteria are briefly outlined at the end of this section. Applying the same principle of distribution of burden to expenditure tax, estate duty, wealth tax, and gift tax, we found that the combined per capita burden of these taxes on the agricultural sector in 1958-59 was Rs 0.13 which constituted 0.06 per cent of the per capita income of the sector. Since stamps and registration differs from other non-agricultural direct taxes in its essential features, a different principle was adopted in distributing its burden between the two sectors. We estimated that the per capita burden of this tax amounted to Rs 0.30 which formed 0.14 per cent of the per capita agricultural income.

In the case of the taxes on commodities and services, the burden of the agricultural sector was estimated separately for each tax although the principle adopted for distribution of burden was broadly the same. We found that the per capita burden of taxes on commodities and services amounted to Rs 10.64 which constituted 5 per cent of the per capita income of the agricultural sector. On the basis of the National Sample Survey data on consumer expenditure, we also estimated the burden of commodity taxation of different rural expenditure groups. The per capita burden of commodity taxation of the lowest expenditure group (i.e. households with a monthly consumer expenditure in the range of Rs 1-50) amounted to Rs 4.39 and that of the highest group (i.e. households with a monthly consumer expenditure of over Rs 500) to Rs 50.80 annually. We were not, however, able to relate the per capita burden of each expenditure group to its per capita income due to lack of data. Though unsupported by any data, these estimates leave the impression that, in terms of per capita income, the burden of commodity taxation of the higher rural expenditure groups is less than that of the lower expenditure groups.

According to these estimates, the gross total burden of agricultural taxation in 1958-59 was Rs 4244.47 million. On the per capita level, the gross burden amounted to Rs 14.52 which formed 6.8 per cent of the per capita income of the agricultural sector.

We may briefly indicate the procedure followed in distributing the burden of various taxes between the agricultural and the non-agricultural sector. The problem of distributing the burden did not arise in the case of land revenue and agricultural income tax since these are exclusively agricultural taxes. However, in the case of these taxes, we had to estimate the size of the agricultural population for the whole country and for each state. In regard to expenditure tax, estate duty, wealth tax, and gift tax, the burden was distributed between the two sectors in the ratio of the incomes of the high-income groups within the two sectors. This method was adopted mainly because these taxes stipulate high exemption limits and are meant to tax the economically upper strata of society. In respect of stamps and registration, it was found that there is a significant correlation ($r = 0.83$) between per capita tax from this source and the proportion of urban population in each state. Hence it was deemed appropriate to distribute the tax burden on the basis of a linear regression with per capita tax as the dependent variable and the proportion of urban population as the independent variable. In the case of taxes on commodities and services, the burden was distributed between the rural and the urban sector in the ratio of their "monetized" (i.e. cash) expenditures on the taxed goods. The distinction between cash and noncash expenditures is necessary because taxes are paid only on cash purchases. The respective shares of the rural and the urban sector were further reapportioned between the agricultural and the nonagricultural sector.

NET BURDEN OF AGRICULTURAL TAXATION

We estimated that the total share of the agricultural sector in the public expenditure on agriculture and rural development, irrigation, multipurpose river valley projects, veterinary service, community projects, national extension service and local development works, education, and medical and public health services, amounted to Rs 2237.88 million in 1958-59. Subtracting this amount from the gross burden, we found that the net burden of taxation of the agricultural sector in 1958-59 was Rs 2011.56 million. The per capita net burden amounted to Rs 6.88 which constituted 3.2 per cent of the per capita income of the agricultural sector.

In estimating the agricultural sector's share of the public expenditure on the above-mentioned items, we did not consider the spillover effects since there is no way of measuring them. In the case of the expenditure on education, we made use of the data on the number of students from the rural and urban sectors attending schools, colleges and universities, and on the expenditure by the government for each type or stage of education. In respect of the public expenditure on medical and public health services, the expenditure was distributed between the rural and the urban sector in the ratio of their consumer expenditures on medicine.

Is Agriculture Inadequately Taxed?

In connection with the role of taxation for economic development, many economists have contended that agriculture in India is inadequately taxed. However, none of them has examined the problem in its entirety. The question whether the agricultural sector in India is inadequately taxed or not was, therefore, examined from three points of view: (1) inadequate taxation in the absolute sense, (2) inadequate taxation in the relative sense, and (3) inadequate taxation from the point of view of nationally accepted economic goals.

Inadequate taxation in any absolute sense implies some norm of "taxable capacity" and hence the concept is unacceptable to many economists. However, bearing in mind the limitations of any concept of absolute taxable capacity, we made an attempt to examine if we could speak of the agricultural sector being inadequately taxed in any meaningful sense. First, it was found that direct taxation of agriculture has varied from 1.1 per cent of the income from agriculture (in 1950-51) to 1.7 per cent (in 1959-60). Direct taxation of agriculture has, thus, remained almost static at the level of below 2 per cent of the income from agriculture. We further noted that even this apparent stability was maintained as a result of land reforms. Second, a "crude index of economic well-being" was constructed for the agricultural sector for each year from 1948-49 to 1958-59. This index consisted of two components, one relating to food consumption and the other to nonfood consumption. The component of well-being relating to food consumption was derived from two factors: (1) the proportion of rural consumption expenditure on food, and (2) an index of food output weighted by annual population increase. The component relating to nonagricultural consumption was derived from (1) the proportion of rural consumption expenditure on nonfood items, and (2) an index of the terms of trade of the agricultural sector (i.e. relative prices of agricultural and nonagricultural products). Since one would expect the agricultural sector to contribute more in taxes when its economic well-being is higher, we correlated changes in the yield from direct taxes on agriculture to changes in the index of well-being. It was found that no significant correlation existed between the two.

The familiar argument put forth against raising the level of agricultural taxation in India, namely, that the per capita income of the agricultural sector is so close to the subsistence level that this sector cannot bear any more tax burden, was also examined. The Reserve Bank of India has estimated that in spite of the low income of the agriculturists they do save nearly 3 per cent of their disposable income. Further, according to the National Sample Survey, 10.36 per cent of the consumption expenditure of the rural households go for nonsubsistence expenditures as those on ceremonies, intoxicants, amusements, etc. The income distribution within the agricultural sector is far from being equal. Therefore the argument that per capita income is so low that there can be no further taxation of agriculture loses much of its force. If we exclude agricultural labourers from our discussion, the per capita income figure changes by about 9 per cent. It was found that the nonlabour agricultural population had a per capita income of Rs 173.3 in 1956-57 as against a per capita income of Rs 158.5 for the whole agricultural sector. We further showed that, within the landowning, nonlabour agriculturists, income distribution is highly unequal. It was found that, while on the one hand 43.42 per cent of the landholders own only 5.2 per cent of the land, on the other hand 0.46 per cent have 11.2 per cent of the land. It was shown that the implementation of land reforms is not likely to alter the present pattern of distribution of landownership to any substantial extent. We also referred to a recent study by the Reserve Bank of India on income distribution in India, which confirms our finding. Thus all the available evidence strongly suggests that the agricultural sector is inadequately taxed.

We next examined whether the agricultural sector can be said to be undertaxed in a relative sense, i.e. in comparison to the nonagricultural sector. While direct taxation of agriculture forms less than 2 per cent of its income, it forms nearly 4 per cent in the case of the nonagricultural sector. We found that the gross burden of taxation of the nonagricultural sector in 1958-59 was Rs 5747.7 million and the net burden Rs 4571.5 million. The per capita net burden of taxation of the nonagricultural sector amounted to Rs 36.25 which formed 7.2 per cent of the per capita personal income of the sector (the per capita gross burden was Rs 45.58 which formed 9.2 per cent of the sector's per capita personal income). Thus, if we use tax as percentage of income as a measure of the burden of taxation, the agricultural sector is undertaxed. This criterion, though most widely used and useful for several purposes, is not perfect. Hence an attempt was made to frame a more valid test.

The method suggested by Henry J. Frank was found unsatisfactory since (1) the method is arbitrary, and (2) the ordinal significance of the comparison loses much of its validity when we have only two observations. An alternative method which consists of two linear functions, one for the agricultural sector and the other for the non-agricultural sector, based on thirteen observations, was therefore applied. The thirteen observations related to thirteen states of the Indian Union.[1] The two variables used for deriving the regressions were per capita personal income and per capita personal tax. On the basis of the estimated per capita tax burdens of the agricultural and nonagricultural sectors and their per capita personal incomes, linear regressions were derived for both the sectors—agricultural sector: $Y = 5.270 + 0.034X$; nonagricultural sector: $Y = -67.420 + 0.212X$ (where $Y =$ per capita tax and $X =$ per capita personal income). We also derived "lines of equal proportionate burden" based on the proportion of total tax in total income for the entire agricultural and nonagricultural sectors of the economy. We found that the line of equal proportionate burden cut the regression line of the agricultural sector from below at a per capita income of Rs 221. Thus, intra-sectorally, the agriculturists with incomes above Rs 221 are undertaxed relative to those with incomes below Rs 221. Assuming that the average size of an agricultural household is about six and, further, designating households with an annual income of Rs 0-1500 as low-income group, households with incomes of Rs 1501-3000 as middle-income group, and those with incomes above Rs 3000 as high-income group, we found that the middle- and high-income groups in agriculture are undertaxed relative to the low-income group. If incomes within agriculture were approximately equally distributed, our finding that agriculturists with an annual per capita income of over Rs 221 are relatively undertaxed would have little practical validity because the average per capita income of an Indian agriculturist (in 1958-59) was slightly less than Rs 221. But our analysis of landownership in India has revealed a high degree of inequality in the distribution of landholdings. Assuming that agricultural incomes are distributed proportionately with the distribution of ownership of land, and also assuming that the pattern of land distribution in 1958-59 was substantially the same as in

---

[1] In 1958-59 the Indian Union consisted of fourteen states, including Jammu and Kashmir. We excluded Jammu and Kashmir from our analysis since very little data were available on the economy of this state.

1954-55, we estimated that, out of a total (estimated) agricultural population of 292 million in 1958-59, about 100 million agriculturists had per capita annual incomes over Rs 221. While we may readily admit that all these estimates are rough, the evidence that emerges from our analysis is too strong to be dismissed as purely accidental. We, therefore, concluded that within the agricultural sector the higher-income groups are undertaxed relative to the lower-income groups.

The tax performance of the nonagricultural sector gave a completely different picture. The line of equal proportionate burden cut the regression line for the nonagricultural sector from above at a per capita income level of Rs 523, thus indicating that the tax system governing the nonagricultural sector, including direct as well as indirect taxes, conformed to the principle of progressive taxation. We have seen that this presents a sharp contrast to the situation in agriculture in which the lower-income groups are overtaxed relative to the higher-income groups. Our analysis of the tax performances of the agricultural and the nonagricultural sector also strongly indicated that, as between the high-income groups in the agricultural and nonagricultural sectors, the agricultural high-income groups pay less in taxes relative to nonagriculturists of similarly high incomes.

We also considered if the agricultural sector is inadequately taxed from the point of view of nationally accepted economic goals. The most important nationally accepted economic goal is the achievement of rapid economic growth within the framework of a democratic society. According to the Reserve Bank's estimates of savings in the Indian economy, the rural households save on the average only 2.6 per cent of their disposable income as against 14.1 per cent in the case of the urban households. Even with such a high percentage of saving by the urban households, the aggregate average saving-income ratio for the household sector is only 5.8 per cent. This shows that the saving behaviour of the rural household sector is the crucial element which influences the aggregate saving behaviour of the Indian economy. (The household sector accounts for 80 to 86 per cent of the total saving in the economy.) No sectoral marginal saving-income ratios have been estimated by the Reserve Bank, but the available evidence seems to suggest that the marginal saving-income ratio of the agricultural sector is low. The Third Five Year Plan aims at an average annual rate of growth of nearly 7 per cent. The realization of this target would require, among other things, mobilization of domestic savings of the order of 11.5 per cent of the national income. During 1960-61, the last year of the Second Five Year Plan, domestic savings formed only 8.3 per cent of the national income. An increase in domestic savings from 8.3 per cent of the national income to 11.5 per cent would mean a 38.5 per cent increase in the level of saving. Now, since 80 per cent of the domestic savings comes from the households, rural and urban, any substantial increase in domestic savings has to come from the household sector. Such an increase will call for a massive effort on the part of the planners to step up savings. Can domestic savings be substantially stepped up through voluntary savings? If not, what are the alternatives? It was argued that, under the conditions prevailing in underdeveloped economies like India, it is too much to hope that voluntary savings will be forthcoming in sufficient quantities. Under the circumstances there are broadly two alternatives: (1) increased external assistance, and (2) increased involuntary or forced saving. India is already planning for the maximum external aid during the Third Five Year Plan period. However, even if the entire amount of foreign aid envisaged in the Third Five Year Plan is realized, there will still exist a gap in domestic resources which has to be filled if the planned rate of growth is to be achieved. There are two forms of forced saving, inflation and taxation. In view of the rise in prices that took place during the Second Five Year Plan period and in view of the fact that the foreign exchange reserves of the Reserve Bank are not satisfactory, it is necessary to limit deficit financing in the Third Five Year Plan (according to the Planning Commission) to a total of Rs 5500 million over the five-year period. The other kind of involuntary or forced saving is taxation. In the light of our analysis of the situation prevailing in India, taxation is the most effective, and perhaps the most feasible, tool of increasing domestic savings in India. In the Third Five Year Plan, additional taxation of Rs 17100 million constitutes the most important single source of domestic resources. The objective of raising this amount through additional taxation cannot be achieved without taxing the agricultural sector more, for, obviously, the entire additional taxation of Rs 17100 million cannot be levied on the nonagricultural sector which already is relatively more heavily taxed. The agricultural sector in India is thus inadequately taxed from the point of view of achieving rapid economic development.

EFFECTS OF INCREASED AGRICULTURAL TAXATION

We examined the likely effects of increased taxation of agriculture on (1) consumption and saving, (2) agricultural output, and (3) marketed surplus of agricultural (food) produce.

As far as effects on consumption and saving are concerned, if previously the agriculturists' entire income was spent on consumption, then, the effect of increased taxation will be to reduce their consumption. If we assume that previously the agriculturists saved a portion of their incomes, there are now three alternatives before them. (a) They might pay the tax entirely out of consumption and continue to save the same amount. (b) They might maintain the same consumption and pay the tax entirely out of saving. (c) They might pay the tax partly out of consumption and partly out of saving. It is hard to say which of these alternatives will, in practice, be followed and by which group of agriculturists. However, as a rough approximation, we may conclude that (1) the upper-income groups—the landlords and peasant proprietors of relatively large holdings—are more likely to maintain their consumption and reduce saving in order to pay the increased tax; (2) the middle-income groups are likely to pay the tax partly out of consumption and partly out of saving; and (3) the lower-income groups are likely to pay the increased tax almost entirely out of consumption.

As regards the effects of increased agricultural taxation on agricultural output, we pointed out that, while the income effect makes the agricultural taxpayers work more, the substitution effect makes them work less. For the economy as a whole, the net effect will depend on the relative positions of the different groups in the income scale. We reached the conclusion that, as far as output effects are concerned, it is reasonable to assume that in an overpopulated agricultural sector as that of India, the output effects of a marginal increase in taxation will not be unfavourable.

Regarding the effects of increased agricultural taxation on the marketed surplus of agricultural produce, we pointed out the crucial importance of marketed surplus in the process of economic development. The marketed surplus of agricultural output constitutes the supply of "savings" for economic development. An increase in agricultural output by itself does not promote economic development unless it results in an increased marketed surplus. This is an especially difficult problem in underdeveloped economies where the existing levels of consumption are extremely low. Several writers have pointed out that in recent times there has been a fall in the proportion of agricultural (food) output marketed.

We offered an explanation for the inelastic marketed surplus of agricultural output in terms of the fixed monetary commitment of the subsistence farmers. The agriculturists' need of money income is almost fixed. Their limited monetary commitments may consist of purchases of manufactured articles and direct taxes. The subsistence farmer's demand for manufactured articles, however, is meagre. One could limit it to three or four articles of essential consumption such as salt, certain types of (cheap) clothing, kerosene, etc. Further, he pays very little taxes, direct or indirect. Now, since the monetary commitments of these farmers are more or less fixed, they adjust the sale of their surplus in such a way that they get just enough money to meet the monetary commitments. From these premises it follows that by increasing the monetary commitments of the farmers they may be compelled to exchange more of their produce for money. Increasing direct taxes is one way of increasing the monetary commitments. Compared to other ways of increasing the monetary commitments of the farmers, taxation has the added advantage that it increases the forced saving of the community and at the same time increases also the marketed surplus which is of crucial importance for economic development.

Towards an Improved System of Agricultural Taxation in India

After having shown how important agricultural taxation is for economic development in India, we finally turned to the question as to how the present system of agricultural taxation should be reorganized. Before suggesting concrete measures of reform, we considered the objectives which agricultural taxation may be asked to serve in the context of India's economic development. Among the "external" objectives, we discussed the following objectives with special reference to Indian conditions: (1) to alter the distribution of income, wealth, and landownership, (2) to promote economic stability, (3) to stimulate desired changes in the private allocation and use of agricultural resources, and (4) to mobilize and redirect resources via government. We argued that, among these possible objectives of agricultural taxation, the pivotal place should be given to the last one. Among the internal (conventional) objectives, we discussed (1) equity or impartiality, and (2) administrative and compliance requirements. In respect of administrative and compliance aspects of agricultural taxation we emphasized that, though India is in a better position compared to other underdeveloped countries, there is much yet to be accomplished, as, for example, the revision of land cadastres and assessments.

A critical evaluation of the existing system of agricultural taxation brought out the following general points: (1) The most conspicuous characteristic of the Indian agricultural tax system is its inflexibility which invariably operates in favour of the taxpayer. (2) Taxes are not "personalized" by introducing allowances for the taxpayers' marital and dependency status and for other personal circumstances that bear upon their taxpaying capacity. (3) Several categories of persons and incomes are not taxed.

In respect of individual taxes we made a rather detailed appraisal. We observed that the greatest defect of the land revenue system is its inflexibility. The same rates have remained in force for decades although agricultural prices and incomes have increased considerably. Further, the tax base is not clearly defined and is not uniform as between different states—even as between different parts of the same state. As far as incentive provisions are concerned, they are almost completely lacking. Incentive taxation works through differential taxation and not by keeping the general level of taxation low.

Land revenue is a proportional tax based (as it obtains today) on the size of the holding and, therefore, violates the principle of the ability to pay. Since land revenue is a tax on land owned, tenant cultivators do not have to pay any land revenue. In respect of agricultural income tax we observed the following: (1) Since the exemption limit is at least Rs 3000 in most cases, the vast majority of agriculturists is unaffected by this tax. On the average it takes from ten to thirty acres of agricultural land to realize an income of Rs 3000. Thus at least 78 per cent of the landowners are outside the jurisdiction of this tax. (2) The remaining 22 per cent of the landowners hold about 72 per cent of the agricultural land. A considerable proportion of these landholders actually evade the agricultural income tax.

RECOMMENDATIONS

After reviewing the proposals for reform of the agricultural tax system put forth by various experts we presented our own recommendations. The recommendations were divided into two parts, one consisting of immediate and the other of long-run measures.

Immediate Measures

(1) In view of the extremely low rates of land revenue prevailing at present, the land revenue rates should be immediately raised. Each state may be divided into a limited number of zones on the basis of soil conditions and within each zone a distinction made between dry and wet lands and also between other relevant categories. The size of each holding could, thus, be expressed in standard acres. Once this process is complete, the land revenue rates could be revised in terms of percentage increases in the existing rates. Holdings below the size of 2.5 acres (standard acres) may be exempted from any upward revision of rates. The minimum increase of 25 per cent may be applied in the case of the next group of holdings, i.e. holdings of 2.5-5.0 acres. The maximum increase may be limited to 200 per cent in the case of the largest holdings (i.e. holdings above 60 acres). In between, the percentage increase in the land revenue rate will vary with the size of the holding. Such a rate schedule is meant only as a rough pattern; minor modifications could be introduced to suit the special conditions existing in each state or region. If land revenue rates are revised along this pattern the burden of land revenue will be a little less than 2 per cent of the net income from farming in the case of the lowest category of holdings and a little less than 10 per cent in the case of the largest-sized holdings.

(2) In the case of holdings which come within the purview of the agricultural income tax, the tax—land revenue or agricultural income tax—which would yield the highest revenue may be applied.

(3) If, in any state, there has been during the last one or two years an adequate revision of land revenue rates, the new rates will not apply in such cases.

(4) With the implementation of these short-term measures, there should be no further enhancement of the rates of taxation of essential consumer goods like kerosene, inferior textiles, matches, etc. which figure prominently in the budgets of low-income groups.

Long-run Measures

1. *Reform of Land Revenue System.* (*a*) The potential income from each holding under average conditions of production should be the tax base of land revenue. The potential output of each holding should be estimated on the basis of a soil classification according to productive capacity. It may be expressed as a proportion of the average per acre output of the region concerned.

(*b*) The assessment should be made applicable to the entire holding of the household.

(*c*) Though land revenue as a land tax will be limited to potential income from land, if in individual cases substantial nonagricultural incomes are detected, such income should be added to the taxable agricultural income and the whole income taxed at the appropriate higher rate.

(*d*) Under the new system, tenant farmers also should be subject to the land tax.

(*e*) The appropriate marginal rates of tax should be applied to the entire landholding of the household on a consolidated basis.

(*f*) A basic minimum exemption should be allowed in all cases irrespective of the size of the household or the status of the agriculturist. The exemption limit should be fixed at a certain level of income and not at a size of holding of land.

(*g*) Besides the basic exemption, each taxpayer may be allowed a personal deduction for additional dependents over and above the number taken into account in fixing the basic exemption.

(*h*) Land revenue rates should be made progressive with increases in income.

(*i*) As a measure to promote economic development, certain approved categories of saving and investment may be given credit in calculating the taxable income of the farm household.

2. In order to make the total tax burden of the landowning agriculturists more equitable, a property tax may be levied on all holdings of land.

3. Special levies on land such as irrigation and betterment duties may be done away with since the need for these levies is taken care of by other taxes proposed under this scheme.

4. A capital gains tax may be levied on all land sales. Such a levy will make up for the loss of revenue caused by the proposed abolition of irrigation and betterment levies.

5. Visible public expenditures, the benefits of which have no direct effect on agricultural productivity such as hospitals, roads and

bridges, schools, etc., should be financed as far as possible through separate local levies and not from the general revenue of the state.

6. With the implementation of the proposed land revenue reform, a separate agricultural income tax has no place in the tax system of India. As a matter of fact, the new land revenue will be, in a meaningful sense, an income tax, the salient features of an income tax being incorporated into the land tax. Exceptions to this rule may be allowed in very special cases. For example in Assam and Kerala, where a considerable portion of the nonsubsistence agricultural sector is organized along plantation lines, and where the agricultural income tax has been enforced rather effectively, there may be some logic in letting the present agricultural income tax continue.

7. At present agricultural land is exempted from taxation under estate duty and wealth tax. There is no reason why there should be a discriminatory treatment in favour of agricultural land as a form of wealth and against other forms of wealth such as buildings, stock, etc.

8. Finally, since it is hoped that adequate revenue will be raised as a result of the above proposals, it is desirable that taxes on essential commodities of mass consumption should be reduced to a bare minimum lest the lower strata of the society should be put to extreme hardship.

bridges, schools, etc., should be financed as far as possible through separate local taxes and not from the general revenue of the state.

6. With the implementation of the proposed land revenue reform, a separate agricultural income tax has no place in the tax system of India. As a matter of fact, the levy and revenue will be, in a meaningful sense, an income tax, the salient features of an income tax being incorporated into the land tax. Exceptions to this rule may be allowed in very special cases. For example in Assam and Kerala, where a considerable portion of the non-subsistence agricultural sector is organized along plantation lines, and where the agricultural income tax has been enforced rather effectively, there may be some logic in letting the present agricultural income tax continue.

7. At present, agricultural land is exempted from taxation under estate duty and wealth tax. There is no reason why there should be a discriminatory treatment in favour of agricultural land as a form of wealth and against other forms of wealth such as buildings, stock, etc.

8. Finally, since it is hoped that adequate revenue will be raised as a result of the above proposals, it is desirable that taxes on essential commodities of mass consumption should be reduced to a bare minimum lest the lower strata of the society should be put to extreme hardship.

APPENDIXES

APPENDIXES

A NOTE ON THE USE OF NATIONAL SAMPLE SURVEY DATA ON CONSUMER EXPENDITURE IN THE DISTRIBUTION OF THE BURDEN OF INDIRECT TAXATION BETWEEN THE RURAL AND URBAN SECTORS

THE consumer expenditure data collected from the Fourth Round of the National Sample Survey[1] formed the basic data on the basis of which the burden of indirect taxes was distributed between the rural and the urban sector. The geographical coverage of the fourth round consisted of the whole of Indian Union excluding Jammu and Kashmir, Andaman and Nicobar Islands, and some parts (northeastern) of Assam. Data on consumer expenditure were collected from 12422 sample households of which 8543 were selected from 946 sample villages, 3183 from 49 sample towns and cities, and 694 from the 4 large cities of Calcutta, Bombay, Delhi, and Madras.

One important feature of the fourth round was the use of two sets of questionnaires with two different reference periods, a week and a month for a number of items, which were otherwise identical. The findings of the above report are based on particulars collected from the sample households belonging to the latter group, i.e. those with a month as the reference period.

The NSS conducted seven rounds of collection of data on consumer expenditure. We have chosen for our purpose the report on the fourth round mainly for the following reasons: (1) In the case of the fourth round, for items of consumption such as clothing, other durable and semi-durable articles, rents and taxes, a year was taken as the period of reference. On the other hand, in the seventh round, for all items the period of reference was a month preceding the date of inquiry. This writer thinks that for the above-mentioned items of consumption it is more logical to take the year as a period of reference rather than a month since it is most likely that there will be considerable month-to-month variation in the expenditure on these items. (2) For the fourth round, we have detailed information on the consumer expenditure pattern of rural and urban households. Under food, eleven items and, under nonfood, nineteen items are listed in the report on the fourth round. In the case of the fifth to seventh rounds the report gives information on only six items of food and two items of nonfood. It should be remembered that our purpose in using the NSS data is to find out the ratio in which the burden of commodity taxation should be distributed between the rural and urban sectors of the economy, and also between the different income groups within the rural sector. Commodity taxes are levied on a very large number of articles in India. So the more complete the list of items on which information relating to consumer expenditure is available, the better suited it is for our purpose. Hence we chose the report on the fourth round of the National Sample Survey.

---

[1] Conducted by the Directorate of National Sample Survey during April-September 1952, data processed by the Indian Statistical Institute, Calcutta, and the report published by the Government of India in April 1959.

LIMITATIONS OF NSS DATA

The NSS data is impressive in many respects. In coverage it is unique and in the excellence of the processing almost the maximum degree of precision possible was achieved. The NSS findings, though the most comprehensive and the most reliable on the subject, are, however, not without their limitations.

1. During the period of the investigation (April-September 1952) food control was still in force; the government initiated a policy of progressive decontrol in the middle of 1952 and food controls were completely abolished in July 1954. The existence of food controls, even if partial, must have had the effect of somewhat distorting the rural-urban income as well as the consumer expenditure pattern, especially the pattern of expenditure on food, of the rural and the urban households.

2. The wide fluctuations in the price of food grains, which occupy a very important place in the consumer expenditure pattern of both urban and rural households, and the persistent upward tendency of food prices since 1956 limit the validity of any conclusions based on conditions which prevailed during a period of "controls."

3. The fact that in the NSS report very little imputation for the value of house rent has been made for the rural households, as against adequate imputation for urban rent, further distorts the rural-urban consumer expenditure pattern.

4. Since the rural population seldom keeps any record of household expenditure, it is hard to elicit correct information from them. Further, a month which is the period of reference of the fourth survey (of course, for certain items, a year was used as the period of reference) is by no means the income period in the rural sector. Money income accrues to the rural households, mainly depending on the crops they raise, at certain definite periods or seasons. Most of the cash purchases are made then. This pattern of cash income and expenditure is not taken into due account by having a month as the period of reference.

In spite of all these limitations, we are compelled to use the NSS data in the absence of any alternative data of comparable coverage or accuracy.

DIVISION OF THE BURDEN OF COMMODITY TAXATION BETWEEN RURAL AND URBAN SECTORS

The basic material we have used in order to split the total burden of indirect taxation between the rural and the urban sector is contained in Table 35 which is reproduced from the NSS report on the fourth round.

TABLE 35

PATTERN OF CONSUMER EXPENDITURE AS PERCENTAGE OF TOTAL EXPENDITURE AS OBTAINED IN THE FOURTH ROUND OF NSS SURVEY
(*all-India*)

Items	Percentage of total expenditure	
	Rural	Urban
1. Food grains	40.57	20.66
2. Pulses	3.82	2.52

Items	Percentage of total expenditure	
	Rural	Urban
3. Edible oil	2.10	2.76
4. Vegetables	2.10	2.86
5. Milk and milk products	6.30	8.27
6. Meat, egg, and fish	1.96	3.20
7. Fruits	1.12	1.82
8. Refreshments	1.03	3.53
9. Salt	0.28	0.17
10. Spices	1.77	1.82
11. Sugar	2.10	2.22
12. Food total	63.15	49.83
13. Pan (betel leaves)	0.70	1.18
14. Tobacco	1.91	1.92
15. Intoxicants	0.61	0.44
16. Fuel and light	5.41	5.45
17. Clothing	7.18	8.21
18. Bedding	0.56	0.47
19. Footwear	0.61	0.74
20. Amusements and musical instruments	0.42	1.24
21. Education	0.79	2.93
22. Medicine	1.59	2.93
23. Toilet	0.70	1.25
24. Petty articles	0.79	0.98
25. Conveyance	1.31	2.49
26. Services	5.22	6.56
27. Furniture	0.19	0.27
28. Domestic utensils	0.23	0.20
29. Sundry equipment and ornaments	1.21	2.22
30. Ceremonies	5.69	4.71
31. Rent and taxes	1.73	6.02
32. Total nonfood	36.85	50.17
33. Total	100.00	100.00
34. No. of sample tehsils	478	53
35. No. of sample villages	946	406
36. No. of sample households	8545	3877

SOURCE: National Sample Survey, Fourth Round: April-September 1952, No. 18, "Tables with Notes on Consumer Expenditure," Tables 2-1 and 2-2, pp. 4, 5.

From Table 35 we can calculate the ratio of the expenditure on any given article between the rural and the urban sector. Since indirect taxes are proportional, the tax varies directly with expenditure. Hence we can divide the tax burden between the two sectors in the same ratio as the expenditures on the taxed commodities or services. The ratio is given by:

Total rural consumption expenditure multiplied by expenditure on the commodity as a proportion of total rural expenditure. Total urban consumption expenditure multiplied by expenditure on the commodity as a proportion of total urban consumer expenditure.

The total rural consumption expenditure can be derived by subtracting rural savings from rural disposable income. Similarly the total urban consumption expenditure can be derived from subtraction of urban savings from urban disposable income. These data are given in the Reserve Bank of India study on "Savings in the Indian Economy."[2] The proportion of expenditure on each commodity or category of commodities is given by the NSS study.

If the entire purchases of the households consisted of cash payments, we could immediately distribute the tax burden of each commodity. But we know that these households themselves produce several of the items of consumption. Also, they resort to payments in kind. Hence we should know the extent to which expenditures are monetized, i.e. the proportion of cash purchases in total consumption expenditure. Information on the extent of monetization was collected by the NSS for each sector and for each commodity or category of commodities. This is given in Table 36.

The tax burden from indirect taxation was divided between the rural and urban sectors on the basis of information contained in this table as well as in Table 37, in the ratio of monetized expenditures.

I. *Central Excise Duties.* (1) Motor spirit and tyres and tubes. The revenue from these commodities comes from three sources: noncommercial (private) vehicles, public service vehicles, and goods vehicles. From the revenue statistics for the previous years we know the ratio of the revenue from these three sources. The total excise from motor spirit and tyres and tubes in 1958-59 was divided among these three sources, and the revenue from each source then divided between the rural and urban sectors. It was assumed that 15 per cent of the revenue from private vehicles comes from the rural sector and 85 per cent from the urban sector. In the case of revenue from public service vehicles, it was distributed between the two sectors in the ratio of expenditure on conveyance. In the case of revenue from goods vehicles, the ratio of total monetized expenditures of the two sectors was used. (2) Kerosene. It was assumed that 30 per cent of the rural and 5 per cent of the urban expenditures on fuel and light is spent on kerosene. (3) Sugar. The revenue from the excise duty on sugar was distributed in the ratio of the monetized expenditures of the two sectors on sugar. (4) Matches. It was assumed that 7 per cent of the rural, and 2 per cent of the urban, expenditure on fuel and light was spent on matches. (5) The revenue from the excise duty on steel ingots was distributed between the two sectors in the ratio of the monetized expenditures on the unlisted items in Table 38. (6) In the case of tyres and tubes, the same ratio as in the case of motor spirit was used. (7) Tobacco. The revenue was distributed in the ratio of the monetized expenditures of the two sectors on tobacco. (8) Vegetable

---

2 *Reserve Bank of India Bulletin* (August 1961), p. 1203.

TABLE 36

PROPORTION OF IMPUTED VALUE OF THE PART OBTAINED IN KIND
TO VALUE OF TOTAL CONSUMPTION OF HOUSEHOLDS IN THE
FOURTH ROUND

(*all-India*)

Items	Proportion of imputed value		Monetized expenditure as percentage of total expenditure	
	Rural	Urban	Rural	Urban
1. Food grains	72.6	21.3	11.12	16.26
2. Pulses	66.5	12.6	1.28	2.20
3. Edible oil	23.3	4.4	1.61	2.64
4. Vegetables	40.2	5.3	1.26	2.71
5. Milk and milk products	70.5	20.3	1.86	6.59
6. Meat, eggs, and fish	28.8	7.5	1.40	3.00
7. Fruits	46.2	11.1	0.60	1.62
8. Refreshments	9.0	6.8	0.94	3.29
9. Spices, salt and sugar	23.7	9.1	3.17	3.83
10. Pan (betel leaves)	7.8	3.7	0.65	1.14
11. Tobacco	17.9	3.0	1.57	1.86
12. Intoxicants	29.9	3.4	0.43	0.43
13. Fuel and light	70.2	24.1	1.61	4.14
TOTAL, ABOVE ITEMS	—	—	27.50	49.71
TOTAL, ALL ITEMS	44.3	9.2	55.70	90.80

SOURCE: NSS, *op. cit.,* p. 13.

products. The revenue was distributed in the ratio of the combined monetized expenditure on toilet and edible oil. (9) Coffee and tea. Ratio of the expenditures on refreshments was used. (10) Cotton cloth. The ratio for clothing was used. (11) Artificial silk. The ratio of the monetized expenditure on the unlisted items in Table 38 was used. (12) Cement. Same ratio as in (11) was used. (13) Footwear. The ratio of monetized expenditures of the two sectors on footwear was used. (14) Soap. The ratio of expenditures on toilet was used. (15) Woollen fabrics. The same ratio as for clothing was used. (16) Electric fans. Electric fans are very expensive in India and are a luxury for the rural people. Moreover, rural electrification is still in its infancy. On the basis of these considerations it was assumed that 2 per cent of the revenue from this tax comes from the rural sector and the rest from the urban. In any case, the revenue from this tax is nominal. (17) Electric bulbs. The case of electric bulbs is slightly different from electric fans. In the case of electrified homes, electric bulbs are a necessity, unlike electric fans. Therefore, the rural sector must be bearing a larger share of the burden arising from taxation of bulbs. The revenue was distributed in the ratio of 10:90 between the rural and the urban sector. (18) Electric batteries. Some rural people use electric batteries, though not to the same extent as the urban people. Since factories do have to pay the tax on batteries, it enters as a cost item in the manufacture of goods. The ratio was thus assumed to be 25:75 as between the rural and urban sectors. (19) Paper. The NSS report has included expenditure on paper under education. Hence the ratio of expenditures on education was used. (20) Paints and varnishes. The rural people seldom buy any paints and varnishes. Most of them have very small huts built of mud walls. We cannot get any guidance from the NSS data in respect of these items. Therefore it was deemed reasonable to distribute the revenue between the rural and urban sectors in the ratio of 10:90. (21) Vegetable nonessential oils. The ratio of the monetized expenditures on toilet and edible oil was used. (22) Refined diesel oils and vaporizing oils. The ratio of the expenditures on conveyance was used. (23) Industrial fuel oils. The ratio of the monetized expenditures on the unlisted items in Table 38 was used. (24) Rayons and synthetic fibres. The same ratio as in the case of artificial silk was used. (25) Motor cars. Very few rural people own or use motor cars. Hence, the ratio was assumed to be 5:95 as between the rural and the urban sector. In any case, the revenue from this tax is insignificant. (26) Coal cess. The ratio for the combined expenditure on conveyance and fuel and light was used, since coal is used by railways as well as by households. (27) Cess on copra. Copra is used to make both edible oils and soap. So the ratio of the combined expenditure on toilets and edible oil is used. (28) Cess on oils and oil-seeds. Same ratio as (27) is used. (29) Miscellaneous. The revenue from miscellaneous excise duties was distributed in the ratio of the monetized expenditure on the unlisted items in Table 38.

II. *General Sales Tax.* From the table on the percentage-wise pattern of consumer expenditure of the rural and urban sectors, we eliminate those items on which the two sectors are not likely to pay any sales tax. In the case of the rural households, we assume that sales tax is paid on monetized purchases of edible oil, salt, spices, sugar, tobacco, intoxicants, clothing, and toilets. Further, we assume that the rural households pay sales tax on 50 per cent of their monetized purchases of fuel and light, medicine, petty articles, utensils and sundry equipment, since these articles are likely to be bought from village artisans and vendors who usually do not charge any sales tax. It was thus calculated that the rural households pay sales tax on 17.04 per cent of their total expenditure on consumption. In the case of the urban sector, it was assumed that sales tax is paid on the entire monetized expenditures on edible oil, refreshments, salt, spices, sugar, tobacco, intoxicants, fuel and light, clothing, bedding, footwear, amusements and musical instruments, medicine, toilets, petty articles, furniture, domestic utensils, and sundry equipment. It was further assumed that the urban households pay sales tax on 25 per cent of their monetized expenditures on food grains, pulses, and milk and milk products, since these articles are either totally exempt from sales tax or the tax is applicable only to merchants with turnover over a minimum. It was thus calculated that the urban households pay sales tax on 40.96 per cent of their total consumption expenditure. According to this procedure, the rural share of the revenue from sales tax amounted to 55.39 per cent of the total.

III. *Import Duties.* The burden of taxation of imports was distributed between the two sectors in the ratio of the monetized expenditures on the unlisted items in Table 38. This seemed to be the most reasonable procedure since the bulk of the imports consists of the unlisted items.

IV. *State Excise Duties.* These taxes are levied almost exclusively on alcoholic beverages and narcotics. Hence the tax burden was distributed between the two sectors in the ratio of the monetized expenditures on intoxicants.

V. *Sales Tax on Motor Spirit.* The same ratio as for the central excise duty on motor spirit was used.

VI. *Tax on Railway Fares.* The tax burden was distributed between the two sectors in the ratio of the expenditures on conveyance.

VII. *Motor Vehicles Tax.* The same ratio as for the tax on motor spirit was used.

VIII. *Entertainment Tax.* The revenue from this tax was distributed between the two sectors in the ratio of the expenditures on amusements.

IX. *Electricity Duties.* Twenty-five per cent of the total revenue from this duty was assumed to have come from the household use of electricity. Of this 10 per cent was attributed to the rural households and the rest to the urban sector. Seventy-five per cent of the revenue from this duty was assumed to arise from the industrial and commercial use of electricity. This portion was distributed between the two sectors in the ratio of the monetized expenditure on the unlisted items of Table 38.

X. *Other Taxes and Duties.* Most of the revenue under this head consists of the yield from taxes and cesses on tobacco, sugar and passenger traffic. Hence the total revenue from this tax was distributed between the two sectors in the ratio of the combined monetized expenditures on tobacco, sugar, and conveyance.

DISTRIBUTION OF THE RURAL SHARE OF BURDEN OF INDIRECT TAXATION BETWEEN
DIFFERENT RURAL EXPENDITURE GROUPS

The basic material used for distributing the rural share of the burden of indirect Taxation among the different rural expenditure groups is contained in Table 37 which is reproduced here from the NSS report on consumer expenditure pattern.

TABLE 37

EXPENDITURE ON DIFFERENT ITEMS OF CONSUMPTION IN RUPEES
PER PERSON PER MONTH ARRANGED BY LEVELS OF MONTHLY
HOUSEHOLD CONSUMER EXPENDITURE IN RURAL AREAS
(all-India, rural)

	Items	Expenditure level in rupees					
		1-50	51-100	101-150	151-300	301-500	501 *and above*
1.	Food grains	5.20	7.57	9.19	10.82	12.72	15.78
2.	Pulses	0.44	0.71	0.88	1.04	1.34	1.54
3.	Edible oil	0.24	0.35	0.46	0.59	0.74	1.22
4.	Vegetables	0.26	0.35	0.45	0.56	0.75	1.26
5.	Milk and milk products	0.26	0.66	1.36	2.27	3.73	3.92
6.	Meat, egg, and fish	0.19	0.34	0.49	0.53	0.72	0.93
7.	Fruits	0.11	0.18	0.22	0.33	0.44	0.65
8.	Refreshments	0.09	0.17	0.24	0.30	0.38	0.50
9.	Salt	0.06	0.06	0.06	0.06	0.08	0.08
10.	Spices	0.28	0.35	0.39	0.42	0.58	0.61
11.	Sugar	0.16	0.30	0.49	0.67	0.96	1.12
12.	Food total	7.29	11.04	14.23	17.59	22.44	27.61
13.	Pan (betel leaves)	0.09	0.13	0.16	0.19	0.24	0.42
14.	Tabacco	0.23	0.33	0.44	0.48	0.66	1.36

Items	Expenditure level in rupees					
	1-50	51-100	101-150	151-300	301-500	501 *and above*
15. Intoxicants	0.06	0.07	0.15	0.17	0.37	0.27
16. Fuel and light	0.84	1.07	1.21	1.33	1.63	1.77
17. Clothing	0.90	1.22	1.57	1.97	2.66	3.37
18. Bedding	0.03	0.06	0.13	0.20	0.30	0.38
19. Footwear	0.04	0.08	0.15	0.18	0.28	0.34
20. Amusements and musical instruments	0.02	0.05	0.07	0.19	0.19	0.32
21. Education	0.02	0.05	0.16	0.26	0.48	1.19
22. Medicine	0.06	0.16	0.32	0.48	0.93	1.81
23. Toilet	0.08	0.11	0.15	0.18	0.26	0.42
24. Petty articles	0.08	0.13	0.19	0.22	0.29	0.49
25. Conveyance	0.08	0.14	0.30	0.41	0.74	0.97
26. Services	0.12	0.39	0.80	1.65	3.45	8.40
27. Furniture	0.01	0.02	0.04	0.07	0.14	0.19
28. Domestic utensils	0.02	0.03	0.06	0.07	0.13	0.13
29. Sundry equipment and ornaments	0.02	0.07	0.21	0.40	0.79	2.43
30. Ceremonials	0.27	0.54	1.01	1.67	3.33	8.31
31. Rent and taxes	0.09	0.21	0.37	0.57	0.94	1.16
32. Nonfood total	3.06	4.86	7.49	10.69	17.81	33.73
33. Total	10.35	15.90	21.72	28.28	40.25	61.34
34. No. of sample households	2357	2895	1570	1316	304	103
35. Average household size	3.18	4.63	5.66	7.21	9.21	12.24

Source: NSS, *op. cit.*, p. 18, Table (3.4).

In Table 39 we have only the per capita monthly expenditure, arranged by levels of monthly household expenditure. Before we can divide the burden of indirect taxes among the different groups, we need to have information on the total monthly household expenditure of each expenditure group. For each item of consumption this is given by per capita expenditure × household size × number of households.

Table 38 gives us the total monthly expenditure of rural households in each expenditure group on different items of consumption. But, as we have already seen, part of the expenditure expressed in money terms consists of imputed values. Hence, before we can distribute the burden of indirect taxation between the different rural expenditure groups, we have to estimate the extent of monetization of each group and apply the same to each commodity or group of commodities. The NSS has pro-

TABLE 38

TOTAL EXPENDITURE ON DIFFERENT ITEMS OF CONSUMPTION IN
RUPEES PER MONTH BY ALL HOUSEHOLDS ARRANGED BY
LEVELS OF MONTHLY EXPENDITURE

	Expenditure level in rupees					
	1-50	51-100	101-150	151-300	301-500	501 and above
(Average expenditure) Items	(32.91	73.52	122.94	203.90	370.70	750.80)
1. Food grains	38972.99	101467.14	81664.18	102664.06	35613.96	19894.16
2. Pulses	3297.91	9516.73	7819.86	9867.89	3751.79	1941.51
3. Edible oil	1798.86	4691.35	4087.65	5598.13	2071.88	1538.08
4. Vegetables	1948.77	4691.35	3998.80	5313.48	2099.88	1588.51
5. Milk and milk products	1948.77	8846.54	12085.23	21538.58	10443.40	4942.02
6. Meat, egg, and fish	1424.10	4557.31	4354.24	5028.83	2015.88	1172.47
7. Fruits	824.48	2412.69	1954.96	3131.16	1215.72	819.47
8. Refreshments	674.57	2278.65	2132.69	2846.41	1063.94	630.36
9. Salt	449.72	804.23	533.17	569.30	223.99	100.86
10. Spices	2098.67	4691.35	3465.62	3985.11	1623.91	769.04
11. Sugar	1199.24	4021.16	4354.24	5028.83	2015.88	1172.47
12. Pan	674.57	1742.50	1421.79	1802.79	671.96	529.50
13. Tobacco	1723.91	4423.28	3909.93	4554.41	1847.89	1714.58
14. Intoxicants	449.72	938.27	1332.93	1613.02	1035.94	340.39
15. Fuel and light	6296.12	14342.12	10752.30	12619.52	4563.74	2231.47
16. Clothing	6745.73	16352.70	13951.33	18692.07	7447.57	4248.43
17. Bedding	224.86	804.23	1155.21	1897.67	839.95	479.07
18. Footwear	299.81	1072.31	1332.93	1707.91	783.96	428.64
19. Amusements and musical instruments	149.91	670.19	622.03	1802.79	531.97	403.43
20. Education	149.91	670.19	1421.79	2466.97	1343.92	1500.26
21. Medicine	449.72	2144.62	2843.58	4554.41	2603.85	2281.90
22. Toilet	599.62	1474.42	1332.93	1707.90	727.96	529.50
23. Petty articles	599.62	1742.50	1688.38	2087.44	811.95	617.75
24. Conveyance	599.62	1876.54	2665.86	3890.23	2071.88	1218.26
25. Service	899.42	5227.50	7108.96	15655.79	9659.45	10590.48
26. Furniture	74.95	268.08	355.45	664.19	391.98	239.54
27. Domestic utensils	149.91	402.12	533.17	664.19	363.98	163.89
28. Sundry equipment and ornaments	149.91	938.27	1866.10	3742.72	2211.87	3063.55

vided us with information only on the monetization of the rural sector as a whole and not for each group within the sector. We have, therefore, to find out a method of our own. It is to this task we turn our attention now.

We have already referred to the estimate of the annual consumption expenditure of the rural household sector. From this estimate we may derive the per capita consumption expenditure. According to the NSS Report, the average size of a rural household is 5.01. On the basis of these data, we find out the average monthly household expenditure of the rural sector. The NSS Report also furnishes the monthly household expenditure of the highest rural expenditure group.

We make the following assumptions in estimating the degree of monetization corresponding to any given level of household expenditure: (1) The degree of monetization of an expenditure group with an average expenditure equal to that of the rural sector is the same as the average monetization of the rural sector. (2) The highest rural expenditure group has the same degree of monetization as the average urban household. (3) Monetization increases proportionately with expenditure.

Let M_1 be the monetization corresponding to the monthly expenditure of an average rural household. Under our assumptions, this group has a monetization of 55.7 per cent. Let M_2 be the monetization corresponding to the highest rural expenditure group. Under our assumptions, this group has a monetization of 90.8 per cent. Let E_1 be the monthly consumer expenditure of an average rural household and E_2 that of the highest rural expenditure group. Then, the degree of monetization, M, relating to any expenditure, E, is given by the equation $M = 0.053E + 51.35$.

The next step in our analysis is to find out the total cash expenditure of each expenditure group on each item of consumption. This would enable us to distribute the burden of indirect taxation between the different expenditure groups. Using our equation for monetization, we calculate the total cash expenditure of each expenditure group in the sample on each item of consumption. On the basis of the ratio of monetized expenditures of different expenditure groups derived in this manner, the burden of commodity taxation was distributed between the groups as follows.

I. *Central Excise Duties.* (1) Motor spirit. The entire revenue from private vehicles (rural share) was attributed to the highest rural expenditure group. In the case of public service vehicles, the revenue was distributed in the ratio of monetized expenditure on conveyance. Revenue from goods vehicles was distributed in the ratio of the total monetized expenditure for each group. (2) Kerosene. It was assumed that, starting with the lowest expenditure group, each group spends 50 per cent, 45 per cent, 40 per cent, 30 per cent, 20 per cent, 10 per cent respectively of the expenditure on fuel and light on kerosene. (3) Sugar. The revenue was distributed in the ratio of monetized expenditure on sugar. (4) Matches. From hypothetical consumer budgets it was calculated that, starting with the lowest expenditure group, the percentage of expenditure on matches in the expenditure on fuel and light comes to 9.36, 10, 10.96, 7.83, 6.67, and 5.77 respectively. (5) Steel ingots. The burden was distributed according to the ratio of monetized expenditures on manufactured goods. The ratio of manufactured goods was derived by adding up the expenditures on sugar, fuel and light, clothing, amusements and musical instruments, medicine, toilet, petty articles, conveyance, furniture, domestic utensils, and sundry equipment. (6) Tyres and tubes. The ratio was worked out in the same way as in the case of motor spirit. (7) Tobacco. The ratio was based on the monetized expenditure on tobacco by the different expenditure groups. (8) Vegetable products. It was assumed that the lowest two classes do not purchase any vegetable products. Therefore the whole of the rural share of the tax burden was distributed between the highest four groups in the ratio

10:15:30:45 starting with the third group and going upward. (9) Coffee and tea. The ratio of expenditures on refreshments was used. (10) Cotton cloth. The ratio for clothing was used. (11) Artificial silk. The ratio for manufactured goods was used. (12) Cement. The ratio of manufactured goods was used. (13) Footwear. The ratio based on monetized expenditure on footwear was used. (14) Soap. The ratio for toilet was used. (15) Woollen fabrics. The ratio for monetized expenditure on clothing was used. (16) Electric fans. The revenue was distributed between the upper two groups in the ratio 40:60. (16) Electric bulbs. The burden of the tax was distributed among the upper three groups in the ratio 20:35:45. (17) Electric batteries. The ratio for manufactured goods was used. (18) Paper. The ratio of expenditures on education was used. (19) Paints and varnishes. The ratio for manufactured goods was used. (20) Vegetable nonessential oils. The ratio for the combined monetized expenditure on toilets and edible oils was used. (21) Refined diesel oil and vaporizing oils. The rural share of the tax burden from this tax was split up into parts, tax from goods vehicles and tax from public service vehicles. The burden arising from the tax from goods vehicles was distributed in the ratio of the average monetized expenditure of each group. The tax from public service vehicles was distributed in the ratio of the expenditure on conveyance. (22) Industrial fuel oils. The ratio for manufactured goods was used. (23) Rayons and synthetic fibres. The ratio for manufactured goods was used. (24) Motor cars. The entire rural share of the tax burden from this item was attributed to the highest expenditure group. (25) Coal cess. The ratio was derived by adding the expenditures on fuel and light, and conveyance. (26) Cess on copra. The ratio was derived by adding the expenditures on toilet and edible oils. (27) Cess on oils and oil-seeds. The same ratio as in the case of cess on copra was used. (28) Miscellaneous. The ratio for manufactured goods was used.

II. *State Excise Duties.* The tax burden was distributed among the different expenditure groups according to the ratio of monetized expenditure on intoxicants.

III. *Sales Tax on Motor Spirit.* The ratio is the same as in the case of central excise duty on motor spirit.

IV. *Import Duties.* The rural share of the burden of import duties was distributed among the different expenditure groups in the ratio of the monetized expenditures on manufactured goods.

V. *General Sales Tax.* The rural share of the burden arising from the general sales taxation was distributed among the various expenditure groups in the ratio of the combined monetized expenditures on edible oil, salt, spices, sugar, tobacco, intoxicants, fuel and light, clothing, medicine, toilets, petty articles, domestic utensils, and sundry equipment and ornaments.

VI. *Tax on Railway Fares.* The ratio of monetized expenditures on conveyance was used.

VII. *Motor Vehicles Tax.* The same ratio as in the case of the sales tax on motor spirit was used.

VIII. *Entertainment Tax.* The ratio of the monetized expenditures on amusements was used.

IX. *Electricity Duties.* That portion of the rural tax burden arising from the household use of electricity was distributed among the upper four groups in the ratio 5:15:30:50. The share of the tax burden arising from industrial and commercial consumption of electricity was distributed among the different expenditure groups in the ratio of the monetized expenditures on manufactured goods.

X. *"Other" Taxes and Duties.* The ratio of the combined expenditures on sugar, tobacco, and conveyance was used.

APPENDIX II

POPULATION ESTIMATES FOR 1958-59

TABLE 39

STATEWISE DISTRIBUTION OF POPULATION, 1958-59

(Population in millions)

State	Population on March 1, 1961	Annual percentage rate of growth over 1951[a]	Estimated population in 1958-59[b]
Andhra Pradesh	36	1.6	34.82
Assam	12	3.4	11.26
Bihar	46	2.0	44.16
Gujarat	21	2.7	20.05
Kerala	17	2.5	16.19
Madhya Pradesh	32	2.4	30.49
Madras	34	1.2	33.14
Maharashtra	40	2.3	38.16
Mysore	23	2.1	22.02
Orissa	18	2.0	17.27
Punjab	20	2.6	18.81
Rajasthan	20	2.6	19.00
Uttar Pradesh	74	1.7	71.45
West Bengal	35	3.3	32.90
INDIA	437[c]	2.1	418.32

SOURCE: *Reserve Bank of India Bulletin* (June 1961), p. 901.

NOTE: (a) We assume that the trend is linear, i.e. the rate of growth of population is uniform between 1951 and 1961.

(b) The 1961 census gives the population as on March 1, 1961. In estimating the population for 1958-59, we should take the mid-point of the class interval, which is one year in this case. Since the financial year 1958-59 begins on April 1, 1958, and ends on March 31, 1959, the mid-point is September 30, 1958. Between March 1, 1961, and September 30, 1958, the interval is two years and five months. Thus to estimate the population for the financial year 1958-59 from the 1961 census, we have to go back to two years and five months.

(c) Includes the population of Jammu and Kashmir, and the Union Territories, but excludes the population of Manipur, North Eastern Frontier Agency, Nagaland and Sikkim.

Table 40
STATEWISE DISTRIBUTION OF RURAL POPULATION, 1958-59

(Population in millions)

State	Estimated population in 1958-59	Proportion of rural population on March 1, 1961 (in %)	Proportion of rural population in 1958-59* (in %)	Size of rural population in 1958-59
Andhra Pradesh	34.82	82.60	82.71	28.79997
Assam	11.26	92.50	92.61	10.42707
Bihar	44.16	91.57	91.68	40.48999
Gujarat	20.0	74.39	74.50	14.94043
Kerala	16.19	84.97	85.08	13.77376
Madhya Pradesh	30.49	85.71	85.82	26.16682
Madras	33.14	73.28	73.39	24.31958
Maharashtra	38.16	72.08	72.19	27.55097
Mysore	22.02	77.97	78.08	17.19344
Orissa	17.27	93.67	93.78	16.19598
Punjab	18.81	79.90	80.01	15.05007
Rajasthan	19.00	83.95	84.06	15.96991
Uttar Pradesh	71.45	87.15	87.26	62.34362
West Bengal	32.90	76.85	76.96	25.32325
INDIA	418.32	82.16	82.27	344.15604

SOURCE: *Reserve Bank of India Bulletin* (June 1961), p. 901.

NOTE: * For all-India, the proportion of rural population in the total fell from 82.62 per cent in 1951 to 82.16 per cent in 1961. Thus according to our method of interpolation, as explained in the footnote to the preceding table, the percentage of rural population in the total in 1958-59 must be for the whole of India 0.11 per cent higher than in 1961. We further assume that what is true for all-India is true about each state of the Indian Union, i.e. we assume that in each state there was a decrease in the proportion of the rural population at the all-India rate over the period 1951-61.

TABLE 41

STATEWISE DISTRIBUTION OF AGRICULTURAL POPULATION, 1958-59

(Population in millions)

State	Rural population	Urban population	Rural agricultural[a]	Urban agricultural[b]	Total agricultural
Andhra	28.800	6.020	23.833	0.602	24.435
Assam	10.427	0.832	8.629	0.083	8.712
Bihar	40.490	3.674	33.506	0.367	33.874
Gujarat	14.940	5.114	12.364	0.511	12.875
Kerala	13.774	2.415	11.398	0.242	11.640
Madhya Pradesh	26.167	4.323	21.654	0.432	22.086
Madras	24.320	8.817	20.125	0.882	21.007
Maharashtra	27.551	10.613	22.799	1.061	23.860
Mysore	17.193	4.827	14.230	0.483	14.711
Orissa	16.196	1.074	13.402	0.107	13.510
Punjab	15.050	3.760	12.454	0.376	12.830
Rajasthan	15.970	3.028	13.215	0.303	13.518
Uttar Pradesh	62.344	9.101	51.591	0.910	52.500
West Bengal	25.323	7.581	20.956	0.758	21.714
INDIA	344.156	74.164	284.796	7.416	292.212

NOTE: (*a*) We assume that the proportion of agricultural population in total population remained roughly constant at 69.85 per cent throughout the decade. According to the 1961 census, 82.27 per cent of the population is rural. Assuming that 10 per cent of the urban population is agricultural, we find that 82.75 per cent of the rural population is agricultural. We further assume that this proportion applies to each state. (*b*) We assume that 10 per cent of the urban population is agricultural.

DISTRIBUTION OF THE BURDEN OF "STAMPS AND REGISTRATION" BETWEEN URBAN AND RURAL SECTORS

TABLE 42

REVENUE FROM STAMPS AND REGISTRATION, 1958-59

State	Revenue (in million Rs)	Population (in millions)	Per capita tax (Rs)
Andhra Pradesh	34.495	34.820	0.990
Assam	4.811	11.259	0.427
Bihar	28.732	44.164	0.651
Bombay	61.280	58.218	1.053
Kerala	15.542	16.189	0.960
Madhya Pradesh	15.520	30.490	0.509
Madras	43.690	33.137	1.318
Mysore	18.459	22.020	0.838
Orissa	7.115	17.270	0.412
Punjab	22.878	18.810	1.216
Rajasthan	9.600	18.998	0.505
Uttar Pradesh	38.605	71.445	0.540
West Bengal	36.972	32.904	1.124

SOURCE: (1) Government of India (Ministry of Information and Broadcasting), *India 1959, A Reference Annual* (Delhi: National Printing Works, 1959), pp. 400-67. (2) Table 39.

NOTE: The revenue figures refer to the proceeds of the tax collected by the state governments. These figures represent "revised budget estimates" and not "accounts."

TABLE 43

REVENUE FROM STAMPS AND REGISTRATION : RELATIONSHIP BETWEEN PROPORTION OF URBAN POPULATION AND PER CAPITA TAX, 1958-59

State	Proportion of urban population	Per capita tax (Rs)
Andhra Pradesh	.1729	0.990
Assam	.0739	0.427
Bihar	.0832	0.651
Bombay	.2701	1.053

State	Proportion of urban population	Per capita tax (Rs)
Kerala	.1492	0.960
Madhya Pradesh	.1418	0.509
Madras	.2661	1.318
Mysore	.2192	0.838
Orissa	.0622	0.412
Punjab	.1999	1.216
Rajasthan	.1594	0.505
Uttar Pradesh	.1274	0.540
West Bengal	.2304	1.124

SOURCE: (1) Table 42. (2) Table 40.

TABLE 44

REVENUE FROM STAMPS AND REGISTRATION : RELATIONSHIP
BETWEEN SHARE OF AGRICULTURE'S INCOME IN TOTAL INCOME
AND REVENUE FROM THE TAX AS A PROPORTION OF
TOTAL INCOME, 1958-59

State	$\dfrac{Y_a}{Y}$	$\dfrac{T}{Y}$
Andhra Pradesh	.5037	.0035
Assam	.6157	.0013
Bihar	.5515	.0026
Bombay	.2910	.0032
Kerala	.3472	.0037
Madhya Pradesh	.6124	.0016
Madras	.3703	.0044
Mysore	.4563	.0037
Orissa	.5977	.0021
Punjab	.6467	.0028
Rajasthan	.5078	.0020
Uttar Pradesh	.5565	.0018
West Bengal	.3716	.0030

SOURCE: (1) K.N. Raj, "Some Features of Economic Growth of the Last Decade in
India," *Economic Weekly* (February 4, 1961), p. 265. (2) Table 42.

NOTE: Y_a = Income of the agricultural sector; Y = Total income of the state;
T = Total tax (stamps and registration).

RELATIVE TAX BURDEN OF AGRICULTURAL AND NONAGRICULTURAL SECTORS, 1958-59

TABLE 45

STATEWISE DISTRIBUTION OF AGRICULTURAL INCOME, 1958-59

(at current prices)

State	Total population (in millions)	Agricultural population (in millions)	Income from agriculture (in million Rs)	Per capita agricultural income (Rs)
Andhra Pradesh	34.820	24.435	5031.972	205.94
Assam	11.259	8.712	2237.499	256.84
Bihar	44.164	33.874	6025.349	177.88
Bombay	58.218	36.735	5528.127	150.49
Kerala	16.189	11.640	1463.924	125.77
Madhya Pradesh	30.490	22.086	6038.153	273.39
Madras	33.137	21.007	3684.351	175.39
Mysore	22.020	14.711	2298.318	156.24
Orissa	17.270	13.510	2040.104	151.01
Punjab	18.810	12.830	5322.196	414.82
Rajasthan	18.998	13.518	2429.559	179.73
Uttar Pradesh	71.445	52.501	12233.155	233.01
West Bengal	32.904	21.714	4560.358	210.02

SOURCE: (1) *Reserve Bank of India Bulletin* (June 1961), p. 901. (2) K. N. Raj, "Some Features of Economic Growth of the Last Decade in India," *Economic Weekly* (February 4, 1961), p. 265.

Appendixes

TABLE 46
STATEWISE DISTRIBUTION OF THE NONAGRICULTURAL SECTOR'S INCOME, 1958-59

State	Population of sector (in millions)	Income of sector (in million Rs)	Corporate taxes (in million Rs)	Retained earnings of corporate sector (in million Rs)	Personal income of sector $[2-(3+4)]$ (million Rs)	Per capita personal income of sector (Rs)
Andhra Pradesh	9.765	4957.322	9.705	8.28	4939.337	505.80
Assam*	2.547	1396.670	2.213	7.04	1387.417	544.68
Bihar	10.290	4899.664	—**	47.02	4852.644	471.58
Bombay	21.483	13468.741	221.364	102.72	13144.717	611.87
Kerala	4.550	2752.860	11.429	5.36	2736.071	601.41
Madhya Pradesh	8.404	3820.927	7.112	10.83	3802.985	452.52
Madras	12.130	6267.357	49.674	24.66	6193.023	510.54
Mysore	7.309	2738.989	19.029	12.44	2707.520	370.42
Orissa	3.760	1373.229	—**	4.41	1368.819	364.05
Punjab	5.980	2907.575	6.942	6.16	2894.473	484.04
Rajasthan	5.480	2354.869	4.541	2.33	2347.998	428.48
Uttar Pradesh	18.944	9750.246	17.202	22.91	9710.134	512.56
West Bengal	11.190	7711.209	163.831	81.42	7465.958	667.18

SOURCE: (1) Government of India, *Report of the Finance Commission* 1961 (New Delhi, 1962), p. 109. (2) Government of India, *Report of the Direct Taxes Administration Enquiry Committee* (New Delhi: Government of India Press, 1960), pp. 418-9. (3) Raj, p. 267. (4) *Reserve Bank of India Bulletin* (June 1961), p. 901.

NOTE: *In the case of Assam, the source material (No. 2 quoted above) groups Assam with Manipur and Tripura which are two relatively unimportant regions under the direct administration of the Government of India. Since there was no way of separating the corporation tax of Assam from the rest, it was decided to ignore the share, which is likely to be almost nil, of the two regions, Tripura and Manipur.

**In the case of Bihar and Orissa, the corporation taxes could not be estimated because of inconsistencies in the official statistics quoted above (source materials 1 and 2).

TABLE 47

STATEWISE DISTRIBUTION OF TAX REVENUE, 1958-59

(in million Rs)

State	Land revenue	Agricultural income tax	Income tax	Profession tax	Wealth tax	Gift tax +	Estate duty +	Expenditure tax
Andhra Pradesh	83.400	0.50	43.947	—	3.452		2.613	
Assam	24.596	14.40	17.565	0.60	0.310		0.177	
Bihar	114.528	0.90	38.708	—	1.415		0.775	
Bombay	133.783	—	638.456	0.10	44.230		11.414	
Kerala	16.357	23.10	24.538	—	1.333		0.783	
Madhya Pradesh	83.850	0.30	20.513	0.40	1.421		0.369	
Madras	48.110	17.70	106.646	—	5.794		3.395	
Mysore	44.000	8.00	33.541	—	2.625		1.678	
Orissa	23.973	0.40	6.808	—	1.181		0.647	
Punjab	37.252	—	24.091	1.70	0.927		0.480	
Rajasthan	65.972	0.40	13.681	—	0.564		0.284	
Uttar Pradesh	185.149	6.80	49.871	—	2.660		1.097	
West Bengal	67.111	7.30	565.765	—	28.543		4.480	

TABLE 47 (Continued)

State	Stamps and registration (state)	Stamps and registration (central)	Taxes on commodities and services (state)	Central excise duties	Tax on urban immovable property
Andhra Pradesh	34.495	2.670	210.686	266.539	—
Assam	4.811	0.344	84.320	106.673	—
Bihar	28.732	2.052	170.100	215.194	17.7
Bombay	61.280	4.493	516.491	653.413	—
Kerala	15.542	1.112	105.619	133.619	—
Madhya Pradesh	15.520	1.111	112.946	142.888	—
Madras	43.690	3.131	229.417	290.235	—
Mysore	18.459	1.322	150.751	190.715	—
Orissa	7.115	0.508	44.066	55.748	—
Punjab	22.878	1.640	162.575	205.674	4.9
Rajasthan	9.600	0.687	85.941	108.724	—
Uttar Pradesh	38.605	2.761	269.269	340.652	—
West Bengal	36.972	2.650	325.465	411.746	—

SOURCE: (1) Reserve Bank of India, *Report on Currency and Finance*, 1959-60, Statement 55. (2) *Report of the Finance Commission* 1961, pp. 108-9. (3) Reserve Bank of India, *Report on Currency and Finance* 1961-62, Statements 56 and 60. (4) Government of India, *India* 1959, pp. 400-67. (5) *Report of the Direct Taxes Administration Enquiry Committee*, pp. 418-9. (6) *Reserve Bank of India Bulletin* (May 1958), pp. 512-6.

NOTE: (1) The sign — means that the particular tax did not exist in the state concerned. (2) Wherever figures could be had the actual receipts under each tax item have been given. In the absence of actual figures (accounts), revised estimates or budget estimates (if revised estimates could not be had) are given. (3) As explained in the text, the revenues from central stamps and registration and central excise duties have been distributed in the ratio of state duties on stamps and registration and state taxes on commodities and services respectively.

TABLE 48

STATEWISE AND SECTORWISE DISTRIBUTION OF REVENUE FROM
GENERAL DIRECT TAXES, 1958-59

State	Wealth tax		Gift tax, expenditure tax and estate duty		Tax on urban immovable property		Stamps and Registration	
	Agricultural	Nonagricultural	Agricultural	Nonagricultural	Agricultural	Nonagricultural	Agricultural	Nonagricultural
Andhra Pradesh	1.090	2.362	1.205	2.613	—	—	8.457	28.513
Assam	0.098	0.216	0.081	0.177	—	—	1.852	3.302
Bihar	0.447	0.968	0.358	0.775	—	—	10.416	20.366
Bombay	13.963	30.267	5.266	11.414	1.740	15.66	11.668	54.025
Kerala	0.420	0.913	0.360	0.781	—	—	4.057	12.595
Madhya Pradesh	0.449	0.972	0.169	0.369	—	—	4.218	12.413
Madras	1.829	3.965	1.566	3.395	—	—	8.393	38.428
Mysore	0.829	1.796	0.774	1.678	—	—	3.939	15.843
Orissa	0.373	0.808	0.299	0.647	—	—	2.987	4.641
Punjab	0.293	0.634	0.222	0.480	0.490	4.410	5.138	19.402
Rajasthan	0.178	0.386	0.131	0.287	—	—	2.462	7.825
Uttar Pradesh	0.840	1.820	0.506	1.097	—	—	11.133	30.228
West Bengal	9.011	19.532	2.067	4.480	—	—	7.707	31.943

NOTE: The criteria according to which the revenue from each of the above taxes has been divided between the two sectors are already explained in the text.

The sign — means that the particular tax did not exist in the state concerned.

The tax item "stamps and registration" includes both the state and the central taxes under the same head.

TABLE 49

STATEWISE DISTRIBUTION OF THE MONETIZED CONSUMPTION
EXPENDITURE OF THE AGRICULTURAL SECTOR,
1958-59

(in million Rs)

State	Income	Direct taxes	Disposable income	Consumption expenditure	Monetized consumption expenditure
Andhra Pradesh	5031.972	94.652	4937.320	4772.265	2748.825
Assam	2237.499	41.027	2196.472	2123.044	1222.873
Bihar	6025.349	126.649	5898.700	5701.507	3284.068
Bombay	5528.127	166.420	5361.707	5182.465	2985.100
Kerala	1463.924	44.294	1419.630	1372.172	790.371
Madhya Pradesh	6038.153	88.986	5949.167	5750.286	3312.165
Madras	3684.351	77.598	3606.753	3486.179	2008.039
Mysore	2298.318	57.542	2240.776	2165.867	1247.539
Orissa	2040.104	28.032	2012.072	1944.808	1120.210
Punjab	5322.196	43.395	5278.801	5102.331	2938.942
Rajasthan	2429.559	69.143	2360.416	2281.507	1314.148
Uttar Pradesh	12233.155	204.428	12028.727	11626.607	6696.925
West Bengal	4560.358	93.196	4467.162	4317.825	2487.067

NOTE: The procedure of arriving at the monetized consumption expenditure from
personal income is outlined in the text. Disposable income = Income – Direct taxes;
Consumption expenditure = Disposable income – Saving; Monetized consumption
expenditure = Consumption expenditure – Noncash expenditure.

TABLE 50

STATEWISE DISTRIBUTION OF MONETIZED CONSUMPTION
EXPENDITURE OF NONAGRICULTURAL SECTOR,
1958-59

(in million Rs)

State	Income (personal)	Direct taxes	Disposable income	Consumption expenditure	Monetized consumption expenditure
Andhra Pradesh	4939.337	77.435	4861.902	4266.805	3308.907
Assam	1387.417	21.860	1365.557	1198.413	929.369
Bihar	4852.644	60.817	4791.827	4205.307	3261.216
Bombay	13144.717	749.922	12394.795	10877.672	8435.635
Kerala	2736.071	38.827	2697.244	2367.101	1835.687
Madhya Pradesh	3802.985	34.667	3768.318	3307.076	2564.637
Madras	6193.023	152.434	6040.589	5301.221	4111.097
Mysore	2707.520	52.858	2654.662	2329.731	1806.707

State	Income (personal)	Direct taxes	Disposable income	Consumption expenditure	Monetized consumption expenditure
Orissa	1368.819	12.904	1355.915	1189.951	922.807
Punjab	2894.473	50.717	2843.756	2495.680	1935.400
Rajasthan	2347.998	22.176	2325.822	2041.141	1582.905
Uttar Pradesh	9710.134	83.106	9627.118	8448.759	6552.012
West Bengal	7465.958	621.720	6844.238	6006.503	4658.043

TABLE 51

STATEWISE AND SECTORWISE DISTRIBUTION OF REVENUE FROM
TAXES ON COMMODITIES AND SERVICES

(in million Rs)

State	Taxes on commodities and services (state)	Central excise duties	Total revenue from commodity taxation	Share of agricultural sector	Share of nonagricultural sector
Andhra Pradesh	210.686	266.539	477.225	202.9379	244.2871
Assam	84.320	106.673	190.993	108.5155	82.4735
Bihar	170.100	215.194	385.294	193.3195	191.9745
Bombay	516.491	653.413	1169.904	305.7840	864.1200
Kerala	105.619	133.619	239.238	72.0040	167.2340
Madhya Pradesh	112.946	142.888	255.834	144.1880	111.6460
Madras	229.417	290.235	519.652	170.5276	349.1244
Mysore	150.751	190.715	341.466	139.4754	201.9906
Orissa	44.066	55.748	99.814	54.7291	45.0849
Punjab	162.575	205.674	368.249	222.0325	146.2165
Rajasthan	85.941	108.724	194.665	90.5711	109.0939
Uttar Pradesh	269.269	340.652	609.921	308.2961	301.6249
West Bengal	325.465	411.746	737.211	256.6081	480.6029

NOTE: The burden of commodity taxation is distributed between the agricultural and the nonagricultural sector in the ratio of the monetized consumption expenditures of the two sectors.

Table 52

STATEWISE AND SECTORWISE DISTRIBUTION OF THE BURDEN OF
DIRECT AND INDIRECT TAXATION, 1958-59

(in million Rs)

State	Agricultural sector			Nonagricultural sector		
	Direct taxes	Indirect taxes	Total tax burden	Direct taxes	Indirect taxes	Total tax burden
Andhra Pradesh	94.652	202.938	297.590	77.435	244.287	321.722
Assam	41.027	108.520	149.547	21.860	82.474	104.334
Bihar	126.649	193.320	319.969	60.817	191.975	252.792
Bombay	166.420	305.784	472.204	749.922	864.120	1614.042
Kerala	44.294	72.004	116.298	38.827	167.234	206.061
Madhya Pradesh	88.986	144.188	233.174	34.667	111.646	146.313
Madras	77.598	170.528	248.126	152.434	349.124	501.558
Mysore	57.542	139.475	197.017	52.858	201.991	254.849
Orissa	28.032	54.729	82.761	12.904	45.085	57.989
Punjab	43.395	222.033	265.428	50.717	145.217	196.934
Rajasthan	69.143	90.571	159.714	22.176	109.094	131.270
Uttar Pradesh	204.428	308.296	512.724	83.016	301.625	384.641
West Bengal	93.196	256.608	349.804	621.720	480.603	1102.323

BIBLIOGRAPHY

BIBLIOGRAPHY

BOOKS

AMERICAN ECONOMIC ASSOCIATION. *Readings in the Economics of Taxation* (Homewood, Illinois: Richard D. Irwin, Inc., 1959).

BALAKRISHNA, R. *Recent Trends in Indian Finance* (Madras: University of Madras, 1955).

BARAN, PAUL A. *The Political Economy of Growth* (New York: Monthly Review Press, 1957).

CHELLIAH, RAJA J. *Fiscal Policy in Underdeveloped Countries* (London: George Allen and Unwin Ltd., 1960).

DALTON, HUGH. *Principles of Public Finance* (New York: Frederick A. Praeger, Inc., 1955).

DUE, JOHN F. *Government Finance* (Homewood, Illinois: Richard D. Irwin, Inc., 1959).

———. *Sales Taxation* (Urbana: University of Illinois Press, 1957).

DUTT, ROMESH. *The Economic History of India*, Vol. I (New Delhi: Government of India Press, 1960).

GULATI, IQBAL S. *Resource Prospects of the Third Five Year Plan* (Bombay: Orient Longmans, 1960).

HANSEN, BENT. *The Economic Theory of Fiscal Policy* (English edition, London: Allen and Unwin Ltd., 1958).

HARVARD LAW SCHOOL, INTERNATIONAL PROGRAM IN TAXATION. *Agricultural Taxation and Economic Development* (Cambridge, Mass.: Harvard University Press, 1954).

———. *Taxation in India* (Boston: Little, Brown and Company, 1960).

HELLER, WALTER W., BODDY, FRANCIS M., and NELSON, CARL L. (ed.). *Savings in the Modern Economy* (Minneapolis: University of Minnesota Press, 1953).

HICKS, J. R. *Value and Capital* (2nd edition, Oxford: Clarendon Press, 1946).

HICKS, URSULA K. *Development from Below* (Oxford: Clarendon Press, 1961).

———. *Public Finance* (London: Nisbet, 1947).

HIGGINS, BENJAMIN H. *Economic Development: Principles, Problems, and Policies* (New York: Norton, 1959).

INDIAN STATISTICAL INSTITUTE. *Essays in Economic Planning* (Calcutta: Elka Press, 1960).

KALDOR, NICHOLAS. *An Expenditure Tax* (London: George Allen and Unwin Ltd., 1955).

LEWIS, ARTHUR W. *The Theory of Economic Growth* (London: George Allen and Unwin Ltd., 1957).

MILLIKAN, MAX F. (ed.). *Income Stabilization for a Developing Democracy* (New Haven: Yale University Press, 1953).

MUSGRAVE, RICHARD A. *The Theory of Public Finance* (New York: McGraw Hill Book Company, 1959).

NURKSE, RAGNER. *Problems of Capital Formation in Underdeveloped Countries* (Oxford: Basil Blackwell, 1953).

PIGOU, A. C. *A Study in Public Finance* (London: Macmillan and Company, Ltd., 1928).

SCHWARTZ, HARRY. *Russia's Soviet Economy* (New York: Prentice-Hall, Inc., 1954).

——. *The Red Phoenix: Russia Since World War II* (New York: Frederick A. Praeger, Inc., 1961).

SELIGMAN, EDWIN R. A. *The Shifting and Incidence of Taxation* (New York: Columbia Press, 1932).

SMITH, ADAM. *The Wealth of Nations.* Vol. II (London: J. M. Dent and Sons Ltd., 1954).

STAMP, SIR JOSIAH. *Wealth and Taxable Capacity* (London: P. S. King and Son Ltd., 1922).

TRIPATHY, R. N. *Fiscal Policy and Economic Development in India* (Calcutta: The World Press Private Ltd., 1958).

UNITED NATIONS, TECHNICAL ASSISTANCE ADMINISTRATION. *Taxes and Fiscal Policy in Underdeveloped Countries* (New York, 1954).

WALD, HASKELL P. *Taxation of Agricultural Land in Underdeveloped Economies* (Cambridge, Mass.: Harvard University Press, 1959).

GOVERNMENT OF INDIA PUBLICATIONS

CABINET SECRETARIAT. *The National Sample Survey, Report No. 18, Tables with Notes on Consumer Expenditure* (Calcutta: Elka Press, 1959).

CENTRAL STATISTICAL ORGANIZATION, CABINET SECRETARIAT. *Statistical Abstract of India,* 1956-57 (New Delhi: Government of India Press, 1958).

——. *Statistical Abstract of Indian Union,* 1958-59 (New Delhi: Government of India Press, 1960).

——. *Estimates of National Income,* 1948-49 to 1959-60 (New Delhi: Government of India Press, 1961).

DEPARTMENT OF ECONOMIC AFFAIRS, MINISTRY OF FINANCE. *Report of the Taxation Enquiry Commission,* 1953-54, Vol. 1-3 (New Delhi: Government of India Press, 1955).

DEPARTMENT OF REVENUE, MINISTRY OF FINANCE. *Report of the Direct Taxes Administration Enquiry Committee,* 1958-59 (New Delhi: Government of India Press, 1960).

FINANCE COMMISSION. *Report of the Finance Commission,* 1957 (New Delhi: Government of India Press, 1957).

——. *Report of the Finance Commission,* 1961 (New Delhi: Government of India Press, 1962).

PLANNING COMMISSION. *Second Five Year Plan* (New Delhi: Government of India Press, 1956).

——. *Third Five Year Plan* (New Delhi: Government of India Press, 1961).

PUBLICATIONS DIVISION, MINISTRY OF INFORMATION AND BROADCASTING. *India 1959, A Reference Annual* (Delhi: National Printing Works, 1959).

——. *India 1961, A Reference Annual* (Faridabad: Government of India Press, 1961).

ARTICLES AND PERIODICALS

ADLER, JOHN H. "The Fiscal and Monetary Implications of Development Programs," *American Economic Review* (May 1952), pp. 585-600.

Agricultural Situation in India (Vol. XVII, No. 8, November 1962), pp. 886-9.

BANSIL, P. C. "Problems of Marketable Surplus," *Indian Journal of Agricultural Economics* (Vol. XVI, No. 1, January-March 1961), pp. 26-37.

BARDHAN, P. KUMAR. "Agriculture Inadequately Taxed," *Economic Weekly* (Vol. XIII,. No. 49, December 9, 1961), pp. 1829-35.

BOSE, S. K. "Problems of Mobilization of the Marketable Surplus in Agriculture in India," *Indian Journal of Agricultural Economics* (Vol. XVI, No. 1, January-March 1961), pp. 37-46.

FRANK, HENRY J. "Measuring State Tax Burdens," *National Tax Journal* (Vol. XII, No. 2, June 1959), pp. 179-85.

GEORGESCU-ROEGEN, NICHOLAS. "Economic Theory and Agrarian Economics," *Oxford Economic Papers* (Vol. XII, No. 1, February 1960), pp. 1-40.

GROVES, HAROLD M., and MADHAVAN, MURUGAPPA C. "Agricultural Taxation and India's Third Five Year Plan," *Land Economics* (February 1962), pp. 56-64.

Indian Finance, January 12, 1963.

JOHNSTON, BRUCE F., and MELLOR, JOHN W. "The Role of Agriculture in Economic Development," *American Economic Review* (Vol. LI, No. 4, September 1961), pp. 566-93.

KALECKI, M. "Financial Problems of the Third Plan, Some Observations," *Economic Weekly* (Vol. XII, No. 28, July 9, 1960), pp. 1119-22.

KHUSRO, A. M. "Inter-Sector Terms of Trade and Price Policy," *Economic Weekly* (Vol. XIII, Annual Number, February 4, 1961), pp. 289-91.

———. "Taxation of Agricultural Land," *Economic Weekly* (Vol. XIII, Annual Number, February 1963), pp. 275-82.

LITTLE, I.M.D. "A Critical Examination of India's Third Five Year Plan," *Oxford Economic Papers* (New Series, Vol. XIV, No. 1, February 1962), pp. 1-24.

MUKHERJEE, P. K. "Surplus in Agriculture," *Agricultural Situation in India* (Vol. XIV, Annual Number, August 1959), pp. 431-5.

MUSGRAVE, RICHARD A. "On Incidence," *Journal of Political Economy* (Vol. LXI, No. 4, August 1953), pp. 306-23.

NICHOLLS, WILLIAM H. "Agricultural Surplus as a Factor in Economic Development," *Journal of Political Economy* (Vol. LXXI, No. 1, February 1963), pp. 1-29.

OKHAWA, KAZUSHI, and ROSOVSKY, HENRY. "The Role of Agriculture in Modern Japanese Economic Development," *Economic Development and Cultural Change* (Vol. IX, No. 1, Part II, October 1960), pp. 43-67.

PATTERSON, GARDNER, "Impact of Deficit Financing in Underdeveloped Countries: Some Neglected Aspects," *Journal of Finance* (Vol. XII, No. 2, May 1957), pp. 178-89.

POSTAN, M. M. "Recent Trends in the Accumulation of Capital," *Economic History Review* (Vol. VI, No. 1, October 1935), pp. 1-12.

RAJ, K. N. "The Marginal Rate of Saving in the Indian Economy," *Oxford Economic Papers* (New Series, Vol. XIV, No. 1, February 1962), pp. 36-50.

———. "Some Features of Economic Growth of the Last Decade in India," *Economic Weekly* (Vol. XIII, Annual Number, February 4, 1961), pp. 253-71.

RANIS, GUSTAV. "The Financing of Japanese Economic Development," *Economic History Review* (Second Series, Vol. XI, No. 3, April 1959), pp. 440-54.

RANIS, GUSTAV, and FEI, JOHN C.H. "A Theory of Economic Development," *American Economic Review* (Vol. 50, September 1961), pp. 533-65.

RAO, V.K.R.V. "Public Finance, Economic Growth, and Redistribution of Income in India (1951-52 to 1960-61)," *Economic Weekly* (Vol. XIII, No. 34, August 26, 1961), pp. 1373-7.

Reserve Bank of India Bulletin (Vol. XI¹, No. 5, May 1958), pp. 512-6.

——. (Vol. XV, No. 4, April 1961), pp. 547-50.

——. (Vol. XV, No. 6, June 1961), pp. 901-2.

——. (Vol. XV, No. 8, August 1961), pp. 1200-13.

——. (Vol. XVI, No. 9, September 1962), pp. 1348-63.

ROLPH, EARL R. "A Proposed Revision of Excise-Tax Theory," *Journal of Political Economy* (Vol. LX, No. 2, April 1952), pp. 102-17.

SARAN, RAM. "Problems of Marketable Surplus of Food Grains in India," *Indian Journal of Agricultural Economics* (Vol. XVI, No. 1, January-March 1961), pp. 71-8.

SRINIVASAN, M. "Problems of Marketable Surplus in Indian Agriculture," *Indian Journal of Agricultural Economics* (Vol. XVI, No. 1, January-March 1961), pp. 106-13.

UNITED NATIONS, FISCAL DIVISION, DEPARTMENT OF ECONOMIC AFFAIRS. "Taxation and Economic Development in Asian Countries," *Economic Bulletin for Asia and the Far East* (Vol. IV, No. 3, November 1953), pp. 1-15.

REPORTS

KALDOR, NICHOLAS, *Indian Tax Reform, Report of Survey* (Issued by the Department of Economic Affairs, Ministry of Finance, Government of India Press, New Delhi, 1956).

REPORT OF A MISSION OF THE INTERNATIONAL BANK FOR RECONSTRUCTION AND DEVELOPMENT. *The Economic Development of Jamaica* (Washington, 1953).

RESERVE BANK OF INDIA. *All India Rural Credit Survey*, Vol. II, *The General Report* (Bombay, 1954).

——. *Report on Currency and Finance for the Year* 1953-54 (Bombay, 1954).

——. *Report on Currency and Finance for the Year* 1957-58 (Bombay, 1958).

——. *Report on Currency and Finance for the Year* 1960-61 (Bombay, 1961).

——. *Report on Currency and Finance for the Year* 1961-62 (Bombay, 1962).

UNPUBLISHED MATERIAL

KALDOR, NICHOLAS. "The Role of Taxation in Economic Development." Paper presented at the International Congress on Economic Development held at Vienna, Austria, during August 30-September 6, 1962 (mimeographed).

NICHOLLS, WILLIAM H. "The Place of Agriculture in Economic Development." Paper presented at a Round Table on Economic Development held at Gamagori, Japan, during April 1960 (mimeographed).

PANIKAR, P. G. K. "An Essay on Rural Savings in India." Unpublished Ph.D. Dissertation, Vanderbilt University, 1959.

INDEX

INDEX

AGRICULTURAL LABOUR, 22, 62
Agricultural policy, in the Soviet Union, Japan, 3
Agricultural population, estimate of, 62; per capita incomes of, 79
All India Labour Enquiry, 61

BANSIL, P. C., 99
Baran, Paul, 53, 54, 92
Bernstein, B. M., 90

CAPITAL FORMATION, 109, 115
Capital gains tax, 147
Census 1961, 26
Census of Holdings 1954-55, 128
Census of taxation, 121
Classical economists, 21
Compulsory deliveries of grains, 3
Constitution of India, 8, 90
Consumers' taxes, 25
Consumption, levels of, 5; non-subsistence, 59-61
Consumption expenditure, 37, 75

DALTON, HUGH, 51, 52
Deficit financing, 89
Demonstration effect, 89
Direct taxes, burden of, 30-2; changes in the revenue from, 57; combined receipts of, 11, 57, 58; component parts of, 66, 67; exemption limits of, 11; on agriculture, 11, 54; land revenue as part of, 55; non-agriculturists' share of, 68; progressiveness of, 80

EAST INDIA COMPANY, 8
Economic surplus, 53

FACTOR MARKETS, 94
Fiscal division of the United Nations, 126, 128
Fiscal policy, 109, 111
Ford Foundation Agricultural Production Team, 120
Frank, Henry J., 71, 159
Full Employment, 109

GEORGESCU-ROEGEN, N., 94, 95
Gold hoards, 5, 59, 96
Groves, Harold M., 134, 135, 140
Gulati, I. S., 129, 132-4, 140

HANSEN, BENT, 20, 21
Heller, Walter, 25, 92, 112, 121, 126
Hicks, Ursula K., 23, 24, 50, 125, 132, 136-8, 140, 148
Higgins, Benjamin, 119, 120

INCIDENCE, 19, 20, 22, 23-5
Income distribution, 65, 74, 158
Income effect, 97, 113
"Indian Tax Reform," 50
Indirect taxes, 12, 13, 24, 36-45
Industrial Revolution, 4
Inflation, 89, 90
International Bank Mission to Jamaica, 113
Investment Credit Corporation, 117

KALDOR, NICHOLAS, 50, 53, 98, 112, 128, 129, 132, 136-8, 153
Kalecki, Michael, 50, 92
Khusro, A. M., 129, 132-4, 140, 142

LAND REFORMS, 9, 22, 55, 63, 64, 158
Landownership, distribution of, 62, 63,

79, 159; major source of income, 110
Little, I. M. D., 135, 140
Lugard, Lord, 136, 137

MADHAVAN, MURUGAPPA C., 134, 135, 140
"Mahalwari," 8
Marketable surplus, 99
Marketed surplus, 5, 98-107, 111, 115, 162, 163
McCulloch, J. R., 122n
Musgrave, Richard A., 21-4

NATIONAL SAMPLE SURVEY, 19, 20, 37, 38, 41, 48, 61, 74, 155, 158
Negative taxes, 25, 45
Nicholls, William H., 4, 98, 120
Nurkse, Ragnar, 87, 116, 117, 120

PAPANEK, GUSTAV P., 61
Permanent Settlement, 8
Planning Commission, 86, 89, 91, 161
Population, agricultural, 26, 29; estimate of, 26, 27; urban, 38, 156
Positive taxes, 25, 45
Producers' taxes, 25
Public expenditure, financing of, 148, 166, 167; on agricultural sector, 54, 156; on investment, 46, 69; on non-agricultural sector, 69, 70; on social and economic overheads, 48, 50, 156

RAJ, K. N., 50, 72, 82, 86, 135, 140
Rao, V. K. R. V., 50

Reservation demand, 99
Reserve Bank of India, 31, 38, 59, 65, 74, 82, 83, 89, 158, 160, 161
Resources, allocation of, 52, 94; domestic, 2, 51; financial, 5, 76, 81, 108; mobilization of, 116; transfer of, 52, 118
Rural Credit Survey, 27
"Ryotwari," 8

SARAN, RAM, 99
Savings-income ratio, 59n, 82, 83
Seligman, R. A. Edwin, 20-3
Shenoy, B. R., 89
Smith, Adam, 121, 122
Stamp, Sir Josiah, 51, 52
"Standard acres," 142
Subsidies, 114
Substitution effect, 97, 112

TAXABLE CAPACITY, 51-3, 157
Taxation Enquiry Commission, 19, 22, 24, 110, 129-33, 139
Transfer payments, 25

UGANDA SYSTEM, 137, 138
Unemployment, 109
Urban taxes, 33

WALD, HASKELL P., 52, 53, 92, 124, 125, 132, 136, 138, 140
Wicksteed, Phillip H., 99

"Zamindari," 9, 10

DATE DUE